The Wine Queen

Love, Romance, and a Woman's Quest For Success in the California Wine Industry

By Robert Allen Morris

Orchid Springs Publishing, LLC

Orchid Springs Publishing, LLC
329 N. Park Ave., Floor 2
Winter Park, FL 32789

Also by Robert Allen Morris

Available at www.amazon.com in paperback or on Kindle.

Critical Review of the Wine Queen

Reviewed by Valerie Rouse for Readers' Favorite

"The Wine Queen by Robert Allen Morris is a delightful story about a bright, educated young lady with good business acumen. It tells a tale about dedication. The main character, Ann Robinson, always committed herself to her goals and excelled. This is an admirable trait. Author Robert Morris did an excellent job developing the main character and displaying her inner strength and boldness. This feature is one which all readers should uphold. The tone is colloquial and quite easy to follow. I love the emphasis the author placed on the romance portion of the novel. This section was very intense emotionally and I was caught up in the rapture of the heated romance. I identified with Ann and felt that she deserved the attention and love being given. This indicates the creative genius of the author. I love the fact that the author chose to provide a little background on the upbringing of the main character. This allows the reader to understand her personality on a deeper level. The twist at the end was totally unexpected. It is not very realistic, but it is entertaining to read nevertheless. Overall, The Wine Queen is a good read, and I recommend it to all readers." **– Readers' Favorite**

Praise for the Wine Queen

"*The Wine Queen* is a very interesting book with a great story line. The writer is confident, intelligent, assertive, and obviously understands women. He takes us through the looking glass and into the pages by depicting this story from several points of view. He does this through love, happiness, manipulation, tragedy, and professional successes. This book is passionate, witty, and thrilling as it covers a broad range of subjects keeping the reader yearning for more. The exploration of romance, love, and tragic loss associated with it is extremely attention-catching and makes it almost impossible to put down. An absolute must read, particularly for women." - **Sumer Rohrs, Winner of Six National Championships in Track and Field, and the 2009 NCAA Division III Women's Outdoor Track Athlete of the Year.**

"I read *The Wine Queen* and loved it. It had a story line that was informative, exciting, interesting, and attention grabbing. There is something for every type of reader in this book. Once you start reading it is almost impossible to stop turning the pages to see what happens next. I can't wait to see what the author comes up with next. He writes as though he is portraying every character and makes you feel what they are feeling. A must read, especially for young adult and older women everywhere." - **Cathy Bedford, US Department of Agriculture, Farm Service Agency, Retired.**

"*The Wine Queen* was very entertaining and easy to read. The writer moved quickly through the years and did an awesome job of combining romance, history, tragedy and success. It is obvious that the writer has traveled extensively throughout the country. His knowledge of the history of winemaking and of the California wine industry was very impressive. I would highly recommend for people of all ages, particularly women." - **Sandra Rhoden, retired realtor.**

"In *The Wine Queen,* Allen Morris weaves the story of Ann Robinson from a tragic event in her childhood to a successful career. The reader learns about different industries as Ann works hard and climbs the corporate ladder. Ann's career choices take her from the southeast United States to the Napa Valley of California. All the while, her quest for true love continues. This book contains a strong cast of supporting characters who offer friendship and guidance along the way. The story held my interest throughout and I think others will enjoy it, too." - **Candi Erick, Winter Park, FL.**

Chapter One

The man and woman who were about to die stepped off the Cessna 165 Airmaster and walked toward the fishing lodge on the South Fork of the Flathead River in Northwest Montana. "General and Mrs. Robinson, it's good to see you again," said Josh Sims, the head fishing guide. Josh had bright red hair with a beard to match, green eyes, and was wearing a brown long-sleeve shirt that said "Fly-in Fly Fishing."

"How's the fishing been?" Jim Robinson asked.

"Good. Your spot has been particularly hot this season."

"Great. As soon as we have lunch, we're ready to go there."

They all stepped inside the lodge and Jeff Kantor, the owner, a large-framed man who looked to be in his late forties with a jowly face, black curly hair, and a bushy black walrus mustache, greeted them. "Jim, Katharine, it's good to see you again. Welcome to the start of the 1936 trout fishing season."

The expansive cedar log-and-timber-frame lodge had tall beamed ceilings, a large stone fireplace in the common room, and contained a library, a fly-tying area, a tackle and guides room, and a recreation room with a pool table. Mounted cutthroat trout and pictures of fishermen showing the large trout they'd caught adorned the walls. The kitchen had a small dining area, and there was also a hardwood-floored dining room with a large oak table that could seat twenty-four. There were four guest rooms each with a private bathroom in the main lodge, and four two-bedroom cabins that could accommodate four each.

"It's good to be back," Jim said, shaking Jeff's hand. "What's for lunch?"

"I wanted to help set the mood, so it's pan-seared trout that I caught this morning."

"It doesn't get any fresher or better than that," Katharine said with a grin.

"How many are out fishing?" Jim asked.

"Ten, including two other couples. They're all staying out for shore lunches, so it will be just us for lunch. I thought we'd eat at the table in the kitchen." After a lunch of Caesar salads, the fresh-caught fish, roasted garlic potatoes, sourdough bread, and a fine Chardonnay, Jim and Katharine went to their room, where Josh had taken their luggage. They donned bush pants, waders and fishing vests, then got their fly rods and reels and a tackle box with flies.

"Is it really necessary to take that?" Katharine asked as Jim strapped on a gun belt with a .45 Long Colt revolver in the holster; a bone-handled hunting knife was in the sheath on the opposite side of the belt.

"I'd rather have it and not need it than vice-versa," Jim replied.

Josh drove the Robinsons the four-and-a-half miles to their favorite fishing spot in a Chevy pick-up and dropped them off. "I'll be back to get you about an hour before dark," Josh shouted as he left.

Jim Robinson stood six foot two, and at thirty-five, was bulky in the shoulders, round and slim through the middle, with arms as strong as an ash tree and young forked oaks for legs. A graduate of West Point and now a major general in the US Marines stationed at the Pentagon, his thick black hair had not yet started to turn gray. Katharine, three years younger, was five foot six, slender, with jet-black hair, an almost perfect complexion, shrewd hazel eyes and an hour glass figure that made her look good in whatever she wore. She'd met Jim during her junior year at Wellesley College at a school ball honoring military officers. She'd graduated from Wellesley in 1926, and she and Jim were married shortly afterward. Their daughter, Ann, was born two years later. Now eight years old, Ann was staying with Jim's brother, Dave, and his wife, Harriett, while Katharine and Jim were on this fishing vacation.

"Are you ready?" Jim asked.

"Almost. I just need to finish tying this fly on the leader."

"Good. I'll wait and we'll wade out together."

The scenery was breathtaking. A gurgling stream flowed before them, the cotton wood trees were in bloom, a meadow of wildflowers was behind them, and snow-capped mountains were visible in the distance.

They waded out about seventy feet, and Jim pulled out some line and began casting the fly, a little farther with each flick of his wrist. Katharine did the same, and suddenly her fly disappeared. An instant later the water erupted as a trout broke the surface.

"He's a nice one, Katharine. Let him run on the drag when he wants to."

"Okay."

The fish jumped out of the water several more times as she fought it, but it soon tired. She finished reeling the trout in and held it up by the gills.

"I'd say about four pounds," Jim remarked.

"Yeah, although he felt bigger when I was fighting him."

The couple continued to have good luck, and in about an hour-and-a-half, they had caught seven trout. "I'm ready for a break," Jim said as he waded out of the stream and onto the bank.

"Just one more cast and I'll join you," Katharine responded.

The huge silver-tipped grizzly bear seemed to come out of nowhere. "AURRRH," it roared as it rose up on two legs in front of Jim. Two little brown grizzly cubs ducked, cowering and whimpering behind their mother. The massive beast moved toward him at lightning speed, her neck poised to strike him as her musky smell filled the air. Backing away in fear, Jim managed to pull his revolver. But before his finger could close on the trigger, the bear swatted his hand, breaking his wrist and sending the gun twenty feet through the air and into the stream. As big as a great bull as it stood on its two hind legs, the grizzly's incredible speed as it came toward him actually seemed slow. Jim's mind started to race — from Katharine to their daughter, Ann, to fighting, to escaping. The bear roared and loomed over him, its neck ruffled and silver head pointed down at him. Her long ivory-gray claws, each curved a little, closed and unclosed.

Jim's eyes set, stiffened, yet he saw it all clearly. Another whimper from the cubs behind the bear finally set her off, and her right paw cuffed Jim on the side of the head, across the ear and along the jaw, sending his hat sailing as the claws ripped open his scalp. The blow completely knocked Jim off his feet and half-somersaulted him in the air before he hit the ground. He felt very puny. The grizzly became a silver blur to his eyes. Taking Jim in its mouth, the bear jerked him back and forth like a rag doll, but Jim experienced no pain, just disbelief. The grizzly bit into him again and again, its jaws like a sharp vise that stopped at nothing until teeth hit bone. Then came the claws again, rising like shiny knife blades, long and stark. Katharine screamed.

"Katharine, go get help!" Jim managed to yell to his wife.

She began to hurriedly wade out of the stream, but fell as her foot hit a slippery rock. A sharp pain stabbed through her ankle as she tried to stand. Her ankle was sprained. She managed to crawl onto the bank and into the brush, where she hid, still able to watch Jim as he fought the monster bear.

The bear kept pounding on him. He had to break away. To his right was a wall of mountain, to his left a sheer drop, behind him was the stream filled with slippery rocks, and the bear was between Jim and the road they had come on. There was nowhere he could go. Jim tucked into a fetal position as the bear fell upon him, clawing and biting at his back.

Soon it began to tug on his back, feeling as if someone was jumping up and down on him, and Jim found himself growing angry. *Throw it off the mountain. If only I can throw it off the mountain.*

The bear roared above him. Over in the brush, Katharine screamed again.

The grizzly snarled and roared. Her ivory gray claws brought up scraps of Jim's cloth vest and shirt as well as strips of skin from his back. As he hugged the bear, Jim got his knife in his left hand, around and set. He then plunged his knife through the grizzly's tough hide and into its belly just below the ribs.

Blood spurted over Jim's hands and belly, and ran down both his legs and the bear's legs. He wrestled the bear, stabbing it again and again. The great furry grizzly bellowed in agony, pain and rage. He was still inside its reach and it couldn't get a good swipe at him, so she clawed clumsily up and down his back, bringing up more pieces of cloth and skin and red muscle. She pawed and clawed until Jim's ribs began to show.

Jim screamed. He stabbed wildly, frantically, his hunting knife sinking in over and over. The bear's massive, ruffled neck humped up into a striking curve. Then its head plunged down at Jim, seizing his whole head in her red jaws and lifting him off his feet.

Jim was able to get in one more lunging thrust. All six inches of his knife blade sank in just above the grizzly's heart and stayed there. He then felt a sharp pressure on the top of his neck and his head; the bear was biting his skull, chewing into the bone. *This is it*, he thought. The grizzly shook him by the head as a dog might shake a doll, and his neck cracked.

The bear dropped Jim's lifeless body and went toward Katharine's frantic screams, which were growing increasingly hoarse. As the grizzly closed in on Katharine's hiding spot, she tried to run but the bear was upon her in an instant. In a rage, spouting blood from a score of wounds, it picked up Katharine by her leg and shook her violently until the leg popped out of its hip socket. Its own blood still spurting out on all sides and coughing up blood from its victims, the grizzly picked up Katharine again, this time by the rump. Like a great cat chewing on a struggling mouse, the bear tore off half of it. Katharine managed to pull her fillet knife from its sheath. Her last, fading thoughts were of Ann, and what her daughter would do without her mother and father. As the giant bear arched to swat Katharine, she used the last of her strength to thrust in the fillet knife just below Jim's skinning knife, piercing the bear's heart. With one powerful blow from the bear's huge paw, Katharine's neck snapped like a brittle branch. Then the monster bear fell dead on top of her.

It was about an hour later when Josh came roaring up in the truck. He saw Jim lying on the ground, but didn't see Katharine. *Maybe he's had a heart attack*, Josh thought as he went toward him. But when he got close enough to see Jim's mutilated body, he quickly lost the contents of his stomach. Recognizing a bear attack, Josh returned to the truck, got the double-barreled shotgun and loaded it with buckshot before grabbing the microphone for the pickup's radio. "Josh to Lodge," he said tersely into the radio.
"Lodge," Maria, the maid replied.
"Get Jeff! There's been a bear attack!"

"Have you found Mrs. Robinson?" Jeff asked as he examined Jim. Jeff had been a medic in World War I, but his skills and the emergency medical kit he had brought weren't needed - Jim was obviously dead from a crushed skull.
"No, but I haven't looked for her. I was afraid to leave the truck."

About that time, they heard one of the cubs whimpering and Jeff walked toward the sound. Then he saw the monster bear lying on the ground. As he approached it, his Winchester Model 54 .30-06 rifle ready, he saw Katharine's foot protruding from under the bear. He poked the bear's open eye with the muzzle of his rifle to be sure it was dead. "Over here, Josh. Grab the other front leg and let's try to pull the bear off of her. She may still be alive."

After trying to shift the bear's carcass for several minutes, Josh said, "This thing won't budge."

"I have a rope in my truck. Let's hook up the truck to the bear and pull it off."

"Okay."

When the bear was pulled off, it was obvious from Katharine's glazed open eyes that she was also dead.

"I'm going back to the lodge to call Glacier Emergency Services to transport the bodies. You stay here. Radio Ron and Ben to pick up your fisherman."

"Okay. What about the cubs? They'll starve to death without their mother."

"They'll stay near their mother for a few days. I'll arrange for someone from the Los Angeles Zoo to come and get them."

It was six-thirty the next morning at Dave and Harriett Robinson's house in Macon, Georgia when Ann's uncle Dave woke her up, "Ann, I have something to tell you," he began carefully.

"Huh, yeah?" Ann replied sleepily, rubbing her eyes as she sat up in bed.

"This is difficult to say. Ann, your moth..."

"Oh, for heaven's sakes, quit stalling," Harriett scolded as she barged into the guest room. "I told you we should have woke her up and told her last night." She then turned to Ann. "Both of your parents are dead. A bear ate them while they were fishing. So now you've been told."

"What? They're both dead?" Ann buried her head in the pillow and began to sob loudly.

"When you've finished blubbering, you can come and eat your breakfast, although it will be cold by then," Harriett said sharply.

Dave just stood and stared at his wife. He knew she could be callous, but this was not the time for it.

"Well, what are you staring at?" she snarled at Dave.

The most cold, heartless bitch I've ever seen, he thought. "You. You apologize to Ann for your mean, insensitive words, NOW!"

"Fine! I'm sorry, Ann," Harriett said, emphasizing the word *sorry* sarcastically.

"What's going on?" Blanche, Harriett and Dave's nine-year-old daughter asked from the doorway.

"Your mother just told Ann about her parents."

"Oh, that. What's for breakfast? I'm starved."

Like mother like daughter, Dave thought.

Dave Robinson, three years older than Jim, was his half-brother; they'd had different fathers. Dave was five feet nine inches tall and weighed 165 pounds. He was finely manicured, with a prosperous round face, dark brown hair, gray eyes and sincere thin lips. He had been an attorney at the same law firm for ten years now, four of those as a partner, with Steve Taylor, his father-in-law. Harriett constantly reminded Dave what a failure he'd be without her father's help.

Harriett's father, Steve Taylor, who had grown up on a corn and soybean farm in South Georgia, was a World War I veteran and recipient of the Purple Heart and Bronze Star. He had lost his left leg when a home-made bomb exploded too close while he was point man on a night mission. He'd almost died, but had miraculously recovered, and learned to walk with an artificial leg. Deeply religious, he believed that God had saved him for a purpose. After the war he'd enrolled in the University of Georgia and graduated with a degree in psychology with honors. Then it was on to Vanderbilt in Nashville, where he graduated magna cum laude from law school. Steve soon found his calling – in family law - more specifically, as a divorce lawyer. He was very good at it, and his firm quickly became the second biggest in Georgia. Steve was voted "Best Divorce Lawyer in Georgia" by the Georgia Bar Association twice.

Harriett was a large woman, five foot nine and 165 pounds. She had black hair that she usually wore pulled back into a bun, prominent cheek bones, a large nose, and always had a snarl on her face. She was also a heavy drinker, and when she was drunk, even meaner than she normally was. Their daughter, Blanche, was blonde with blue eyes, but that was all that differed between daughter and mother. She had Harriett's sour disposition, which as a nine-year-old, manifested itself in the numerous wicked pranks she played on her classmates. Harriett spoiled her daughter by getting her anything she wanted, and always fought with Dave in front of Blanche about disciplining her misbehavior. Blanche largely ignored her parents and did what she wanted, which frequently got her into trouble.

Harriett had found out she was pregnant a month after she and Dave were married, and Blanche was born seven months later. Dave had graduated from law school shortly after the wedding and they'd moved to Macon, Georgia, where he'd gone to work for his father-in-law. Steve suspected that Harriett had been pregnant before she and Dave got married but decided they couldn't have known, and thus had married for the right reasons. Dave didn't know that he wasn't Blanche's father. In fact, even Harriett didn't know who Blanche's father was. She just knew he was probably one of the members of the Alpha Tao fraternity - most likely one of the blond ones.

The remaining Robinson family consisted of Jim's sixty-eight-year-old mother, Arlene, his seventy-year-old father, Frank, and Arlene's older sister, Beatrice. Katharine's remaining family was her father, Bill, and her younger brother, Ron.

Harriett's family consisted of her parents, Steve, and his wife, Denise. Jim's funeral was to be held in Washington DC, at the Washington National Cathedral, while Katharine's would be held in Des Moines, Iowa, her and Jim's home town. Both would be buried at Jim's family's burial plot in Des Moines.

A few minutes before ten o'clock on the day of Jim's funeral, friends invited by the Robinson family to serve as honorary pallbearers arrived and took their positions at the cathedral entrance. The Robinson family reached the cathedral at the same time and was guided to where they needed to be for the arrival ceremony.

The hearse carrying Jim's body arrived at the chapel entrance shortly after ten. The pallbearers took their places at the rear of the hearse and the honor cordon presented arms. The pallbearers removed the casket from the hearse and as the hymn "God of Our Fathers" was played the procession moved into the cathedral. General Duncan led the procession. He was followed by the special honor guard, the national color detail, the minister, the pallbearers with the casket (which was soon placed on a movable bier just inside the cathedral), the personal flag bearer, the honorary pallbearers, the Robinson family, and then the other mourners.

As the last of the procession entered the cathedral, the Marine band stopped playing and the honor cordon ordered arms. Inside, the national color detail and personal flag bearer left the procession when they reached the doorway of the chapel; a national flag had already been posted in the chapel. The rest of the mourners entered the chapel and took positions around the casket, which the body bearers had placed on a catafalque. The first relief of the honor guard, one officer and four enlisted men, was posted and the pallbearers were dismissed. The Reverend Francis Pickering then conducted a prayer service followed by his funeral sermon. As part of the sermon, Reverend Pickering spoke of the many good things about Jim.

"As we all know, Jim Robinson was a brave soldier, a respected leader among his troops, and a war hero. In recognition of this bravery, he was awarded the Purple Heart, the Silver Star, and second only to the Congressional Medal of Honor, the Distinguished Service Cross. Jim was also highly respected among his coworkers and among his superiors. Jerry Biscoe, one of Jim's colleagues told me last night at the funeral home that Jim was always trying to help others and would often help a coworker solve a difficult problem but wanted no credit.

"Jim was also a family man, loved by his devoted wife, Katharine, now also deceased, and Ann, his daughter, with whom he spent lots of time with in spite of his busy schedule. The world will be a little worse place without Jim Robinson, and he will be missed by all who knew him. Now, let us pray." When the service was concluded, the family left the chapel, followed by the mourners.

Katharine's funeral was held on June 23 at the Methodist Church in Des Moines, the church where she had been baptized in 1915. At her funeral, her brother, Ron described three of her attributes: the love of words, the bonds of home and family, and the spirit of adventure. During his sermon, the minister recognized many of the good things Katharine had accomplished.

"She was not only a devoted and much loved wife, mother, daughter and sister, Katharine gave her time to her community. She established the friendly fellowship club for senior citizens where they could socialize and enjoy arts and crafts together; was president of the Woman's Club and the Garden Club; led the restoration of several historical landmarks; and was a Girl Scout leader. Like her husband, Jim, Katharine will be missed.

"Let us pray. Eternal God, we thank thee for your sovereign order, that those who are leaders in their community do so because you have ordained them for your purpose and plan. And we thank thee that thou hast promised to establish their thoughts as they commit their works unto thee. Omniscient Lord, thou knowest each Christian in detail, the circumstances from which each comes, the future unto which each goes, and the present condition of each. And you have a purpose and plan for each of us. Forgive us, gentle, gracious God, for our indifference, our rejection of your love, your care, your guidance. Awaken us to our need of thee, our poverty of spirit without thee, our blindness when we do not walk in thy light. We pray in His name who is the Light of the World. Amen. Please join me in observing a moment of silence in memory of Katharine Robinson."

Later, during the burial service for Jim and Katharine at the gravesite, the minister told everyone, "Jim and Katharine had God's love and courage to guide them until the very end. They fought the grizzly bear bravely, and together they ultimately killed it."

Harriett whispered loudly to one of her friends, "I don't know what's so brave about being stupid enough to get eaten by a bear. You'd think a 'brave soldier' would know better." A number of people heard her disrespectful remark, including Ann and Dave.

Ann was crying and seemingly ignored it, but Dave whispered a terse, "Shut up, Harriett."

Chapter Two

After the funeral, Ann went to live with her Grandmother and Grandfather Robinson. But due to their ages and failing health, it was meant to be only temporary. Both grandparents comforted Ann and were helpful and supportive while she mourned her parents' deaths. Then, about a month later, the family gathered at the office of Jim and Katharine's attorney, Randy Crews. "I have here Jim and Katharine's last will and testament," he began. "To my parents, Arlene and Frank, I bequeath our home in Bethesda…" The reading continued on and soon got to Ann. "To our daughter, Ann, we bequeath the proceeds of our life insurance policies. These funds are to contribute to the cost of her upbringing until she reaches the age of eighteen, and then to pay for her college education. It is our wish that Ann live with and be brought up by my brother, Dave, and his wife, Harriett."

Ann almost fainted. Harriett smiled and asked, "How much money do the life insurance policies pay?"

"Harriett, not now!" Dave scolded.

"That's okay, Mr. and Mrs. Robinson. The net proceeds come to fifty thousand dollars.[1] It is to be used as follows: two

---

[1] The same as $852,777 in 2014.

thousand three hundred and forty[2] a year for Ann's room and board, and fifteen dollars a month[3] for Ann's allowance from when she's twelve until she reaches eighteen. The balance of the insurance money, twenty-five thousand five hundred and twenty dollars[4] goes into an irrevocable interest-bearing trust that Ann will receive at age eighteen. She can use that for college expenses and to live on while she's enrolled."

"That's *all*?!" Harriett screeched.

Ann moved in with her uncle and aunt in Macon, Georgia one month later, on September 4, 1936, just before school started. The Robinson's red brick house sat on a quarter-acre lot in a neighborhood about a mile from Dave's office. The front door, graced by a small porch with white, wrought-iron chairs, opened into a formal living room that was almost never used. The most popular room in the house was the family room. It was spacious, with stained heart-pine walls, a hardwood floor, large fireplace, sofa, rocking chairs, and two La-Z-Boy reclining chairs. It also had a cathedral-shaped RCA Victor radio in an oak cabinet. At the other end of the house was Dave's home office, where he frequently prepared legal briefs, and went to get away from Harriett. The house had three bedrooms: a master with a bathroom, Blanche's bedroom and a guest room, both of which shared a bathroom. In the usually-deserted basement were a multi-blade reel push lawnmower, Dave's vegetable gardening tools, and a seldom-used shower and sink.

"This will be your room," Harriett explained as she showed Ann the newly arranged space in the attic where she'd moved a small bed, nightstand, and dresser left behind by the family that previously owned the house, no doubt because it had seen better days. Ann spotted a rat running along one of the rafters overhead.

---

[2] The same as $39,910 in 2014.
[3] The same as $257 in 2014.
[4] The same as $436,900 in 2014.

"What about the guest room where I usually stay when I'm here?" Ann asked.

"That's a *guest* room. If you were in there where would our guests stay?"

"I could stay in this space in the attic when you have guests," Ann suggested, knowing Uncle Dave and Aunt Harriett never had guests.

"But then your things would be in the guest room. Now this is your room and that's *final*!"

"Class, please join me in welcoming our new student, Ann Robinson," Ann's teacher, Mrs. Shuler, said on the first day of the 1936-37 school year.

"*Welcome Ann*," all twenty-eight students said in unison.

At recess, a girl in glasses with red hair tied in a pony-tail came up to Ann and asked," Are you Blanche Robinson's cousin?"

"I'm ashamed to admit it, but yes," Ann replied.

"So you don't like her either?"

"No, but her mother, my aunt, is even worse."

"Hi. I'm Cathy Rossi," the red haired girl said.

"It's good to meet you, Cathy."

A heavy-set girl with braces then ran up and asked, "Would you two like to play hide-and-seek with us?"

"Sure," Ann replied.

It was December 16, the day Ann was to play the Virgin Mary in the elementary school Christmas play. She'd gone to bed early to be sure she got plenty of sleep. Then a cold pasty substance and foul smell woke her up. The stench was overpowering. And what was this gooey stuff? She turned on the light, and saw that sardines and honey were all over her and in her bed.

"*Uugh*," she said as she shivered. She looked over at her alarm clock; it was 4:07 a.m. On the floor beside her bed were three empty sardine cans and a partially full jar of honey. She gathered up her bed linens and covers, got a change of clothes, and headed for the bathroom that Blanche shared with the guest room to take a shower. Ann was supposed to use the shower in the basement to bathe, but right now she didn't care. She'd use the shower next to Blanche's bedroom to get off this foul-smelling goo. Before taking a shower, though, she had a task to do.

She took the sardines and honey, crept silently into Blanche's bedroom, and hid them in her cousin's closet.

A few minutes later, upon hearing the shower, Blanche got out of bed, went to her parents' bedroom, and pounded on their bedroom door, shouting, "Mom, Ann's using the shower in my bathroom again."

"What!?" Harriett exclaimed as she came out of her bedroom, massaging her temples to try and easy her headache from getting drunk the night before. Her hair was in large curlers and there was a white paste all over her face.

"Ann's using my shower," Blanche repeated.

"At this hour? Well, we'll just see about that." Harriett tried the bathroom door, but it was locked. "Ann, come out here immediately," Harriett bellowed. There was no answer.

"What's going on?" a yawning Dave asked as he walked into the hallway in front of the bathroom where Ann was taking a shower.

"Ann's taking a shower in Blanche's bathroom," Harriett replied.

"Isn't that where she takes her showers?"

"No, she uses the shower in the basement," Blanche said as Harriett gave Dave a sharp look.

"She bathes in the basement? Why?" Dave asked.

"Well, I've asked her to. I don't want her messing up Blanche's bathroom," Harriett explained.

"Why not just ask her to clean it up? She already does most of the house cleaning around here."

"Well, I..."

"Never mind, Harriett. I want to see what you or Blanche did that made her take a shower so early."

"Why do you think one of us did something?" Harriett demanded.

"Because, Ann wouldn't be up before five a.m. taking a shower unless one of you did something to her." Dave then noticed Blanche was slowly creeping toward her bedroom.

"Come back here, Blanche," he commanded.

Just then Ann came out of the bathroom wrapped in a towel.

"I thought I told..." Harriett began.

"Shut up Harriett," Dave scolded. "Ann, why are you up and taking a shower at this hour?"

"Because someone put sardines and honey all over me and in my bed last night," Ann answered.

"Why I've never heard of something so preposterous," Harriett said with a start.

"Well, here are my bed linens to prove it," Ann said, handing the odorous sheets to Dave.

"Okay, who did this?" Dave asked.

"I think Ann did it, to try and blame me," Blanche replied.

"Do you think I'm stupid enough to believe she'd put honey and sardines all over herself and in her bed just to blame you?"

"Why don't we check both of their rooms?" Harriett suggested. "We might find the evidence of who did it in one of them."

"For once, you've had a good idea, Harriett. We'll start with Blanche's room, Dave announced." When he looked in Blanche's closet, there were the sardine cans and honey.

"Blanche!"

"Ann must have put them in there," Blanche stammered. "I left them in her..."

"Shut up, Blanche!" Harriett shouted.

"Okay, that's enough for me," Dave said. "Blanche, you're grounded for a month. Nothing but school, meals and then into your room. Ann, you move into the guest room. It's about time that room was used."

Blanche fell on her bed crying.

"Dave, I won't stand for such unfair punishment to our daughter."

"Shut up Harriett, or I'll make you move into the attic," Dave threatened.

June 20, 1941. Five years later.

Ann is thirteen and Blanche is fourteen and the family is at Miami Beach on vacation.

"Blanche, your father and I are going out to dinner and then to see the play, *"The Corn is Green,"* Harriett told her daughter as she got ready. "You and Ann stay here in our suite. You've got the radio and plenty of books to read, so you shouldn't be bored."

"Order your dinner from room service," Dave told the girls. "We should be back by ten thirty or eleven. Then tomorrow we're going offshore fishing on the boat I chartered."

"Okay, Daddy. You and Mom have a good time," Blanche replied sweetly.

"Yeah, enjoy yourselves," Ann called after them as they were leaving.

"What do you want for dinner, Ann?" Blanche asked after her parents were gone as she handed Ann the room service menu.

"Let's see, this chicken breast sandwich with potato salad looks good. I'll have that and a Coke."

At seven Blanche picked up the telephone receiver and dialed a number printed on the phone. "Is this room service?"

"Yes it is," the female voice on the phone replied. "Did you want to order something?"

"Yes, I do. I'll have the chicken breast sandwich with potato salad and a Coke." Then Blanche added, "And my mom will have the clam chowder, baked potato, steamed Maine lobster, and a bottle of white wine."

"Blanche, you can't have something that expensive," Ann protested. "And you aren't allowed to drink wine."

"Our house white wine is Gallo Chablis. But we also have a good selection of varietals," the woman said.

"My mother says the house Chablis will be fine," Blanche said, continuing her lie and ignoring Ann, who was shaking her head no.

"Fine, miss. It should be delivered in about thirty minutes."

"You aren't allowed to drink wine because you're underage," Ann repeated.

"Why do you think I told room service it was for Mom?"

"Yeah, but what will she and Uncle Dave say when they get home tonight?"

"Let me worry about that."

"Okay, okay."

Their food arrived at seven forty. After the waiter had left, Blanche asked, "Want some wine, Ann?"

"No thanks."

"Fine, that leaves more for me."

"You're not going to drink that whole bottle are you?"

"I don't know yet," Blanche replied with a smile. She then ate every bite of her lobster dinner and drank most of the wine. Then she called room service again. "Could you harrve som someone come to ro.. room 613 and take our tray from din... dinnerner? It will be sitting outside our do... door."

"Yes, ma'am," the woman on the other end replied.

A few minutes later, Blanche went to the restroom. When she did, Ann quietly called room service. "Please cancel our earlier request to pick up our tray. I still haven't finished eating."

"Okay, just call us when you want it removed," said the room service hostess.

About two hours later, Dave and Harriett returned. When they were outside the door Dave asked, "Whose lobster dinner and bottle of wine is that?"

"I don't know. Maybe the room next door," Harriett replied.

"That room is vacant and so is the one on the other side of us. I think the girls had a party and got drunk."

They entered the suite with Dave carrying the food tray and wine. Ann was reading a novel while Blanche was snoring away. "Okay, the scam's up. Who ordered the expensive dinner and drank the wine?" Dave asked.

"Ask Blanche," Ann suggested.

"Blanche, dear, wake up," Harriett said as she shook her.

"Oh, hi Mom, Dad. How was the play?" a sleepy, hung-over Blanche asked.

"Never mind the play. Whose lobster dinner and wine is that?" Dave asked.

"What are you talking about?"

"This!" Dave replied as he showed her the tray and wine.

"That's Ann's," Blanche said defensively.

"No it's not. I had a chicken sandwich, potato salad, and a Coke."

"She's lying!" Blanche screeched.

"Well, one of you is and it's easy to find out who it is. Ann, let me smell your breath," Dave requested.

"Sure," Ann said. She then let out a short breath as Dave sniffed at it.

"No alcohol there. Okay, Blanche, your turn."

"Dave Robinson, I can't believe you don't trust your own daughter," Harriett said.

"Not when she lies to me so much."

"Okay, okay. I ate the lobster and drank the wine," Blanche confessed. "What's wrong with that? You two went out and had fun, so we should be allowed to have some too."

"Not by drinking alcohol and ordering expensive dinners at age fourteen," Dave replied. "Tomorrow, Blanche, you will not be allowed to go fishing with us. You will stay in this room. And I will order your meals and beverages, and tell room service not to bring you anything else."

"I *hate you!*" Blanche yelled as she ran into the bedroom she shared with Ann and slammed the door.

"Dave, if Blanche can't go fishing, then Ann shouldn't be allowed to go either," Harriett demanded.

"Why? Ann didn't do anything wrong."

"You're always against Blanche."

"Shut up, Harriett, or I'll cancel the rest of the vacation and we'll go home."

It was Wednesday, May 19, 1943 and Blanche's sixteenth birthday. Harriett and June, one of Harriett's friends, were in the living room drinking tea. "I can't wait until Blanche gets home from school and sees the red Alfa Romeo convertible we're giving her for her sixteenth birthday," Harriett said.

"You're getting her an Italian sports car? Isn't that a bit lavish for a first car?"

"She deserves it. She's a wonderful daughter."

Blanche and Ann got home at three thirty, and Blanche asked, "Mom, whose cool car is that outside?"

"It's yours! Happy birthday, Blanche!"

"It's mine!? Neat!"

"Here are the keys. Have fun!"

I give her a week before she wrecks it, Ann thought.

"Isn't Blanche going to come to her birthday dinner?" Dave asked at seven as he was sitting down to roast prime rib, scalloped potatoes, a green bean casserole and freshly baked biscuits that Ann had prepared. A birthday cake that Harriett had baked was on the counter.

"Now Dave, she just got her new sports car and she's out having fun with her friends."

"Why didn't you wait to give it to her until after her birthday dinner? That way, we could have all been able to be part of her big day."

"Because she would have seen the car outside when she came home from school."

"Not if I drove it to work."

"What would the other partners say when you came to work in a red Alfa Romeo?"

"When I told them it was for Blanche's sixteenth birthday, probably that she was spoiled, which she is."

"Dave, you just never..." The ring of the phone interrupted their conversation.

"Are you Dave Robinson?" a stern voice asked on the other end of the line after Dave answered.

"Yes."

"This is Officer Smallwood. We have your daughter, Blanche, and two other teenagers in jail."

"Why?"

"Blanche wrecked her car and was driving drunk. The two boys in the car were drinking, too. Blanche didn't have her blouse or bra on."

"Are she and the others okay?" Dave asked.

"Yeah, just shook up. But the car has too much damage to be driven. I suggest you come and get Blanche. I'll call the parents of the boys so they can come and get them."

"Thanks, officer."

"Officer? What was that call about?" Harriett asked. "Our wonderful, deserving daughter was just caught driving drunk and topless with a couple of boys. She wrecked her new car."

"I can't believe that."

"I doubt that Officer Smallwood lied to me just now."

"What were you thinking, Blanche?" Harriett asked sympathetically when they got home.

"You and Dad just never want me to have any fun at all, do you?"

"No, we just want you to learn to be responsible," Dave offered.

"Well, I'm sure she's learned her lesson. Everybody makes at least one mistake," Harriett observed.

"Yeah, but all Blanche does is make mistakes. But that's okay. I'm going to fix the car and give it to Ann on her sixteenth birthday," Dave announced. "I'm getting an old, rusty pick-up truck that won't go more than forty-five miles per hour for Blanche to drive."

"I'm going to get the Alfa Romeo for my sixteenth birthday?" Ann asked excitedly.

"Yep."

"You can't be serious!" Harriett replied.

"Well, I am," Dave affirmed.

"Fine, then you'll sleep in your home office from now on."

"Promise?"

"Hummmph!" Harriett grunted and left the room.

"Gee thanks, Uncle Dave!"

"You more than deserve it, Ann."

Within a week of getting the 1935 Ford pickup, Blanche wrecked it while driving drunk with three boys in the truck. Nobody was hurt, but Dave said that Harriett had to drive Blanche around until she went off to college.

Chapter Three

At school one day, Eric Carver, a senior, stepped between Ann and her friends and leaned against the lockers, blocking their way. Ann glanced up, startled. A shy smile lit her face. He was tall, over six feet, and lean, with a muscular, athletic look about him. He had thick, curly blond hair, an infectious smile, pronounced cheek bones and an engaging set of crystal-blue eyes that had caused female hearts to flutter from seventh grade onward.

Ann's cheeks blushed pink and Eric felt himself tighten with sexual need. He liked that he could unsettle her. Normally her creamy complexion and trim features made her seem aloof. But Ann had grown into a beautiful young woman. She was taller than most of the other girls at school and somehow seemed emotionally stronger, even with her shyness. Ann's hair was jet-black and flowed over her shoulders, her face soft, with the angles and shadows of a model. Her lips were full and generous, and her eyes always seemed to dance with excitement. Most males who met her for the first time realized that she was one of the most beautiful women they'd ever seen. Modeling companies were already coming around and inquiring whether she'd do a photo shoot, but she'd told them she wasn't interested.

"Will you go with me to the movies on Friday?" Eric asked. Her wide-set eyes were deep chocolate brown and when she turned them on him, he knew he had to have her. She twitched her full lips like a tease and he wanted to kiss her.

"Yes," she said. "I'll go with you."

When he'd left, Gloria said, "Eric Carver just asked you out! I'd die for a date with him!"

"So would all the girls in school," Jean observed. "What's your secret, Ann? Other than being gorgeous?"

"I don't know."

"No, no, no! I won't have Ann going out with some football jock. They all just have one thing on their mind," Harriett said when Ann told her aunt and uncle she was going on a date with Eric.

"Eric's not like that. He's captain of the football team, president of the student body, and has excellent grades. All the major universities are approaching him with football scholarships. He'll probably have his pick of where he wants to go."

"Harriett, I know Eric's father. I met him at our club. He played golf with us once and I think he's a decent man."

"No!" Harriett insisted.

"Fine, then Blanche has to stop dating also," Dave countered.

"What? That's not fair. She's older and wiser than Ann."

"Blanche is one year older. And how is a C average and constantly in trouble with the school wiser than Ann's A average and her being president of most of the school's student organizations?" Ann was president of the Future Business Leaders of America, their school's chapter of the National Honor Society, the debate team, was head cheerleader, and on the student council.

"You've just never understood Blanche."

Yes I have. She's a lazy manipulative bitch like you, Dave thought.

Blanche had long straight blonde hair and dull blue eyes. Her face was heart-shaped, with a wide forehead and a widow's peak, small narrowly-spaced eyes that always looked nervous, a thin nose, and a narrow jaw with a pointed chin. Her eyebrows were darker than her hair and more straight than arched. She was now five foot five and weighed about 120 pounds. Her fingernails were stubby because of her nervous habit of biting them. She was popular with the boys at her school, but only because she slept with most of them.

"Don't you ever wonder why Blanche never dates the same boy twice and sometimes two or three come by together to take her out?"

"She's just dating a lot of people to be sure she chooses the right husband."

No, she's the school whore, thought Ann.

"Well, what is it? Does Ann get to go out with Eric, or is Blanche also prohibited from dating?" Dave asked again.

"Okay, Ann can go," Harriett relented. "But I want her home by nine."

"The movie doesn't start until eight," Ann said.

"Home by eleven," Dave replied.

It was six p.m. on Friday and Eric was at the front door of the Robinson's house, ringing the doorbell. "Hi Eric," Dave said as he opened the door. "Come in, Ann's expecting you."

"Thank you, sir."

"Hi, Eric," Ann said as she walked in dressed in a black skirt and white blouse, wearing tennis shoes, and her hair pulled back into a pony-tail.

"Mr. Robinson, we're going to dinner at Morrison's cafeteria, then going to see *Double Indemnity*. We should be back before eleven."

"I hear that's a good movie, but I haven't seen it," Dave offered.

"It stars Fred MacMurray and Barbara Stanwyck," Ann added.

"Have a good time," Dave said as Eric and Ann walked out the front door.

"Oh, I like your car," Ann observed as Eric opened the door to his green Porsche so she could get in. "I think convertibles are really neat. I have an Alfa Romeo."

"It was a sixteenth birthday present from my grandfather," Eric explained.

"So tell me about yourself," Eric said after he and Ann had gotten their food at the restaurant.

"My parents were both killed by a grizzly bear while they were on a fishing trip when I was eight."

"That's horrible!"

"Yeah, I still miss them. They were great parents. Now I live with my Uncle Dave and Aunt Harriett, I make good grades, and I enjoy being in various clubs."

"Yeah, I guess. President of every major club at our school."

"What about you? Tell me about yourself."

"My dad, George, is an accountant and my mom's a housewife. I have a little sister, Gloria. I've always enjoyed sports and I've just accepted an athletic scholarship to Notre Dame. I want to major in accounting like my dad."

"Congratulations! Notre Dame's a great school."

They enjoyed the movie, and as promised were back at the Robinson's home by eleven. "I really had a good time tonight," Eric said. Then he tilted up Ann's chin and gave her a tender kiss. "I'll call you," he said as he left.

"Well, what was the date with Mr. wonderful like?" Blanche asked after Ann came inside the house.

"It was fun. He's interesting. Not the kind of boy who'd want to be in a back seat with you, Blanche."

We'll just see about that, Blanche thought.

The next Wednesday, Harriett called out to Ann after answering the phone. "It's that that Eric boy."

"Hi, Eric."

"Ann, would you like to go see our basketball team play on Friday night?"

"Sure."

"Good. I'll pick you up at six. We'll get a burger and go to the game."

After the game they walked back to Eric's car. As he opened the door for her, she said, "Tonight was fun."

"I think so too," Eric replied after he got in on the driver's side. His broad shoulders seemed to fill the small sports car. She was so close. Close enough to touch the muscled forearm or the strong hand that gripped the gear shift. And she wanted to do just that. For the first time, she knew real desire. Oh, she'd been thrilled by flirtations before, even titillated by chaste kisses, but sitting here in the warm car with Eric, after the adrenaline rush of the basketball game, she wanted more.

He inserted the key into the ignition but didn't start the engine. Could he feel the desire coming off of her like waves of heat? He turned and pulled her to him. The gear shift dug painfully into Ann's side, but she didn't care. Eric's lips slid over hers with a ferocity that buoyed her girlish lust into full-blown passion. His kiss was demanding, and Ann responded. She was lost in the white-hot sensations drumming through her from his touch, his lips, and the sound of her pulse racing in her ears.

Laughing voices broke up the moment as a group of students found their car nearby. Eric leaned away, still holding her shoulders in his grip.

"I've wanted to do that since I first asked you out," he said.

"Me too." Ann didn't trust her voice to explain more. She knew Eric wanted to have sex with her. And, if not her, he could have his pick of any girl. But he had chosen her.

He started the engine, put the Porsche into gear and roared out of the parking lot.

Later, on the steps of her aunt and uncle's house, Ann's shyness returned.

"It's chilly tonight," she said, rubbing her arms. But Eric wasn't ready to retreat to polite small talk.

"God, you're beautiful." His finger traced a line from her ear across her cheek, to her lips. Ann kissed Eric's finger and his mouth followed. His lips were gentler this time. His tongue flitted against her teeth, as if asking permission to enter. She opened her mouth to him. He pulled her against his hard chest and she surrendered to the need to touch him. She ran her hands across the breadth of his shoulders and into his thick, blond hair. Their kiss deepened. He explored her mouth with a sweet, searching tongue. The new well of passion inside her was both frightening and exhilarating. She felt the need to press every inch of her body against his - to feel his skin on hers. But before she completely lost herself to this lure, she pulled away.

For a long, penetrating minute, Eric stared into her eyes. They'd opened a door, and soon she'd have to decide if she wanted to go through it.

"Well, then," she said, "I guess that's goodnight."

He leaned in for one more lingering kiss.

"WHA WHAT'S GO, GOING ON OUT HE HEEREE?" Harriett screeched drunkenly as she turned on the bright porch light and strode out through the front doorway.

"I'm giving Ann a good night kiss," Eric explained.

"I kno knoww what you want to gi give her. All you bo boys are alike. You only want one thing from a gi girl. Well, fro from now on, Ann's off li limits to you," she said drunkenly. "Now ge get out of heeree."

"Bye, Ann," Eric said sadly as he left.

THE WINE QUEEN

Ann slammed the door with Harriett still outside, and locked it, then ran to her room and fell onto her bed sobbing.

"Did Mr. Wonderful break your heart?" Blanche asked cynically as she opened the door and came into Ann's room.

"Leave me alone."

"Whatever you say *miss broken heart*," Blanche replied cynically as she left the room.

Meanwhile, Harriett was ringing the doorbell. Finally, Dave, who'd been working on a legal brief in his study, answered it.

"Harriett? What are you doing out here?"

"That little bi bitch locked me outt."

"Harriett, you're drunk again. Blanche locked you out?"

"No, A Ann did. And I I'm not dr drunk. Just feeling go good."

"You're drunk, Harriett. Now why would Ann do that?"

"Because I ca caught her and that Eric having se sex."

"Where?"

"Out he heere!"

"On the front porch? Harriett, you're not only drunk, you're delusional. I want to hear Ann's side of this story."

Dave went to Ann's room, walked to the door, and knocked lightly. "Ann? It's Uncle Dave."

"Go away!" Ann sobbed.

"I just want to talk. To find out what happened."

"Okay," she replied, her face stained with tears.

Dave came into the room as Ann got a tissue and dried her eyes. Then she began to nervously twist the tissue in her hands.

"What happened?"

"Aunt Harriett's drunk again. She saw Eric kissing me good night and came out and shouted at us. Then she made him leave and told him he couldn't see me again. Oh, Uncle Dave. It was so embarrassing, I just want to *die*!" Ann shouted. Then she began crying again.

"There, there. It will be okay," Dave comforted. "Don't worry. I'll speak to Harriett and make her apologize to Eric."

The next morning when she was sober, Dave confronted his wife. "Harriett, you will apologize to Eric when he comes to dinner tomorrow night. That is, if he'll still speak to us after what you did."

"You're having that *boy* over to dinner?" Harriett said, massaging her temples to ease the headache from her hangover.

"That *boy* has one of the highest grade point averages in the senior class and is headed to Notre Dame on a football scholarship."

"Fine," Harriett relented. "But I'm not cooking."

"Good, I wouldn't want to make him sick. Ann can cook like she does most of the time."

Dave then phoned Eric. "Eric, its Dave Robinson, Ann's uncle," he said when Eric answered the call.

"Hey Mr. Robinson. I'm sor..."

"I wanted to invite you over for dinner tomorrow night. My wife wants to apologize for her behavior earlier."

"That's not necessary, Mr. Robinson."

"No, we insist."

"Okay," Eric agreed

Dinner the next night went smoothly, and Harriett apologized. Eric and Ann began seeing each other regularly after that.

On Thursday, Eric came up to Ann at the school cafeteria and asked, "So, *Uncertain Glory* is playing at the Fox drive-in. Would you like to go Saturday night?"

"Isn't Errol Flynn in that movie?"

"Yeah, he plays the main character."

"Sure, I'd like to go."

"Good, I'll be by to get you at six. We can get a burger and a Coke before we go."

The movie had been running for about half an hour when Eric said, "Come here," and pulled her closer to him. Looking into her eyes, Eric lost control and took her in his arms, their lips meeting in a passionate kiss that went through him like a lightning strike. Her lips were so lush and delicate, searching his with determination. "Ann, I think I'm in love with you," Eric blurted. Then he slid his hand under her bra.

"Eric, I told you, sex is off limits," she said, pulling his hand out of her blouse.

"But why, Ann? I've got a condom, so you won't get pregnant."

"That's no guarantee, and besides, I'm not ready for sex yet."

"Do you know how many girls would be willing to have sex with me if I took them out?"

"I don't care. I'm not one of them."

"I'm ready to go home, then."

"I tell you what. You can feel me up, but that's all."

"Okay!"

Eric then slipped his hand inside her bra. As his fingers began to massage her supple breast, the gasp she made echoed in his head. He continued to caress gently, feeling her fingers dig into the muscles of his shoulders as desire shot through him. Then her hand slid down to his groin and she began to massage.

Suddenly he was moaning as intense surges of ecstasy washed through him.

"Eric. Are you okay?"

"Yeah. I just came in my pants. I'll be right back," he told her as he headed to the rest room.

The high school prom was three weeks away and Eric had asked Ann to go. Blanche was going with Josh, a senior who mostly hung out with a gang of boys who smoked and spent most of their free time at the pool hall downtown. Harriett had spent lavishly on Blanche's prom dress, which was a different one than she'd worn the year before. With the help of her home economics teacher, Ann had made hers. The local newspaper had gotten wind of the fact that Ann was making her prom dress and did a story on it, featuring the gorgeous teenager in the dress on the front page of the Sunday social section the week before the prom. After that Ann was again bombarded by calls from agents interested in getting her to model professionally, which she still refused to pursue.

"She's always so lucky," a jealous Blanche told her mother at dinner one night. Ann was absent, as she was at an honor society meeting at school.

"Don't worry, you have a better dress than Ann does," Harriett said reassuringly.

"Then why didn't they put me in the newspaper?"

Because you didn't make your dress like Ann did, Dave thought. *You're plain looking and your dress makes you look cheap.*

Finally the night of the prom arrived. Three boys came by to get Blanche at six thirty, two of whom were dressed in jeans and T-shirts. Josh had on a green suit, but was wearing tennis shoes. At seven the doorbell rang again and Dave answered it. "Hey, Mr. Robinson," Eric said as he switched the plastic container holding Ann's corsage to his left hand so he could shake hands.

"Come in, Eric. Ann, Eric's here," Dave shouted from the base of the stairs.

A few minutes later, Ann came down the stairs and Eric almost fell off the couch. He couldn't believe that this beautiful creature was the girl he'd been dating. He'd seen her picture with the dress in the newspaper, but she looked so much better in person. Her dress was a floor-length lime charmeuse-a-line with a deep V-neck and a crisscrossing back, detailed with a kick train, rhinestones, and glass and seed beads with sequins.

"You look incredible," Eric said as he handed her the corsage, amazed he could find his voice.

"Thank you Eric," Ann replied as she pinned on the corsage.

THE WINE QUEEN

"We should be home around midnight," Eric told her uncle as they left. Since the incident at the drive-in, Ann had been thinking a lot about having sex with Eric, but it still didn't feel right. However, she was still aware there was no shortage of girls who would gladly have sex with him. She really liked Eric a lot, and maybe in time that would turn to love. She was even thinking about applying to Notre Dame so they could stay together.

They arrived at the prom just before seven thirty. The school's gymnasium had been decorated in blue, white and pink, and bouquets of flowers were generously displayed throughout. There were tables for four set up, a band was playing on the stage, and couples were dancing.

"Well, look who just arrived. Cinderella and Prince Charming," Blanche said cynically as she walked up to them.

"Hey, Ann," Cathy Rossi, still Ann's best friend, said, cutting off Blanche. "Wilford and I are over there. Why don't you and Eric join us?" Wilford was one of Eric's friends and also on the football team.

"Okay. Eric, let's sit with Wilford and Cathy."

"I'll be there in a minute," Eric said, as Blanche stopped him to whisper in his ear.

"If you want to have sex with me tonight, meet me outside the ladies' room at nine," she said.

"What was that about?" Ann asked.

"What?"

"Whatever Blanche whispered that made you smile."

"She told me a dirty joke."

"That sounds like my cousin."

"Tell us the joke," Wilford suggested.

"I'd rather dance with Ann," Eric said. They'd never danced before, and Ann was looking forward to it.

On the dance floor Eric's warm hands found the bare skin of Ann's back. The music was slow and pulsing. He pulled her close. With every move of his athletic body, Ann's senses flared.

She felt like a beacon of heat. Even her full-length gown couldn't hide the way her body was responding to Eric. She was certain that everyone knew, that everyone could see how aroused she was. "You're the most beautiful, desirable woman here," Eric whispered in her ear. The heat of his breath sent a shiver down her neck and into her stomach. He leaned his head against hers and they looked at each other in that secret, longing way that only young lovers have. His hips shifted left and right. His powerful thigh brushed up against hers with every beat of the music. She stared into his beautiful blue eyes, thrilled to find her desire reflected there. Maybe sex tonight wouldn't be such a bad idea.

"Let's get pictures," Ann suggested when she and Eric returned to the table, handing Cathy the camera she'd brought.

"Okay," Cathy agreed and she took Eric and Ann's picture. Then Ann took one of Wilford and Cathy.

"I'll send it to you when I have them developed," Ann told her friend.

The table cloths were red and black, the school's colors. The meal was served buffet-style. Ann and Cathy had the baked chicken, and Eric and Wilford the roast beef.

"Looking forward to Notre Dame?" Wilford asked Eric before stuffing a fork full of potatoes in his mouth.

"Yeah," Eric replied. "But it will be difficult to start as a freshman again, both in school and on the team."

"Where are you going to school, Wilford?" Ann asked, cutting a bite-sized piece of chicken breast and sliding it into her mouth.

"The University of Georgia. Go Bulldogs."

"Ann, I've been meaning to tell you. In June, our family is moving to Napa, California," Cathy said. "My senior year will be at Napa High."

"Why are you moving?" asked Ann.

"Dad and Mom are going to start a winery. Dad learned winemaking as a young man in Italy, and has always dreamed of owning a winery."

"I'll miss you, but maybe I can visit sometime," Ann suggested.

"That would be great," Cathy replied.

After they'd eaten, Ann and Eric had their picture taken by the official photographer. Then when Wilford headed to the restroom, Eric followed. Once they were inside, Eric asked, "Would you do me a favor?"

"Sure. What?"

"Ask Ann to dance at nine."

"Okay. Why?"

"Because I'm sneaking away with Blanche."

"Blanche Robinson? Going to get some, huh?"

"Yeah. My first."

"Well, she's a good place to start. Man, she's like a wildcat."

"Is it any good?"

"Hey, man, there's only two kinds – good and better."

Per his and Eric's plan, just before nine Wilford asked, "Ann, would you like to dance?"

"Okay."

"Guess that means you and I will dance, Eric," Cathy remarked.

"First, I need to go to the rest room." Eric stood up and walked away. Blanche was waiting for him near the gymnasium's door, and they left in Eric's car.

"Where to, Blanche? Miller's Pond?" Eric asked as he and Blanche drove away from the prom.

"First, to The Burger Hut for a soda, then to my house." She replied.

"Your house?"

"Yeah, my parents are gone, so we'll have the house all to ourselves."

"What if Ann comes home since I'm not at the prom anymore?"

"I fixed it with my friend, Joan. She'll take her out with some friends for a milk shake." It was all a lie, as Blanche knew that Joan would bring Ann back home so she'd see Blanche having sex with Eric.

"Okay," Eric agreed reluctantly.

"Where's Eric?" Ann asked later when she and Wilford returned from their dance.

"I haven't seen him since he went to the bathroom," Cathy replied.

"Wilford would you go check on him?" Ann asked, worried. "He may be sick."

"Okay." Wilford went to the restroom, but he knew where Eric was. He returned to the table after a few minutes.

"I ran into Charlie and he said he saw Eric leaving with Blanche," he reported, covering up his part in Eric's disappearance.

"Blanche!? Why, that bitch!" Ann screamed.

"Ann, let us take you home," Cathy offered sympathetically.

"Thanks, but I don't want to ruin your evening. I'll ask my Uncle Dave to come get me. He's at his office getting ready for court on Monday," Ann replied as she headed to call her uncle.

As Ann waited on her uncle, she thought sadly about her relationship with Eric. *Oh, well, it's good this happened now and not after I fell in love with him.* But her sadness then turned to anger as she thought, *I bet Blanche took him to our house since Uncle Dave and Aunt Harriett aren't there.* Then she realized, *Great. Now maybe Uncle Dave can catch her in the act.*

"Where's Ann?" Joan asked as she walked up to their table. Joan, one of Blanche's friends, knew about her plan to have sex with Eric.

"She left with her uncle," Cathy replied

"Her uncle?"

"Yeah."

THE WINE QUEEN

About fifteen minutes later, Joan tried calling Blanche at her parent's house to warn her, but nobody answered the phone.

Meanwhile, Dave had arrived to pick up Ann. "What happened to Eric?" he asked as he and Ann walked to the car.

"One of his friends said he was sick and had to leave," Ann replied.

When they were inside her house, Blanche answered Eric's unspoken question. "On the sofa."

"The sofa? Why not in your room?"

"Because I want to do it on the sofa." She then continued thinking, *so Ann will walk in on us when Joan brings her here.*

Then the phone rang. "Aren't you going to answer the phone?" Eric asked.

"Do you want me to answer the phone, or do this?" she replied, also thinking, *it's probably Ann calling to see if my dad's home.*

"Let's do *this*!" Eric answered. At this point, he would have done almost anything she wanted. His fingers fumbled with the strap of her dress and she slid out of it. He gasped at the sight of her in her bra and panties. His hands shook and his breath became ragged as he unhooked Blanche's bra and her small breasts jiggled out. He then slid down her panties so she could step out of them. Her sexiness gripped Eric like a powerful drug that he craved.

"Now it's my turn," she said with a sly grin, like a cat that had just cornered a mouse. She then placed his hand between her thighs, and as he messaged her, he began to tremble. Blanche took off his jacket and loosened his bow tie, then teased open the top button of his shirt and slid her fingers against his warm skin. Eric shivered with excitement. *This is going to be fun*, she thought. He was close to losing control completely. Blanche enjoyed this power she now held over such a strong, masculine boy.

"You can wait," she said, sensing he was about to turn the tables. "It's still my turn."

Eric's belt came off next. Then she unzipped his pants and slipped her hands down and around his hips to grasp his hard buttocks. The pants and belt clattered to the floor. She licked his smooth chest and bit. Hard. Eric groaned and buried his face in her hair, pulling her closer.

"Wait," she giggled. "These come off first." She snapped the elastic of his boxer shorts, his erection straining against them. Eric shrugged them off. For a long heated moment they stared at each other drinking in their nakedness. Blanche licked a finger and traced it along the downy trail leading down from his navel. Eric groaned again and crushed her in his arms. His lips closed on hers in a bruising kiss.

Oh yes, this was going to be fun, she thought again.

Eric climbed on top of Blanche, and as he began, he exploded into waves of pleasure. "Damn!" Blanche said, disappointed that it was over so soon after it began.

Then the front door opened and Dave shouted, "What in the hell is this?"

"Eric!!" Ann shrieked. Eric jumped up and ran out the back door, trying to dress all the while and never saying a word. They soon heard his car start and the tires squeal as Eric drove away hurriedly.

"Blanche, I'm disgusted with you," Dave said once Eric was gone.

"This was my first time, Daddy. Honest," she pleaded with him as she dressed.

"Yeah, right. She's the school whore, Uncle Dave," Ann declared.

"Ann's lying. She's just jealous because she caught me with Eric. This was my first time."

"If that's true, why are you always going out with so many boys at once?" her father asked.

40

"We're just friends."

"Blanche. I'm not an idiot. I was young and in high school once and I remember the type of girls who went out with several boys at once."

"Fine. You never believe anything I say anyway."

"That's because you hardly ever tell the truth."

Just then Harriett came home. "What's everybody doing home?" she asked.

Chapter Four

It was Ann's senior year in high school. Blanche was already a freshman at Heritage Christian University in Florence, Alabama, a town of about fifteen thousand. Heritage Christian was Dave's idea. He thought that going there might strengthen Blanche's character and improve her morals, but so far, Blanche had focused on only three things: sleeping with most of the male students, getting drunk, and skipping classes.

Dave effectively handled the divorce of a somewhat famous athlete with the Atlanta Chargers football team, and the high profile divorce was covered by all the major newspapers. Word spread of Dave's ability to help minimize the pain and loss for both parties in a divorce, and to negotiate settlements that were fair to both sides. Dave was soon bringing additional business to Taylor, Robinson and Crane from all over the state, and his income tripled. Harriett demanded that they build a new custom-designed house, which Dave did in Oak Brook, a new upscale gated community in the suburbs of Macon. Harriett became even more high-and-mighty than before, and she started smoking, a habit she picked up from the new friends she'd met at the country club they had recently joined. She'd spent the previous summer vacationing in Europe with her new-found friends.

Ann had a summer job at Jonas and Morris, an accounting firm in Macon. Her boss was Loretta Bailey, who was, at thirty-two, the youngest female partner in the firm. She and Ann had hit it off from the start and soon became friends. Ann had a plan and Loretta fit it perfectly. Ann had noticed Loretta accepting a date with a man who looked old enough to be Loretta's father, about average height, balding, and slightly overweight. Ann had inquired and the man wasn't wealthy or highly successful. Just average, and divorced. Loretta was single, about five foot eight and 125 pounds, with red hair and inquisitive green eyes. Her figure made her look good in anything she wore, and when she entered a room, the male heads always turned in her direction.

Ann and Loretta were just finishing lunch one Friday in August when Loretta lit a cigarette and asked, "What type of guy are you attracted to, Ann?"

"I'm still not sure. But I know he should be smart, ambitious, romantic, and interested in having a family. And if he's dating only one woman, he should be faithful to that relationship. I was dating Eric Carver, who is now at Notre Dame on a football scholarship, but that's over."

"What happened?"

"Let's just say we had two different versions of what being faithful in a relationship means. What about you? What type of men are you interested in?"

"When I first went off to college, it was the jocks. You know, the athletes. But I soon got tired of listening to them brag about themselves and having to compete with other women for their attention. Then it was the intellectual type. But I got bored with their constant talk about technical things like osmotic pressure, light-wave theory, the life cycles of celery leaf minor, mating habits of root weevils, and so on. Then it was the over achievers. But they're so focused on working sixteen hours a day, that they don't have the time for a serious relationship.

"Now I think I'd like to find an older man who has achieved most of his goals. Who's kind, respects women, treats them as equals, and has already been married and raised a family. That way, he's already an experienced husband and father. He will know how lucky he is to find someone who treats him well. If you're better looking than the women he's had or could have relationships with, he'll treat you like a queen and go out of his way to make you happy. He'll never be unfaithful since he can't find anyone who will be with him that's as young and good-looking as you. My mother did that. She married my father, the finest man I have ever known," Loretta said as she crushed out her cigarette.

"I think I know just the man for you," Ann said.

"Who?"

"My uncle Dave."

"Isn't he married?"

"Yeah, but he's on the verge of getting a divorce."

"Why?"

"Because my aunt is an evil, manipulative bitch." Ann then spent the next half hour telling Loretta about Harriett. Then she said, "I'll tell you what. Let me arrange for you to meet my Uncle Dave, and you can see if you're attracted to him."

"Okay."

Ann was the president of her school's Young Professionals Club. So she arranged for Loretta and her Uncle Dave to make presentations at the first meeting of the school year, at seven p.m. on September 9.

Dave was talking to Ann before the meeting started when an incredibly beautiful woman dressed in a black skirt and red blouse walked up to them and smiled. "This is my uncle, Dave Robinson. Uncle Dave, Loretta Bailey, the youngest partner at the Jonas and Morris accounting firm."

Dave's smile froze on his face as he shook Loretta's hand. She was gorgeous, and nearly tall enough to look him straight in the eye. He couldn't help thinking that she'd fit perfectly in his embrace with her head tucked under his chin. While Loretta chatted with Ann, Dave took in her tiny features, striking eyes, and fiery hair that feathered over her shoulders. For the first time in a long while, Dave felt desire tingling up from his gut. Then the beautiful Loretta was grinning at him. He realized that he'd been staring and she'd asked a question he hadn't even heard.

Loretta's talk was about being successful as a woman in a man's profession. Dave didn't hear much of it, as he was too mesmerized by her. Dave's talk was about balancing work and family responsibilities in a demanding job, which he somehow stumbled through.

"Both of you did superb jobs tonight," Ann said. "Uncle Dave, why don't you take Loretta and me to the Macon City Diner for coffee and doughnuts?"

"That's a great idea, Ann," Dave replied.

After they'd arrived at the diner and ordered, Loretta said, "Your father-in-law fought in World War I and lost a leg, didn't he?"

"As a matter of fact, he did," Dave replied. "He was awarded the Purple Heart and the Bronze Star. Why do you ask?"

"I'm not sure, but I think he fought with my grandfather, Colonel William Bailey."

"I don't know. Steve never talks about the war," Dave replied. "But it would certainly be a rare coincidence if my father-in-law and your grandfather did fight in the war together."

"Mr. Taylor thinks of Uncle Dave as the son he never had," Ann said. "And Uncle Dave's brought a lot of business to Taylor, Robinson and Crane."

"Yeah, I read about that divorce you handled with Jason Stone from the Atlanta Chargers," Loretta replied. "It must take a special talent to negotiate settlements that are fair to both parties."

"Thanks. Let's talk about you, Loretta," Dave suggested. "A partner at thirty. I'm impressed. What's your secret?"

"A lot of seventy- hour weeks, and trying to look beyond the numbers to better understand the client's needs."

"My secret is the same as yours. Long hours and understanding clients' needs."

"You must have an understanding wife to deal with your busy schedule."

"I don't think I'd call..." Dave started.

"She's a selfish, manipulating witch who doesn't deserve a fine man like my uncle," Ann interrupted. "He's just too nice to say it."

Four Months Later

"I've missed you terribly, Loretta told Dave as she climbed into his Mercedes and he kissed her. It was just starting to rain.

"I've missed you too," he replied.

"Was your trip to Savannah successful?"

"Yeah. I secured a $1,000 retainer to represent the wife of Jim Johnson, a doctor whose family owns Southeast Agribusiness. His wife caught him cheating on her with his nurse."

"Guess what?" Loretta asked, changing the subject.

"What?"

"As of today, I have successfully gone a month without smoking. For the baby. And for you and me."

"Oh, Loretta, that's great! You're going to make a great mother."

"I sure hope so."

"Are you going to confront Harriett tonight and tell her about us?"

"Yeah, or if she's asleep when I get home tonight, first thing in the morning, just like I told you last Monday when we were having lunch."

Loretta decided not to tell Dave that the detective she'd hired to spy on Harriett had called her about an hour ago and said that Harriett was having dinner at the Blue Haven restaurant with her lover, Jerry Anderson. Jerry was the tennis pro at Dave's country club, and also a part-time detective. Loretta's detective told her that he'd overheard Harriett telling Jerry that she wanted to tell Dave about their affair, and that she knew about Dave and Loretta. Loretta also decided not to show Dave the pictures her detective had taken of Harriett and Dave kissing and in bed together, because she wanted Dave to be visibly surprised in front of Harriett when he discovered that she was cheating on him.

"Here is a magnetic tape recording device," Loretta said as she handed Dave a metal box.

"A tape recording device?" Dave asked after looking inside. "I've never seen one before."

"They record sounds, such as people talking. Tape recorders are not sold commercially to the public yet, but my father says the FBI has used them for several years. This is a new type, much smaller than most tape recorders so it will fit into a briefcase. It is powered by flashlight batteries. One tape is good for an hour. There are two tapes in there with the recorder, and instructions on how to use it. Put it in your brief case and tape your confrontation with Harriett tonight and any follow-up tomorrow."

"Okay," Dave replied as he tried to concentrate on the winding road ahead just outside of Macon, the rain pelting down.

Loretta leaned over and kissed him on the lips. The car swerved, and she exclaimed, "Dave, watch out!"

There was a loud *thump* as the car lurched upward, and there was a dragging sound as Dave slammed on the breaks and pulled onto the narrow shoulder of the road.

"What was that?" Loretta asked.

"I don't know. I'll get my flashlight so we can see," Dave said while Loretta got out and walked to the front of the car.

Dave walked to where Loretta was peering into the darkness under the car and shined the light. "It's a large limb," Dave observed. "It probably fell from that oak tree."

"Can you get the car off it?"

"I don't know," Dave replied as he looked around for another limb to use as a lever to pry the limb loose.

"How about the car jack? Couldn't we lift up the axle enough to remove the limb?"

"Yeah, that might work." Half an hour later they pulled into the parking lot at Loretta's apartment, both of them dirty with mud and grease. "Don't you want to come in and take a shower?"

"No, I don't have any clean clothes to change into. Besides, it's already late and I need to get home."

"Call me tomorrow and tell me how it went," Loretta said as she kissed him good-bye.

It was after midnight when Dave quietly slipped into his recently-built elegant house in the dark, trying not to wake Harriett. Just in case he encountered her, he'd read the instructions about how to use the recorder, put a tape into it, turned it on, and put it into his brief case.

As it turned out, he did run into his wife. "Dave! What happened to you? You look like you were run over by a truck!"

"I ran over a tree limb and had to use the car jack to get it off. I didn't think you'd still be up, much less dressed." Harriett was dressed impeccably in a patterned blue blouse and a white pleated skirt that fell several inches below her knee. On her feet were stylish low-heeled pumps. Harriett's brunette hair was now cut short, and curved over her ears. The fine lines around her mouth and her dark, piercing eyes, with slightly puffy pockets under them were beginning to show her forty-six years, her recently acquired smoking habit, and the heavy drinking.

"Well, look who just came sneaking in," a male voice said from behind Dave.

"Jerry Anderson? What are you doing here?" Dave asked, looking around. Jerry was tall and lean with broad shoulders, muscular arms, and eyes that were dull blue, but shrewd-looking.

"Harriett and I were out."

"Yeah, but we wanted to get back to hear the important news," Harriett said in a tone Dave didn't like.

"What news?"

"You know, you were going to tell Harriett about your affair with that accountant slut. The one you got pregnant?" Jerry offered.

"What?"

"And Harriett was going to tell you about her affair with me," Jerry sneered.

"What in the hell is going on here?" Dave asked.

"It's actually quite simple," Harriett began. "Jerry's my detective, and he's had you under surveillance."

"Yeah. I've got pictures of you and Loretta kissing in your office, in your car, and at her apartment. And I overheard you and Loretta discuss telling Harriett about Loretta's pregnancy when you and Loretta were having lunch at the Empire Café."

"So I know all about you and Loretta," Harriett said with a laugh. "And by the way, Jerry and I became lovers long before you started having your affair with Loretta."

"That's right," Jerry added as he put his arms around Harriett and kissed her.

Dave knew he should have slugged Jerry, but he really didn't care anymore whether Harriett was faithful or not.

"Now, honeykins, go take a shower and get on to bed so you'll be nice and rested when we have that little talk in the morning," Harriett ordered.

"Fine, but I want that son-of-a-bitch out of my house," Dave said, pointing at Jerry.

"Let's watch that temper," Harriett replied. And who owns this house is now subject to negotiation, isn't it?"

"I have to be going anyway," said Jerry. "So I'll just leave you two love birds to work out your problems."

"I'll call you tomorrow," Harriett said as Jerry left.

No wonder Harriett's been so cold toward me, Dave thought after he'd finished his shower and was alone in his bedroom. *Let her have her lavish dinner parties and boring country club friends - and her lover. Loretta, now there's a beautiful, sensual woman. Her skin is like cream, unbearably soft and fragrant. She'd do anything to please me in bed.* Dave felt that making love to her was like riding a cloud filled with lightning bolts into a dream, a dream that he craved like a powerful drug.

The more Dave thought about Harriett's behavior, about how their nineteen-year marriage had all been a farce, and how she was probably planning to blackmail him with her knowledge of his affair, the angrier he became. Once he would've never thought he could truly hate someone; but he hated Harriett now.

To hell with living a lie, I'm tired of sneaking around to be with Loretta. I want a divorce, Dave thought. *I'll figure out some way to get one without letting Harriett and her father destroy my career. Maybe the news about Harriett and Jerry can help somehow.*

The next morning Dave got up, shaved, put the other tape in the recorder, turned it on, slipped it back into his brief case and went downstairs.

"Would you like some breakfast, Mr. Robinson?" Maria, their recently-hired housekeeper, asked when Dave walked into the kitchen.

"Just some coffee and toast."

"And he'll have it in the dining room with me," Harriett demanded. After Maria brought Dave's coffee and toast, Harriett said, "That's fine Maria. Please close the door so we can have some privacy."

"Yes, ma'am."

"Harriett, I"

"Shut up and listen to me. I don't want a divorce. I like our lives, our friends, our standing in this community and the convenience of our marriage. You keep having your affair, and I'll have mine."

"But I do want a divorce," Dave demanded.

"Okay. I'll call Daddy right now and tell him all about your girlfriend. Then you can kiss your job with his firm, most of your assets and your career good-bye."

Harriett's father, Steve, hated irresponsible fathers who cheated on their wives, who never spent time with their kids, and who were always late with or failed to make alimony and child support payments after a divorce. He also hated unfaithful wives, who coldly manipulated their husbands for personal, social, or financial gain. Steve's behavior in a recent client conference with Mauree Anderson showed his passionate belief in his work. Maureen, the successful chief financial officer of Wondrous Facial Products, Inc., was also a loving and devoted wife and mother of two. She had caught her deadbeat, unemployed tennis pro and part-time detective husband, Jerry Anderson, who had a drinking problem, in bed with a voluptuous girl young enough to be their daughter.

Maureen had agreed to marriage counseling. But it was only a few weeks later when, coming home from a business dinner, she spotted Jerry and his mistress checking into a local motel on a night he'd told Maureen that he was visiting his mother. Maureen filed for divorce and hired Steve as her attorney. As Maureen told her story, Steve, who now had silver hair, a tiny goatee, and active gray eyes became enraged. Jumping up, he hobbled across the room, Bible in hand, and shouted, "He'll get his divorce all right, and his twenty-three-year-old bimbo girlfriend, but that's all. The sorry ##@# will be bankrupt by the time I'm through with him!!" He could be just as passionately disdainful and vindictive toward cheating wives, especially if they had children and were manipulating their husbands.

"Fine. I'll tell your father about you and Jerry," Dave stated.

"And you think he'd believe you?" Harriett sneered. "I've got proof of your affair. But what proof do you have about Jerry and me?"

"None," Dave admitted glumly. *Except maybe this tape recording* , he thought hopefully. *If this tape recording devise worked, then I'll have proof of Harriett's affair, but she also has proof of mine. If Steve finds out about all of this, he's likely to disown Harriett, and also fire me. So what good will the tape recording really be?*

"Okay, so now we understand each other. Let's get on to the real problem here. Loretta, or more specifically, the baby. Are you sure it's yours?"

"Yeah. I think she's in love with me. But then who really knows? I thought you were in love with me once, too."

"Let's stick to the subject. Can you convince her to get an abortion?"

"No way. Loretta wants this baby."

"What about adoption?"

"She won't consider that, either. She wants to have our baby and for us to be a family together."

"Stupid girl. She probably believes you when you tell her you love her."

I do love her, Dave thought.

"I know a man who will take care of our problem for two thousand dollars, and it will look like an accident or a robbery. He's very skilled and thorough."

"You mean have Loretta killed?"

"She's left us no choice. His phone number is 5-1255," she said, looking in a little gray book. "Write it down. Call it and say you want a party catered. He'll advise you how to proceed from there."

"What are you doing with the phone number of a hit man?" Dave asked in a panic.

"Jerry gave it to me."

"Oh, that's great. What a wonderful guy. Harriett, I'm not going to have Loretta..."

"Handle this, Dave, or I'll handle it myself!" she shouted, handing him the phone number she'd written down.

"Go to hell!" Dave yelled back as he stomped out of the house, slamming the front door behind him.

Dave was lost in his thoughts as he drove through the late morning traffic toward his office. *Is Harriett out of her mind? I'm not going to have Loretta murdered. Maybe she's just bluffing. But what am I going to do?*

He got to his office just before ten. "Mr. Robinson, Miss Bailey called – twice." Debra, his secretary, told him.

"Thanks. I'll call her right now."

Loretta picked up on the first ring. "It's almost ten o'clock. I thought you were going to call me earlier," she said with an urgent tone in her voice.

"Harriett and I just finished discussing everything."

"So you told her?"

"Yeah. Could we meet for lunch at your place?"

"Of course, darling. And Dave?"

"Yes."

"I love you, more than you know."

"I'm taking a long lunch today," Dave told Debra as he left the office at eleven thirty. "Reschedule all my meetings that are before three."

"Okay, Mr. Robinson."

"Hi, darling. Your favorite lunch is ready," Loretta teased as she answered the door to her apartment.

Dave gasped at the sight of her. All she was wearing were pink, lacy see-through bikini panties and bra, that he'd bought for her. *God she's sexy*, Dave thought as she put her arms around him. Dave didn't bother with, "Hello." His first kiss pushed Loretta away from the door. His second thrust them down the hallway. By the third, they were in her bed, clothes already discarded in a trail on the floor. He brushed back her hair, planting kisses from her ear, along the soft flesh of her jaw to her mouth, where she opened up to greet him. His lips covered hers in tender possession. Loretta felt every teasing touch of his tongue. His nakedness was a sensual weight down the length of her body. She wrapped herself around him, touching every bit of his flesh and still it wasn't enough. She needed more. He broke off the kiss to run his blazing lips across her breasts and down her stomach. She arched to greet his touch. He turned his head and the stubble of his beard scraped her skin, sending ecstatic shivers up her spine.

"This is how it's meant to be," Dave said, rising on his elbow to look her in the eye. "Just like this. Always." And his lips claimed her again.

Afterward, in the warm glow of their love, Dave held her close and whispered, "I love you, Loretta. I want to marry you and be a father to our baby."

His words were a balm that soothed her soul. For so long she'd wished for this, never truly believing it could happen. But here he was, her one true mate. She was safe in his arms and he loved her. She was so happy, she couldn't speak. Instinctively, her hand crept over the tiny life growing in her belly.

"Hey," said Dave, pulling away to wipe the tear that slid down her face. "You're crying!"

She sniffled and smiled through the blur of tears.

"Tears of joy, my love. I've never been happier."

Dave kissed her lips, her cheeks and her salty tears. She tucked her head back in the warm hollow of his chest and he whispered to her about the wonderful life they would soon have together. As she drifted off to sleep, her last thoughts were that it was time for her plan.

The ringing alarm woke them. It was 2:20 p.m. "Can't you take off the rest of the afternoon?" Loretta asked sleepily.

"I wish I could, but I have a three o'clock with an important client whose wife wants to negotiate settlement terms." Dave replied as he went into the bathroom.

"So what was Harriett's reaction when you told her about us?"

Panic shot through Dave as he remembered Harriett's horrible plan. She said she wouldn't give me a divorce," he told her, trying to act calm. "In fact, she wants me to have you killed. She even gave me the phone number of a hit man that she wants me to hire for two thousand dollars."

"What? Has she lost her mind?"

"Yeah, I think so.

"Did you tell her about the baby?"

"She knows everything."

"What are we going to do?"

"I'll talk to her again tonight. After she's had more time to think about everything, she may listen to reason."

"Were you able to tape any of it?" Loretta asked.

"Yes. What should we do with the tapes?" he said as he handed them to her.

"I need to think about it. We can decide later."

"Okay."

"I love you," she said softly as Dave was preparing to leave. "As long as we have each other, we can deal with anything."

"I love you too, Loretta." Then he kissed her tenderly, wondering what he was going to do about the incredible mess he was in.

When Dave returned to his office, Debra told him, "Mr. Robinson, your three o'clock called and is running about fifteen minutes late. But Mr. Taylor wants to see you in his office."

Dave hurried to his father-in-law's office. "What's up, Steve?" Dave asked nervously, trying not to think about the events of the last twenty-four hours.

"You know, Dave, I think of you as my own son. You're doing a wonderful job here and our clients rave about how pleased they are with your work. We're different, you and I. I'm a passionate bull dog, and there will always be a need for that But you have a talent for helping both sides in a divorce reach an amicable agreement, and while there are never any winners in a divorce, your approach certainly minimizes their pain and that of their children. I think that's the wave of the future."

"Thanks, Steve. Coming from you, that means a lot." But Dave only partially heard his father-in-law's accolades. His emotions were raging as he tried to decide whether he should just to tell Steve about everything that was going on between him and Harriett and live with the consequences.

"Dave, I want to make you the managing senior partner, second only to me. I'm ready to start slowing down some, and I will rest easy if I know you are there to take up the slack. When I retire, the law firm will be all yours."

"Steve...I, I don't know what to say. This is a special honor, and an incredible opportunity."

"Let's toast this with a drink." Steve buzzed his secretary. "Nancy, bring us that eighteen-year-old bottle of Glenlivet and two glasses. He then turned back to Dave. "I'll announce this at next Monday's partners meeting."

"Harriett, it's Loretta Bailey," Loretta said as she called Dave's wife about an hour after he had left and she'd had time to listen to the tapes.

"Who?"

"You know, Dave's pregnant mistress. I think you would absolutely love to listen to what I've just heard and to see what I know about you and Jerry Anderson."

"What lies has that spineless bastard been telling you?"

"Dave didn't tell me anything. I've got proof. Or maybe you'd prefer if I just shared it with 'Daddy.'"

"Why, you little bitch, if you..."

"Why don't I plan to drop by your place. Say around fiveish?"

"Suit yourself," Harriett replied coldly, trying to hide her concern. "I take it you know where we live? We recently moved."

"Yeah. You live in Oak Brook in the house Dave finished building last spring."

It was just before five when Loretta drove up to the gated entrance to Oak Brook. "Loretta Bailey here to see Harriett Robinson," she told the uniformed guard.

"Mrs. Robinson is expecting you," he said as he pushed a button opening the twin black iron gates. "The Robinson's house is the fourth on the left. Number 117 is on the mailbox out front."

"Thank you."

The brick drive on the five-acre estate was lined with magnolia trees, and various other colored shrubs and plants adorned the beautifully-landscaped emerald green lawn. She turned onto the circular drive of the Robinson's house; a fountain in the drive's center sprayed glistening water thirty feet into the air. The house was a sprawling two-story structure of white stone with a tile roof. There were four white stone columns that supported a covered marble entry-way, adorned at the front by bronze statues of a German Shepard on each side. Loretta felt dwarfed by the giant columns at the entrance.

When she rang the doorbell next to the twin ten-foot oak doors with stained glass windows, she was greeted by the uniformed Maria. "Miss Bailey, Mrs. Robinson will meet you on the terrace," the maid said.

As Maria led Loretta through the house, she saw an interior that was breathtaking, with Persian rugs on rich brown hardwood floors, sixteen-foot ceilings, a twin spiral staircase, and original paintings decorating the walls. She arrived on the terrace to find a table with a pot of hot tea waiting upon it.

Maria poured two cups of tea, and then left, quietly closing the French doors behind her.

"So, you're Dave's pregnant mistress," Harriett said coldly as she strode onto the terrace with the presence of a Broadway legend convinced of her ability to dominate an audience.

"And you must be Dave's soon-to-be ex-wife," Loretta replied as she set the tape recorder on the table.

"What's that?" Harriett asked, pointing to the device. "My father tells me these are the newest rage at the FBI these days: a magnetic tape recording device small enough to fit into a brief case. I'll demonstrate," Loretta said as she hit the play button. The tape began with the confrontation between Dave, Harriett, and Jerry the night before, and the recording was very clear. Loretta then spread the photos she had of Harriett and Jerry together out on the table as the tape continued to play.

Harriett lit a cigarette with trembling hands and looked like she might be sick. Loretta stopped the recorder, removed the tape, put in the second tape, and hit the play button. This tape began with the conversation from that morning when she ordered Dave to have Loretta killed. "Oh, my God!" Harriett said, her hardened exterior crumpling.

The tape finished and Ann said, "Oh, and I have another present for you." She then gave Harriett a photo of Harriett's father, Steve, standing next to a man Harriett didn't recognize. Both were dressed in Marine khakis and Steve was on crutches. The caption beneath the picture read, "Blood brothers. I owe my life to you, Bill."

"Where did you get this?"

"My grandfather gave it to me. That's him in the picture, Colonel William Bailey."

"Your grandfather is the man who saved my father's life in the war?"

"Yep," Loretta smiled. "Oh, and there's one more thing. Here." She handed Harriett a front page from a newspaper that had a picture of her father, Steve, with Maureen Anderson. Jerry was in the background. The headline read, "Steve Taylor Triumphs Again."

"What's this?"

"The sensationalized divorce of your lover boy, Jerry, from a prominent resident of our community. I believe you were in Europe at the time and missed it all. Jerry was the recipient one of your father's attacks on dead-beat dads and unfaithful husbands. Your father ruined Jerry and he's broke. That's probably why Jerry hooked up with you - for your money. Gee, I wonder what Daddy will think when he realizes that his daughter is having an affair with a deadbeat he loathes, and that she is cheating on a man he loves like a son?"

Harriett looked as if she was going to faint.

"Now here's my *deal, Harriett! First Part.* If anything happens to me, two copies of this tape will be sent out: one to the *Macon Telegraph* and the second to Police Chief Yarborough. My dad and Dave will handle the rest. If your hit man is successful in killing me, a third copy will go out to him along with one thousand dollars and instructions to kill you, upon which he will receive another thousand dollars. My dad will handle the details. Then tape recordings will go to the recipients of the first two tapes, recordings of me explaining that I had you killed for killing me. That way, Dave and my dad won't be suspects."

The color drained out of Harriett's face as she put her head in her hands and started sobbing, trying not to lose the contents of her stomach.

"*Second Part!* You'll convince 'Daddy' that you don't love Dave anymore and you want to go away and find yourself. You'll give Dave a reasonable divorce, and divide your jointly owned assets in half, except... Dave will get this house."

"Hey, Aunt Harriett," Ann said cheerfully when she got home from her honor club meeting shortly after Harriett's confrontation with Loretta. "I hear you and Uncle Dave are getting a divorce."

"Who told you that?"

"Loretta's my boss from last summer, and we're also very good friends. In fact I introduced her to Uncle Dave because I thought he needed someone like her in his life. She called me at school after she met with you and told me everything."

"Why, you bitch!"

"No, Harriett. You're the bitch. And maybe bitches win in the short term but not in the end. Maybe you can go live in California with your bitch daughter."

"In California? What are you talking about?"

"Blanche hasn't told you? Probably because she was afraid Uncle Dave would cut her off financially. Her friend Joan told me that Blanche got pregnant and she and her boyfriend moved to California. I doubt if she really knows who the father of her baby is, what with all the booze Joan says Blanche has been drinking and all the guys she's been sleeping with. Apparently her boyfriend's father is a Baptist minister. No wonder they moved to California. I doubt seriously that a grandchild born five months after his son's marriage would be popular for a Baptist minister in Alabama."

"*WHAT!?*"

"Why don't you call Joan and ask her yourself. I'll write her phone number down for you."

Harriett just stared, unable to speak - for once.

Chapter Five

Ann scored a 1560 out of 1600 on her SAT and had kept her straight-A grade point average for the rest of her senior year. Plus she was president of most of the major student organizations at her school. She wanted to go to Yale, but they weren't co-ed, so she applied to Wellesley which was where her mother had gone, Stanford, and the University of Georgia. She was accepted at all of the schools and chose Wellesley. It was her first day at Wellesley. First-time students were asked to arrive a week before classes started in order to get settled in, learn their way around campus, buy their textbooks, and so on. As Ann left her dormitory, Cathy Rossi said, "Hi, Ann."

"Cathy! You've come all the way back east to go to college? After your family moved to California to start a winery, I thought you'd go to Stanford or UCLA."

"I was accepted to Stanford, but decided I wanted to be farther from home. To really leave the nest."

"How's California?"

"Great. The weather's perfect most of the time."

"I take it your dad has started his winery."

"Yeah, he named it Columbia Creek Winery, for the creek that runs through the property. We just made our first wines. You should come visit us at one of the breaks."

"I'll do that."

"Freshman assembly is tonight at seven, and it's mandatory that we all attend."

"I know and I'll be there. Thanks."

Cathy was tall and attractive, with long red hair, inquisitive green eyes and a dimpled chin. "What dorm room are you in?"

"Buckman, five A. You?"

"McCarty, two C."

"Several of us have formed a study group and we plan to meet every other night. Would you like to join?" Ann asked her friend.

"Sure."

"Great. We're meeting in the library at seven on Thursday night."

"I'll be there."

At 6:55 Ann arrived at the auditorium in Green Hall where the freshman assembly was scheduled to take place. Someone unlocked the door and students began filing into the cool, dimly lit auditorium and taking their seats. Ann and Cathy went down near the front, to the third row, where they were able to find two seats together.

A short, middle-aged heavy-set woman in horn-rimmed glasses and graying hair pulled into a bun walked up to the podium, tapped the microphone, and asked, "Can everyone hear okay?" A "Yes" came back in unison from the audience. "Good afternoon. I'm Dr. Janet Anderson, First-Year Dean. Welcome to orientation week. In your freshman and sophomore years, you will complete your general education in arts and sciences. Beginning in your junior year, you'll concentrate on your major. The studies are rigorous and demanding. If you haven't already, I suggest you join a study group to share the load of homework and preparing for classes and tests. How many of you have already purchased your text books for the first semester?"

About a fourth of the class raised their hands. "Young lady, there in the third row, with the red hair."

"Yes, Dr. Anderson," Cathy answered.

"When you purchased your textbooks, what did you find?"

"Homework assignments for each of my classes."

"Homework assignments. And it's important that you complete them before going to your first class. Now, if everyone would look to her right." Everyone did. "Now look to your left." They all did. "Our experience shows that by the end of the year, two of you will not be here anymore. Are there any questions?"

There was only silence. "Fine, then we are adjourned."

It was May of Ann's sophomore year and she was heading for a summer job interview at the student union. She looked at her watch nervously as she realized she was running about five minutes late. *That damned phone call from Ron, who just wouldn't take no for an answer.* "Sorry, I'm late. I'm Ann Robinson," she said as she walked into the room.

"George Johnson, and that's okay. Let's see," George said as he looked at her resume. "Grade point average of four-point-oh, outstanding freshman of the year award, part-time fashion model, and working weekends at a local orphanage. Your background is impressive. Tell me about yourself, Ann."

"So, I spent last summer as a fashion model in New York, but I didn't like it," she explained as she finished. "The people are too flaky and artificial. I'm really interested in agriculture, although I have no farm experience."

"Why are you interested in agriculture?"

"Because it's a risky business that requires exceptional management skills to be successful. From what I've read, weather and diseases cause supplies to fluctuate, which makes both costs and prices unpredictable. I think I would like the challenge agriculture offers."

"Ann, Southeast Agribusiness is one of the largest firms in the Southeast. We have large dairy, tobacco, and peanut farms, and about one hundred twenty thousand acres of timberland near Savannah where we also run several thousand head of cattle. Your job would be as a financial analyst, working on budgets and financial plans. You salary would be one-hundred dollars per week. Are you interested?"

"Yes, when would I start?"

"The week after classes end."

"Good, that gives me time to go to Savannah and find an apartment."

"Hi, I'm Jim Johnson," the tall, finely manicured man with a ruggedly chiseled face, dark hair, and hazel eyes said as he introduced himself to Ann. She'd been working at Southeast Agribusiness for just over two weeks.

"Ann Robinson. Are you related to the owners?"

"I'm their son."

"Which part of the business do you work in?"

"I don't. I'm an endocrinologist."

"Not interested in the family business?"

"Yeah, but more interested in practicing medicine. Maybe I'll find a wife who will take over the business while I practice medicine," Jim said with a flirty smile.

Jim and Ann soon started dating, and over the next year she fell in love with him. In June of 1949, after her junior year in college, he asked her to marry him and she accepted. He had presented this romantic notion to her that he would run his medical practice and that she would ultimately take over managing the family agribusiness company, and that they would live happily ever after as partners in life.

"Fixing one of your great lasagnas for me tonight?" Jim asked her one afternoon over the phone.

"Sorry, but one of the Holstein heifers is having her calf tonight, and I need to be there to help deliver it."

"I understand. I'll take a rain check until tomorrow night.
"You've got a date."

Just as Ann was getting ready to leave her office to go to the dairy barn where the cow was to have her calf, the assistant manager of one of their dairies called and said, "Ann, the Holstein just gave birth to a fine bull calf and everything's okay. He came earlier than we expected. So you can head on home if you'd like."

"Great, I'll get a shower and off to bed early for a change."

When Ann arrived at her apartment she saw that Jim's car was parked outside and there was loud music blaring from within the apartment. "Jim, is that you?' Ann asked, as she walked through the door. She walked into the bedroom, and Jim and Theresa, his nurse, were in bed together. Two empty bottles of wine were on the dresser along with two partially filled glasses.

Jim laughed, and said, "Hi, honey. There's room for you in here too."

"*GET OUT!! BOTH OF YOU!!* Here, take your damn engagement ring!" she shouted, throwing the ring in Jim's face.

"Now, honey, let me expla..."

"*GET OUT NOW!*"

When Jim and Theresa left, Ann fell onto her bed sobbing. Ann was devastated and stopped dating, believing that she could never trust a man in a romantic relationship again.

In June of 1950, Ann graduated Summa Cum Laude from Wellesley. She was also inducted into the Phi Beta Kappa scholastic honor society, and for her scholarship, leadership and service she was inducted into the Alpha Sigma Nu honor society, too.

Ann's first job was with the National Farm Equipment Company. She was an assistant dealer management representative for the southeast, which included dealerships in Florida, Georgia, Alabama and Tennessee. Her responsibilities were to visit the dealerships and make sure their financial records were accurate and up-to-date, describe any new equipment being introduced, and tell them what they had to do or change to conform to company policy.

On August 6, 1951, Ann once again ran into her friend Cathy Rossi, at the American Farm Economics Association's (AFEA) annual meetings at Clemson University in South Carolina. They had arrived about twenty minutes early for the selected papers session on finance and were standing outside the auditorium door, which hadn't been unlocked yet. The American Farm Economics Association divided their annual professional meetings into various topics such as economic development, management, marketing, natural resources, finance, etc. Papers written on these subjects by economists were reviewed, and the best were selected for presentations in the various sessions at the annual meetings.

"Why Cathy Rossi! How long has it been?" Ann asked, surprised to see her.

"Over two years, I think."

"What are you doing here?"

"I came to hear the paper that develops a financial model for asset replacement. I'm working on my master's in agricultural economics at the University of California at Davis and may use the model developed in this paper as part of my thesis. What about you?"

"One of our engineers at National Farm Equipment is interested in the asset replacement model described in this session and how it quantifies the value of technological change. Since Clemson is in my territory, he asked me to attend this session."

"Where do you live now?"

"In Atlanta. Marietta, actually, which is a northern suburb of Atlanta. And still not married. How about you?"

"Are you kidding? I'm still having too much fun being single. Cathy's social life in college had been an endless string of casual sexual affairs with male students at Boston College, Harvard, and MIT. "Have you finally changed your conservative ways?"

"No," Ann replied resolutely. "Since that incident with Jim, I've been a little soured on romantic relationships."

"I think men are all ultimately unfaithful to any relationship. But it's a man's world in the workplace, so why not use your sexiness to help advance your career, and just have a good time with them in your social life."

"We've always differed about that, Cathy. It's my skills and productivity that will advance my career, not my looks or my sex. And in my personal life, I'm looking for that special someone who will view me as his equal and his partner in life. My interest is in finding *that* man, not in having casual sex in my social life."

"You're living in a fantasy, Ann, because the type of man you're looking for just doesn't exist in the real world."

"I guess you have your philosophy and I have mine." "Yeah, and I'm getting ready to enjoy some of the benefits of my philosophy tonight if the author of this paper we came to hear isn't too bad looking."

"What do you mean?"

"My thesis committee chairman, Ron White, was also the thesis committee chairman for Ray Collins, the author of this paper on asset replacement, and they're good friends. Ron told me that Ray is having serious problems in his personal life, and Ray's wife now sleeps in a separate bedroom and doesn't have sex with him anymore. In fact, Ron said it's been that way since their son, Tommy, was born about a year ago. I'm going to come to Ray Collins' rescue, unless he's a real dog in the looks department."

"Have fun," Ann said with a touch of disdain in her voice, remembering that once Cathy decided to get a man into bed, no man seemed to be able to resist her.

By this time, the door to the building had been unlocked and people were filing into the auditorium and taking their seats. Ann and Cathy went down near the front, to the second row where they were able to find two seats together.

A short, middle-aged balding man walked to the podium, and said, "Testing, testing. I believe our sound system is working. Good afternoon. I'm Dr. Horace French, chairman of the session on finance, our first session in the 1951 AFEA meetings' selected papers series. We have four excellent papers this afternoon. The first one is entitled 'Optimal Asset Replacement Under Technological Change' by Ray Collins. It develops a financial model for deciding when to replace depreciable assets that are used as part of the operation of a farm or business such as farm machinery, trucks, and cars, or even perennial crops such as sugarcane and citrus trees.

"Mr. Collins holds a bachelor's degree in agricultural economics from the University of Florida and a master's degree in agricultural economics from the University of California at Davis. He is currently employed as director of financial planning for the National Agribusiness Company in Lakeland, Florida. As most of you probably know, the AFEA's selected papers program seeks to recognize the contribution of new knowledge to the field of agricultural economics. Most papers are the result of many years of work, usually by two or more authors who have worked together to solve some business problem. Mr. Collins's paper is the only one in our selected papers program with only one author, and more important, he solved this problem while also managing a number of other responsibilities at his job. I understand the National Agribusiness Company is already using his model to make their asset replacement decisions. I give you Mr. Ray Collins!"

As Ray walked across the stage toward the podium, Ann gasped at the sight of him. Dress at the meetings was casual, and Ray had on khaki pants, a blue Polo shirt, and brown loafers. Probably in his late twenties, he looked very young compared to the other authors, who were now seated on the stage. Ray was six feet tall with thick, curly black hair, broad shoulders, and was a lean and muscular 195 pounds. He had a face that many women found fascinating, his dark features strongly sculpted and fiercely handsome, with the rugged good looks of a movie star. Ray was one of the most attractive men that Ann had ever seen. She glanced over at Cathy, whose attention was also focused on Ray, a look of fascination and intrigue in her eyes that gave Ann a twinge of jealously as she thought about what Cathy had planned for Ray that night.

"Good afternoon, ladies and gentlemen. It's certainly an honor and a pleasure to be here," Ray said as he began his presentation.

Cathy leaned over and whispered in Ann's ear. Wow! He's gorgeous! I'm moving to the front row." And then Cathy swooped into the only available seat in the front row.

As Ray started his presentation, he walked away from the podium and faced the audience, moving about the stage as he made various points or explained examples. He was speaking completely from memory, relying on no notes. The audience was silent, and everyone's attention was riveted on Ray. When he came to the financial models and to the estimated savings from using the analysis developed in his paper, he had math and calculations on a blackboard to make it easier for the audience to follow. But he presented the majority of the paper as if he were telling an interesting story, making each member of the audience feel as if Ray were talking only to him or her. And his real-world examples, analogies, and easy-to-follow logic made what was a very complex series of mathematical equations easy to understand.

Ann realized that it was more than just his unbelievably good looks, or the tremendous intellectual skills he had to have for his paper to be selected for this competitive and demanding program - particularly as young as he was - or the fact that this was by far the best presentation she'd ever heard that made

Ray so fascinating to her. There was a power and a self-confidence about him that was mysterious and exciting, and very captivating. And then somehow, in the course of his presentation, his eyes briefly met hers. It was only for a moment, no more than a few seconds. And yet Ann became dizzy with emotion as she realized how incredibly attracted to him she was. *Stop thinking that way,* she thought to herself. *He's a married man with a family and definitely off- limits.*

Ray soon finished his presentation and opened up the floor for questions. After he had answered a handful of them, he thanked the audience. Everyone gave him a standing ovation and Ann got up and left the auditorium.

She went straight back to her hotel room, where she sat in a shocked daze. No man had ever had this effect on her before. Ray was not like any man, or any person she'd ever seen, and she didn't know what to make of what she'd experienced on this August afternoon in Clemson, South Carolina. There was one thing she was sure of, though. He was the most exciting man she had ever encountered, and he left her feeling as she had never felt before. She had finally found her male equal, and it was exciting, confusing, and angering to her. *Why did he have to be married and have a family?* And then she remembered Cathy's plans, and started to loathe Cathy and what she was planning to do. *Maybe he won't succumb to her,* Ann thought. But then she thought, *he's male, he's human, and he probably hasn't had sex for almost a year. No man ever resists Cathy, so get real.*

Ann was up early the next morning and had breakfast at six thirty. She was looking forward to getting on the road and back to her office at National Farm Equipment's regional offices in Atlanta, and likewise getting Ray Collins out of her mind. She had gone back to her room to gather up her luggage just after seven o'clock when the phone rang.

"Hello, Ann? It's Cathy."

"Yeah. Well I'm in a hurry to get on the road, Cathy, so what is it?" Ann replied rudely, hating that she was feeling jealous of what she knew Cathy had probably done with Ray the night before.

"I wanted to tell you about my dinner with Ray Collins last night."

"Skip it, Cathy. I can already imagine, and I don't have time for the details."

"Ann, he didn't touch me!"

"What?"

"Ray wouldn't touch me. I tried everything I knew to get him to go to bed with me and he refused. He was polite about it, and said he was honored that I had offered, but he said he would always be faithful to his marriage vows and could not be with me."

Ann's stomach began to tighten as what she was hearing sank in.

"Ann, I was dressed in a tight, sexy, little black cocktail dress and matching fishnet stockings, and I could tell he was attracted to me. I even told him that Ron told me about his marital problems, and that I wanted to show him some of the best sex he'd ever have. But he just politely refused. What happened after that was what was so incredible!"

"What happened?"

"Ann, he understood me and what I was all about. With a caring and kindness I've never experienced, he began to talk about his views of ethics, honesty, family, and commitments. He explained his views of the sanctity of marriage, the responsibilities a husband and wife have to each other and to their children, and how he believes that parenthood is a couple's most important responsibility. He explained that his marriage vows are to God and to his children, as well as his wife, and if she chooses to dishonor them, that is no reason for him to do so as well.

"He told me he understands how easy it is to get disillusioned about morality and honesty in today's world, but that I shouldn't give up hope, that I will meet someone someday who will make the wait worthwhile. He told me that I'm beautiful and smart, and that those are rare gifts that I should cherish. He explained that my professional successes would come from building valuable job skills and professional alliances, not sexual ones. That I should be proud of myself and my accomplishments. And finally, that I'm too good and valuable of a person to be trying to use sex to achieve my goals in life.

"Ann, I've never met anyone like Ray. He's made me think long and hard about myself and about my life. Now I think I've been wrong about a lot of things, certainly about men, if there are anymore like him. But one thing that I'm not wrong about is the personal life that Ray probably has. Ann, there is a sadness and a longing in his eyes that even he can't hide. He won't talk about it, but I sense that his wife treats him like dirt. And if that's the case, how anyone could treat this wonderful, special man like that, I'll never understand."

Ann was speechless. Once she had regained her composure, she said, "Thanks for the description of your dinner with Ray last night, Cathy. I thought he might be someone special when I saw him giving his paper yesterday. I'm glad that my first impressions were correct. Sorry to rush, but I must be going."

But she didn't go. Rather, she sat in her hotel room, overwhelmed by her thoughts. She now realized that, for the first time in her life, she'd finally encountered the man, or the type of man, she wanted as a partner in life. And she was intensely interested in him, or at least the idea of who she thought he was and was all about. If she had the chance to spend time with him, she felt she would quickly fall in love with him. But he was married with a family. A family that he was committed to preserving, which was one of the things she admired most about him.

Chapter Six

In the weeks and months following her encounter with Ray Collins at the AFEA meetings, Ann was excited to finally know that the man of her dreams really existed, but depressed that he was married with a family and thus unavailable. And although she tried, she just couldn't get Ray out of her mind.

In January she got in touch with Cathy Rossi and asked her friend to set up a meeting for her with Ron White. The meeting was supposedly to explore Ann's interest in working on her master's degree in agricultural economics, and although that was an idea that Ann was considering, her real interest was in getting to know someone that was friends with Ray Collins. She had finally accepted the fact that, somehow, she had to get to know Ray better. But because she was so intensely attracted to him, she felt that at this time she had to avoid meeting him, or she would quickly find herself hopelessly in love with a married man. She felt that a good way to get to know Ray under the circumstances was through one of his friends. Also, because Ray was having marital problems, she wanted a way to keep track of how Ray's personal life was doing. If his marriage were to break up, she wanted to know about it as soon as possible.

After Cathy introduced Ann to Ron, he gestured to an open chair.

"Have a seat," he said, trying to hide his astonishment at Ann's beauty. "Can I get you anything to drink? Coffee? A soft drink?"

"No, thanks. I'm fine," Ann replied.

"Me, too," Cathy said.

"Cathy's told me a lot about you, Ann," Ron began. "How do you like working for National Farm Equipment?"

"Pretty well, although I don't like all the travel. My responsibilities cover Florida, Georgia, Alabama and Tennessee."

"Cathy told me you were promoted recently."

"Yes. The company has been good to me."

"So what makes you think you would like to study agricultural economics?"

"I never really thought about it until I attended the AFEA meetings at Clemson last August to hear a paper about asset replacement at the request of one of our engineers. But when I saw the advanced analytical methods that agricultural economists are trained to use, and the types of business problems they can solve, I wanted to learn more about the field."

"Was that the paper on asset replacement by Ray Collins?"

"Yes, it was."

"Ray Collins was one of my students. But don't let his paper mislead you. There aren't many agricultural economists, including those with PhDs, that have Ray's business problem-solving skills. He's sort of in a class by himself."

I definitely agree with that, Ann thought. "Cathy said you were good friends with Ray," Ann said as she began to steer the conversation to discussing Ray.

"Yes, and his is a friendship I really value. In fact, I was just talking with him on the phone yesterday. He and his wife,

Connie, just found out that they will be having their second baby in August, and both of them are very excited about it."

Ann suddenly felt sick and her face became pale. "Are you okay, Ann?" Cathy asked.

"Yes, but if you will excuse me, I would like to go to the rest-room."

"It's down the hall and on the right," Cathy told her. "I can show you if you'd like."

"That's okay, I can find it," Ann said as she left. Tears were already welling up in her eyes as she entered the ladies' room and went into the privacy of a stall. And then she began to cry softly. *What could I have been thinking? Ray is committed to keeping his marriage and family together, and he's done it. Somehow, he and Connie have resolved their problems, and now their marriage is restored. They'll probably live happily ever after.*

Then Cathy came into the restroom. "Ann, are you okay?"

"Yeah, I just have some nausea. Probably something I ate. But I don't feel like continuing our meeting today. I'd just like to go to my hotel and lie down. Would you tell Dr. White that I'm sorry, but I don't feel well and would like to call and schedule another time to continue our meeting?"

"Sure, Ann. Would you like me to drive you to your hotel?"

"Thanks, but I'll be fine."

"Call me," Cathy said as she left to go back and cancel the rest of their meeting with Ron.

Ann went back to her hotel room and sat on the bed, alone with her thoughts. She soon began to sink into a deep depression, realizing that there would probably never be an opportunity for her to have a romantic relationship with Ray Collins. She cried herself to sleep that night.

The next morning she awoke with a commitment to finally forget about Ray Collins, and concentrate her efforts on her career and her social life. Maybe she would start dating again. *What better way to forget about Ray?* She thought.

One of Ann's neighbors, Bob English, was a partner in an Atlanta law firm, and recently divorced. He had asked her out once a while ago, but she had refused. There was a meeting of her condominium association that coming Wednesday night and she would probably see Bob there. If he asked her out again, Ann decided that she would accept.

"Hi, Ann. How's my favorite female executive doing?" Bob asked her as they were going into the clubhouse to start the association meeting. Bob English was in his mid- thirties, five foot ten, and had sandy colored hair that was beginning to thin. Although he'd told Ann that he was recently divorced, he was actually separated and pursuing a divorce. The hang up on the divorce was Bob's refusal to accept custody of their two children for two years while his wife, Joan, finished her college degree at the University of Chicago, where she'd been in school before they were married. She'd withdrawn from college after she and Bob had married to get a job that would help pay for his law school education. Joan had been in love with Bob until she had found out about his affair with his twenty-two-year-old secretary. She had forgiven him, but then a second incident with Joan's best friend was all it took to shatter her feelings for him. Bob was trying to avoid custody like the plague, because once he was really single, he was planning to "make up for lost time" on the dating front. Joan had conceded the custody issue, reasoning that he really wasn't a very good father anyway. But if she had their son and daughter while she went back to get her degree, and later had a job, then she wanted enough money in the settlement to pay for a live-in nanny to care for the children. Bob was also balking on the money issue, although Joan's attorney said she would win.

"I'm curious if you tried out that new restaurant you were telling me about last time," Ann replied to Bob's question with a slightly flirtatious tone in her voice.

THE WINE QUEEN

"No, I haven't. I was still hoping that I could convince you to try it out with me."

"When did you have in mind?"

"How about Friday night?" Bob suggested excitedly.

"You've got a date."

"Great!"

"Bob?"

"Yes, Ann."

"What time?"

"It's about eight."

"No, Bob. What time will you pick me up for our date?"

"Oh, I'm sorry, Ann. How about seven?" he suggested, embarrassed.

The night of their date, Bob was twenty minutes early and Ann was still dressing when he rang the doorbell. She answered the door in her robe, and said, "I'll be ready in a few minutes, Bob. Have a seat and make yourself at home."

"Take your time, we're in no hurry."

The restaurant was in an old restored Georgia mansion that had been the home of a large plantation in the nineteenth century. Much of its historical appearance had been preserved, right down to the Civil War musket ball holes in some of the walls. The menu was French, and the decor elegant.

"We'll have the Gallo Burgundy," Bob said as he selected a lower priced wine. Ann thought, *I really wanted to have seafood and a white wine.*

When the waiter came to the table with the menus Bob said, "We only need one menu," as he reached for the menu the waiter was handing Ann. "My wife's cleaning my clock badly in this divorce so I've really got to watch the pennies. Then to the waiter he said, "We'll each have the house salad and dressing, and the grilled pork loin with asparagus and garlic potatoes."

A short while later, Bob had to blow his nose. It was loud enough that several heads turned. "Waiter, we need another napkin over here," he shouted loudly to the waiter across the room.

How disgusting, Ann thought. *Oh well, I didn't expect to find the right man on the first date I've had in over three years.*

"So how's life as a professional business woman?" Bob asked.

"Much like it is as a professional business man, I suppose. It has its challenges and its rewards."

"I bet that with your looks, guys are always hitting on you."

"Sometimes. But the ones who know me understand where I'm coming from and there's usually not a problem."

"Where are you coming from with me, Ann?"

"To enjoy a nice restaurant and interesting conversation."

"How about after we finish dinner?"

"I think it's too soon to know," Ann replied as she thought, *Boy, was this a mistake.*

"Well, I already know," Bob said, putting his hand on her knee.

At that Ann got up and said, "This date's over, Bob!" Then she went to the restaurant's lobby and had the manager call her a cab. When Bob came up to try to apologize, she said, "Look, let's just admit that this was not a good idea."

"But the least I can do is take you home!"

"I'd rather just take a cab."

"You professional women! You think you're better than everyone, and all of you just hate men!"

"Is there a problem here?" the restaurant manager asked, responding to Bob's loud comments.

"We're fine. Mr. English was just headed back to his table," Ann explained as Bob headed back toward the dining room.

It was about a month later when Jerry Hamilton, the engineer that had asked Ann to go hear Ray present his paper, was in the Atlanta office and ran into Ann. Jerry was in his early thirties and single. He had wavy blond hair and a mustache, and was just over six feet tall. He served four years in the US Army, where he was a Special Forces instructor before getting a degree in mechanical engineering from Georgia Tech. He was a heart throb to many of the single women in the Atlanta office, but he had only been interested in dating Ann. Although he'd asked her out several times, she'd always refused.

"Hi, Ann," Jerry said as he tapped on her open office door before he walked in at 11:55 a.m.

"Hi, Jerry. It's good to see you again," Ann said, greeting him warmly.

"I just wanted to thank you again for those notes you took from that paper Ray Collins presented at the AFEA meetings. They were very helpful. In fact..."

"Jerry, I've got a one o'clock meeting and was planning to get an early lunch. If you'd like, you can join me and we'll continue our conversation."

"Great."

They went to the cafeteria on the lobby floor of the office building. After they had ordered clam chowder and turkey breast sandwiches, the special of the day, Jerry restarted their conversation. "As I was saying, Ann, those notes you took at Ray Collins's presentation were very useful. I called him to ask some more questions, and he was very cooperative and helpful."

"You talked to Ray Collins?" Ann asked, her interest level increasing significantly.

"We not only talked over the phone, he also agreed to help us use his model for some estimates we're trying to develop as part of National Equipment's strategic plan, if we wanted to meet with him. So a week later, my boss, Ted, and I flew to Tampa and drove to NAC's offices in Lakeland to meet with Ray." By this time Ann was fascinated with what Jerry was telling her.

"NAC has no interest in keeping the analytical techniques Ray developed for his paper confidential, which is why they let him present it at the AFEA meetings. To them, the real value of those models is in the savings they achieve by using them. We met in Ray's office and told him our primary interest was in predicting the effect widespread use of his asset replacement principles may have on the farm machinery market. Ann, what we saw next was amazing.

"We had hoped that he could help us understand how to apply some of the analytical components of his model to the macroeconomic situation, so that a team of engineers could develop models to forecast the economic impact of his model on our market. We had expected it would take about a year and several hundred thousand dollars in research until we saw what Ray did over the next hour. And he made it look so easy! By the time he was finished, he not only gave us a specific prediction of the impact his asset replacement principles would have on the national demand for farm machinery, but he also presented another set of equations that we can use in our research and development process so that any new technology we develop makes economic sense as an immediate replacement for existing equipment. Thus we now have a better way to improve the market success of our R&D efforts!"

Ann was awestruck. Apparently, Ron White had been correct about Ray's business skills. He was in a class by himself, maybe even a financial genius. She quickly regained her composure, looked at her watch, and said, "Thanks for sharing that with me Jerry, but it's time for me to get back for my meeting."

"Ann, I know you've said no in the past, but I would really like to have dinner with you while I'm in town."

Jerry was then shocked when she said, "Sure. When?"

"How about tonight? I'll pick you up at your place at six thirty, if you'll give me directions on how to get there."

"You've got a date, Jerry. I need to run to that meeting, but my secretary, Gladys, will give you directions to my condo."

THE WINE QUEEN

Jerry arrived precisely at six thirty, and he and Ann left to go to dinner. On the drive to the restaurant, Jerry asked, "So what made you change your mind about going out with me?"

"It wasn't you specifically. A few years ago, I was engaged, and it turned into a very bad situation, which soured me on dating and romantic relationships. But I'm beyond all of that now and ready to start going on dates again."

"Ann, the thing I like most about you is your intellect and your open-mindedness."

"Thank you, Jerry."

They soon arrived at the restaurant and ordered their meal. "I think I share your admiration of Ray Collins, Jerry. He gave a very impressive presentation at Clemson."

"He's a very impressive guy." Suddenly Ann noticed that Jerry's eyes were redder and it looked as if he was holding back tears.

"Jerry, is something wrong?"

"I'm in love with an older married woman."

"What?"

"I know that being as open-minded as you are I can share all this with you, which is why I've wanted to go out with you. So I could have someone to talk to."

"How old is she?"

"Forty-six."

"Does she have children?"

"Yes, four; two in their twenties from her first marriage and a boy fourteen and girl twelve from her second."

"Jerry, my advice is to break it off with her."

"I know, but we're so much in love, and I'm in agony when I think about her sleeping with her husband." And then he began to cry.

"Jerry, please, get ahold of yourself," Ann said with a comforting tone in her voice.

"It's just that she's so beautiful and smart and sweet. I've never met anyone like her before," Jerry sobbed.

Although Ann dated other men over the next few months, none were attractive to her. They were either liars trying to get her into bed, or crybabies who saw her as a mother figure, or thought they were God's gift to women and wanted to brag about their sexual exploits, or they were simply boring to her. She found herself comparing them to what she envisioned Ray to be, and none ever came close to measuring up.

By January, she had come to a significant decision. She was not going to be able to forget about Ray, and now she accepted that. He was the only man she had any serious interest in. And while she may not be able to have a romantic relationship with him, the two of them could have a professional relationship, which would have to be enough for her. She would go back to see Ron White at UC-Davis and enroll in graduate school. When she finished her master's degree in agricultural economics, she would try to get a job working for Ray. Ultimately, she could even become his most valuable professional colleague, and they would have a wonderful professional future together with rewarding careers. She may never get married, but at least she would be able to share her professional life with the man of her dreams.

"So you've decided to get your master's degree in agricultural economics," Ron White said as he looked through Ann's application file in early March of 1953.

"Yes, I believe it will give me the professional training I need for a career in agribusiness with one of the large food companies, which is where my career interest lies."

"Let's see, you were number one in your class at Wellesley, and graduated summa cum laude in 1950?"

"Yes."

"You were also a member of three national scholastic honor societies, inducted into the Alpha Sigma Nu honor society in recognition of outstanding scholarship, leadership and service, were President of Phi Beta Kappa, editor of Wellesley's student newspaper, listed in the Who's Who of American colleges and universities, and your senior thesis was published in *The Economist* magazine."

"That's correct."

"All that and you had a summer job as a fashion model, two summers as a management intern for Johnson Agribusiness Enterprises, and currently you are the southeastern dealer management representative for National Farm Equipment Company at an annual salary of nine thousand dollars?"

"Yes, sir."

Ron's secretary then walked into the office, interrupting his and Ann's conversation. "Dr. White, Mr. Ray Collins is on the line for you," she said. At just the mention of Ray's name, Ann got butterflies in her stomach.

"Excuse me, Ann, but I need to take this call," Ron said.

"Sure, Dr. White. Do you need privacy?"

"No, you can stay. I will only be a minute or so." He then picked up the phone.

"Hi, Ray. I called you earlier to see if the rumor was true."

"What rumor?" Ray replied from the other end of the line.

"I was talking with John Mercer the other day and he said you had accepted a position as vice-president of financial planning for the Global Soft Drink Company."

"That's right. I start on April sixth."

"Congratulations, Ray. I know that you'll do well there."

"Thanks, Ron. It's a big step for me, and I sure hope you are right."

"Ray, I'm in a meeting, so I've got to run. I just wanted to congratulate you, and confirm our meeting at your office next week."

"I'm looking forward to it, Ron." The two men then hung up.

So Ray's headed to the Global Soft Drink Company, Ann thought. *With his business mind and a much bigger arena to work in, it will be interesting to see what happens.*

"Ann, I take it you are planning to go for a master's degree rather than a PhD, since your interest is a career in business rather than teaching or doing research."

"That's correct. I'm interested in going the business route with my master's degree, and I'd like to have you as my major professor."[5]

"I would be honored. I also think you should complete an application for a graduate research assistantship," Ron said as he handed her the application forms. "That will pay you for doing your master's thesis. With your grades and GRE test score, you'll definitely be awarded one."

"What would it pay?"

"Roughly twenty-two hundred dollars a year."

"Great. I'll complete the application and mail it to you."

In June, Ann received her acceptance to the graduate program in agricultural economics at The University of California at Davis, and was also awarded a graduate research assistantship. Ron White would be her major professor, and she would begin her studies in September of 1953.

---

[5] A major professor to graduate students in agricultural economics supervises the research and writing of the student's thesis, and is also a mentor, teacher, adviser and professional friend for life. Many graduate students in agricultural economics choose their school based on who it offers as major professors.

Chapter Seven

Ann devoted herself to studying and doing well at UC Davis for the next two years. She was headed to a meeting with Ron to discuss her oral exams and defense of her thesis that was scheduled for May 21, 1955. Her thesis was entitled "Risk Management Strategies for Sugar Processors Using the Commodity Futures Market."

"Ann, I have good news," Ron said as they began their meeting.

"What?"

"I talked with Ray Collins on the phone this morning and he said there is an opening for a senior commodity analyst in the sweetener purchasing department at the Global Soft Drink Company at their corporate headquarters in Memphis, Tennessee."

"Is procurement one of Mr. Collins's responsibilities? I thought he was vice-president of financial planning."

"He was when he first started working for GSDC. But he was recently promoted, and is now senior vice-president of finance, with responsibility for purchasing and accounting in addition to financial planning."

"As smart as you've told me he is, I'm not surprised," Ann replied, thinking, *Ray will probably be president of GSDC at some point.*

The position Ray told me about reports to the director of domestic sugar procurement. Sometime during the interview process you will meet with Ray, because he views this position as the springboard to a critical role in procurement at GSDC and wants to be personally involved in selecting the right candidate. Human resources will be contacting you to schedule an interview."

"Oh, that's wonderful!" Ann exclaimed excitedly, thinking, *Finally. I'm ready to meet Ray Collins and get on with my career plan!*

"Ann, Ray has the best business mind I've ever encountered, and he's also as honest and ethical as they come. Bill Taylor, one of my students who graduated from here two years ago got the chance to work with Ray at GSDC and he said it was the best business learning experience he'd ever had. I'm very proud to see that you are getting this opportunity, and with your intelligence and skills, I can only imagine what you'll be able to accomplish after training with Ray Collins."

Ann was so excited about the fact that she would finally be meeting Ray and maybe get a chance to work with him that she was unable to sleep that night. Three days later, a woman from GSDC's human resources department contacted Ann and set up an interview for Monday, June 11. This first interview would be with human resources and with Jack Lovelace, who was director of North American sugar procurement and would be her boss. If they determined that she was a good fit for the position, she would come back for an interview with George Martin, vice-president of purchasing, and with Ray Collins. After that second set of interviews, they would make a decision about whether to offer her the job. As June 9 approached, Ann could barely contain her excitement.

"Ann, can I get you anything to drink?" Sherry Monson, the GSDC human resources manager, asked as she began the interview.

"No, I'm fine."

"Good. We'll talk for a while, then I have some application forms for you to complete. Your meeting with Jack Lovelace is scheduled for eleven and you will also have lunch with him."

After the two of them were done, when Sherry was taking her to Jack's office, she and Ann walked right past Ray Collins in the hallway. This was the first time Ann had seen him since he made his presentation at the AFEA meetings over three years ago, and it was also the first time she'd seen him in a business suit. The sight of him took her breath away and her stomach got those butterflies again. She had forgotten how attractive he was. *God, he looks handsome in that suit*, Ann thought. He was talking to someone, so Sherry only nodded a quick hello without interrupting them.

Ann's interview with Jack seemed to go very well and they went to lunch in the executive dining room. "This position is being created because of a revolutionary idea that Ray Collins, our senior V.P. of finance, has developed, and we think is going to be very profitable. I can't discuss it now because it's confidential. However, Ray wants to interview any candidates that I recommend for this position because this commodity analyst will work directly with Ray on some aspects of that project. Ann, I think you bring a lot to the table. And your master's thesis which quantifies various commodity futures hedging strategies for sugar processors has certainly given you a solid background about the sweetener business. I'll be in touch to set up another interview, this time with my boss, George Martin, and Ray Collins."

Ann was so excited over the job prospect at GSDC that she could hardly stand it. And to be able to work with Ray on her first project! Everything was working out wonderfully. She received her master's degree in agricultural economics on June 18, 1955. Ron White had no doubts that she would get the job at GSDC because she was perfectly qualified for it and the company had had good experiences with his students in the past. However, with the busy schedules he knew that most senior executives had, he figured it might be a month or two before she got through the remainder of the interview process and received an offer. So he offered Ann a position as a research associate in agricultural economics. He wanted her to use the models on risk management and futures trading in sugar markets she had developed in her thesis to analyze trading strategies for soybean futures.

On Monday, July 9, Ann got a call from Jack Lovelace to schedule an interview for her with George Martin and Ray Collins on the following Tuesday, July 17. She would meet with George Martin at ten thirty, then at eleven thirty, she would meet with Ray and their meeting would continue through lunch.

She was beside herself with excitement. *I'm finally going to meet Ray Collins and also have lunch with him!* she thought excitedly. *I'll have to go shopping in San Francisco and get the perfect outfit.* She and her roommate, Beth Davis, who was one semester away from finishing her master's degree in journalism, went shopping that Saturday. Beth didn't know about Ann's attraction to Ray, and Ann had no intention of telling her, or anyone else; her private life was her business and no one else's. But Beth was glad to help Ann shop for an outfit to wear to this very important job interview. Ann went to Brooks Brothers and finally selected a gray wool pinstripe business suit and a light pink silk blouse, black pumps, and a black leather purse. "What do you think?" Ann asked Beth when she was trying on the suit and blouse.

"I think you look fabulous, but then with your figure, you'd look fabulous in anything," Beth replied.

Ann's interview was only three days away and she couldn't think about anything else.

Tuesday morning finally arrived, and she was off to the airport at six a.m. to catch her flight to Memphis. She looked stunning in her new outfit, a fact few men she came within sight of in the airports and on the plane were not aware of.

THE WINE QUEEN

She arrived at GSDC's offices on time and Jack Lovelace came out to greet her. "Ann, there's been a slight change of plans," Jack began. "Ray Collins will not be able to meet with you today because of a family issue." Ann's spirits fell, but she managed to hide her disappointment. "However, he's asked his boss, Harry Davis, to meet with you instead. Harry is the executive vice-president of GSDC and very highly thought of by the company and by the board. He doesn't normally get involved in interviewing for positions at this level, but he agreed to do so in this case as a personal favor to Ray whom Harry respects very much. Harry hired Ray and is his mentor here at GSDC. Harry also has a real skill for spotting business talent, and Ray will highly value Harry's opinion from this interview."

The interview with George Martin went well and Ann could tell that, since she was Jack Lovelace's choice, George was sold on her. Harry Davis would be the determining factor. She was nervous as George Martin's secretary escorted her to the waiting area outside of Harry's office and introduced her to Lisa, Harry's secretary. Ann took a seat and after about five minutes, Harry came out of his office.

"Good morning, Ann. Welcome to the Global Soft Drink Company," Harry said as he gestured her into his office. "We'll visit for awhile, then we'll get some lunch.

Harry Davis stood over six foot four, was mostly bald, had shrewd brown eyes and weighed about 225 pounds, all of it solid. His large, imposing presence intimidated many, but something about him immediately made Ann feel at ease. "Why are you interested in this job at GSDC?" he asked.

"The work I did for my master's thesis got me interested in the sweetener business and I saw the opportunity to pursue that interest and make a worthwhile contribution to the job here."

A perplexed look appeared on Harry's face and she could tell that he didn't accept her answer, which was confusing. "Maybe I should ask the question differently," he said. "Why would someone who graduated first in her class at Wellesley, won just about every academic award there was to win, and who was on a fast track career at National Farm Equipment leave that career to study agricultural economics?"

"I became interested in the business problem solving skills that a graduate education in agricultural economics develops and wanted to acquire those skills," she explained.

"You mean skills like the author of this paper has?" Harry asked as he slid across his desk a copy of Ray's paper on asset replacement.

Ann was shocked, and her stomach began to tighten. "How did you know that I had heard Ray Collins present that paper?"

"I didn't until now. But it's the most likely agricultural economics paper that someone from National Farm Equipment would be interested in." And then Ann knew Harry understood what she was trying to do. *Damn, he was smart!* "How bad is it?" he then asked.

"How bad is what?"

"How bad is it to be in love with a man you can't have?"

"I'm dealing with it," Ann said, deciding not to pretend any longer with Harry.

"Will just working with him be enough? Because you know he'll never be unfaithful to his wife. But then I suspect that's one of the things you admire about him."

"I hope so Mr. Davis."

"That's Harry," he corrected her.

"I've been trying to forget Ray for over three years now and it hasn't worked. If working with him is all I can have, then that will have to be enough."

"What will you do if we decide not to hire you?"

"If you want the best person for this job, then you'll hire me," Ann said with renewed confidence.

"Ron White told me that, other than Ray Collins, you were the best student he'd ever had, with a real talent for business strategy. So let's see what you've got. What have you been told about the job you will be doing?"

"That I will be analyzing sweetener markets and working on futures hedging strategies for those markets. And that Ray Collins has developed an idea that is confidential, but that could be very profitable for GSDC and this position will work on some aspects of that project with Ray. That is why he wanted to interview candidates that Jack and George recommend."

"Now tell me what you think you will be doing."

"Working on implementing Ray's idea and hedging strategies to switch GSDC from sugar to high fructose corn syrup for its sweetener needs."

Damn! She is good, Harry thought. "What makes you think that?"

"Because I know how much more profitable GSDC would be if they could switch from sugar to HFCS. Ray has responsibility for procurement and the problem is solvable, which means that Ray has probably solved it."

"How do you know that the problem is solvable?"

"Because I've also solved it, or at least come close enough to know that someone as smart as Ray could solve it."

At this point, Harry was intrigued with what she was saying, so he asked, "How would you solve this problem?"

Harry was more than impressed as he listened to Ann go through the same hedging strategies in corn and energy markets that Ray had described not two months earlier and the same un-priced approach to business using the same type of cost-based pricing formula Ray had recommended. When she came to the basis problem created by cross- hedging HFCS with sugar futures, she had no solution. Although she had worked on forecasting models to improve the predictability of that basis, she had not yet been able to come up with Ray's exchange for physicals concept. *Given the time, though,* Harry thought, *who knows. She might even come up with that.* When she got to that part Ann simply said, "And I think that Ray has somehow solved the cross-hedging basis problem."

Harry was impressed with what she had told him. She had gone farther toward solving the HFCS switching problem than anyone he knew, other than Ray. He was very impressed with Ann's skills and her business acumen. She was smart, she had incredible business talents, and she was one of the most beautiful women he'd ever seen. She was also in love with Ray Collins, someone that Harry had the highest respect for, and thought of as a son. "Are you ready to have some lunch?" Harry asked, as he saw on his watch that it was twelve thirty.

"Sure," Ann replied, thinking, *What is his opinion of what I just explained to him? Does he agree? Was I correct in assuming that was what I'd be doing? Has Ray really solved that basis problem? Have I screwed this up?*

Later, when they were seated in the dining room, Harry said matter-of-factly, "The job is yours if we can agree on salary. What starting salary did you have in mind?"

Now excited that she may have the job she really wanted, Ann began nervously, "I know that you expected to get a candidate for somewhere around five or six thousand dollars, because that's where most of our graduates that have work experience are starting. But I'd like to start at nine thousand a year, because that's what I was making at National Farm Equipment when I left there over two years ago, and quite frankly, I think I'm worth that in this job."

"I disagree," Harry said forcefully, and Ann's spirits sank. "If you were still at National Farm Equipment, by now you'd be making over nine thousand dollars a year, so I think you should start at ten thousand. As far as I'm concerned, that's the salary you requested," he said with a big grin on his face. "And let's not forget a performance bonus of thirty percent of that base salary and a moving package that covers all of your relocation costs from Davis to Memphis."

"Really?" Ann asked excitedly with a euphoria coming over her that she hadn't felt in a long time. "Oh, Harry, I won't let you or GSDC down!"

"I know you won't. By the way, if Ray moves to another part of the company, would you want to work for him there, or would you stay at this job in the sweetener department?"

"I think you already know what I'd like to do in that situation, but I'll work wherever is best for GSDC."

"Great. One other thing, and this is not part of the job interview, because you've already got the job. Just call it curiosity on my part. How do you feel about children?"

"What?"

"Do you want to have children some day?"

"Yes, but at this point I'm not off to a very good start at moving in that direction."

"Many professional women complain that there's not enough time in the day for their job and also their children. What's your opinion of that?"

"I think it's a matter of setting priorities," Ann replied. "If you decide to have children, then either be a stay-at-home mom until they are teenagers and involved in their own lives, or take a job that gives you time for them. I think raising and training children is an adult's most important and special responsibility, and it shouldn't be taken lightly. That's why it's so important to have a marriage that's a partnership, so both of you will work together to make sure your children are raised in a stable, loving family with both spouses playing equal roles in parenting."

"I feel the same way, Ann. And my wife, Arlene, and I have one of those rare and special partnerships. I'd like you to meet her sometime."

"I'd like to," Ann replied, thinking, *I would certainly like to meet the woman that this man considers his partner in life.*

"Ann, have you ever actually met Ray Collins, or did you just see him present that paper and talk to people who knew him?"

"I've never actually met him," she admitted.

"Would you like me to be the one that introduces you to him?"

"Oh, Mr. Davis - I mean, Harry - that would be great!"

"Fine. We'll have you back to formally offer you the job, and I'll introduce you to him then. Maybe the three of us can have lunch together."

On the plane flying back to Sacramento, Ann's mind was filled with exciting thoughts. She'd never met anyone like Harry Davis. He was so perceptive, smart, and capable. And there was no nonsense about him, either. He cut to the chase and said his mind. She already felt he was like a second father, and admired him tremendously. And he was Ray's boss and mentor! It appeared as if Harry was okay with her career motivations. He even seemed to want to help her!

On July 23, Sherry Monson called and asked if Ann could come to GSDC's offices on Friday, July 29. Ann excitedly agreed, looking forward to meeting Ray Collins and formally receiving the job offer. She and Beth went on another shopping trip, and this time she got a blue wool suit and white silk blouse, and Beth asked, "Are you sure there isn't some new man in your life?"

When Ann arrived at GSDC's offices on the Friday, Lisa, met her in the lobby and took Ann to Harry's office. "Good morning, Harry!" Ann said excitedly as she entered his office and Lisa closed the door behind her.

"Morning, Ann. Did you have a pleasant flight?" Harry said flatly, the enthusiasm she'd heard in his voice from their meeting last week now gone.

Ann immediately sensed that something was wrong. "What's up, Harry?" she asked, searching his face for some clue about what was disturbing him so.

"Ray Collins has resigned. To help keep his family intact, he's moving his wife, Connie, to a more rural, slower pace lifestyle at the recommendation of her doctor. He's sacrificing his career to save his family."

The words hit Ann like a bomb. Suddenly she felt ill, and tears were welling up in her eyes. "Excuse me, Harry. I need to go to the ladies room." Lisa told Ann where the restroom was and Ann hurried down the hallway, tears streaming down her cheeks. She went into one of the stalls and began to cry uncontrollably. Now there would be no career for her to share with Ray. She'd changed the entire professional direction of her life in order to be with him, and now that opportunity was no longer there. What was she to do?

After about ten minutes Lisa came into the ladies room and asked, "Are you okay, Miss. Robinson?"

"Yes, but I don't feel well. Please tell Harry that I'd like to cancel the rest of our meeting, and that I'll call him later."

"Ms. Robinson, Mr. Davis wants to come in and talk with you."

"I'd rather he not"

And then she heard Harry's booming voice. "Lisa, would you step outside and tell anyone who wants to use the restroom that it's temporarily closed?"

"Yes, Mr. Davis."

Next Ann heard heavy footsteps come into the restroom, followed by Harry's voice. "Ann, I know how you must feel, but you can't give up. You're not a quitter. You're a winner. And winners never accept defeat. Plus you've got something that tilts things strongly in your favor – me. And I'm the best thing you could have in your corner. So get control of your emotions, come back to my office and let's work on your new plan."

Then Harry left. Ann realized the fact that so powerful an executive as Harry Davis would take the time or even care enough to help her was rare, and it really moved her. She realized how special he was. Most men wouldn't have had a clue what was going on with her or what she was all about, but Harry understood. And he wanted to help. So she came out of the stall, washed her tear-stained face, fixed her make up and hair, and went back to Harry's office.

After she was settled, Harry got up and closed the door, telling Lisa to hold all his calls and cancel his next meeting. "Ann, I want to tell you where I'm coming from. I think that one of an executive's most important responsibilities is bringing talent into corporations. For me, that means finding people with real skills, hiring them, and training them. Ed Bardwell, and Derrick Mobley - the chief financial officer and the CEO of SDC North America, respectively - were two people I brought to GSDC from small companies and trained."

"Ray was also one of those people, wasn't he?"

"Yes. And because of the brilliance he showed in solving the problems of switching to HFCS, plus a number of other projects he's done that are making hundreds of millions of dollars for GSDC, the board just agreed to offer him the presidency of the Bright Sun Orange Juice Company, a one hundred fifty million dollar[6] subsidiary of GSDC. At thirty-two, he would have been the youngest CEO in GSDC."

"Then I was correct: Ray did solve that problem."

"Yes, Ann. He has the best business mind I've ever seen, and I've seen a lot of brilliant minds. If he had stayed here, I have no doubt that in ten years or less he would have been the CEO of GSDC."

"What happened to his wife that he now feels he has to sacrifice his career?"

"Connie tried to commit suicide by taking an overdose of sleeping pills. Two psychologists have told Ray that the fast-paced lifestyle of a rising executive is too much pressure for her and he should move to some place more like where she grew up, or she will attempt suicide again - and might be successful.

---

[6] The same as $1.3 billion in 2014.

They have told him he needs a job with fewer responsibilities so he can have more time to be with her and their boys."

"You don't believe that, do you?"

"Not one bit."

"Why?"

"Connie was always leaving him and their two sons to 'get away.' And when Ray would schedule extra time to be with her in Florida or other places, she wasn't interested. I can't count the times that he scheduled three-day weekends or other times for them to get away together and would then turn up at the office because she wouldn't go with him. I don't think she loves him, or that she particularly likes the responsibility of being a mother. I think she has been having affairs and this whole suicide thing is just a way to manipulate Ray into getting whatever it is she wants."

"Really!" Ann exclaimed, thinking, *As perceptive as Harry is, and as well as he understands people, I bet he's right about Ray's wife.*

"Ann, I don't think their marriage will last. At some point, Ray's going to discover how she really feels about him and their two boys, and that will be that. I would be surprised if they are still married after another year or two."

At that assessment, particularly coming from Harry, Ann's spirits brightened.

"I think you should accept the job here, develop additional professional skills, and bide your time. You don't really want to be just Ray's professional colleague. If he lives up to your expectations and both of you fall in love, you want to be his wife and partner in life. But you aren't ready to be his equal partner yet. At this point, you could be his wife, but not truly an equal partner for him. For that, you need to develop the additional professional skills that will put you in Ray's league."

"But what if I don't have what it takes to be in Ray's league?"

"Trust me, Ann, you do. And you are the only other person I know who I can say that about. But to get there, you will need the training and professional skills that the job you have been offered here will provide, plus you'll need one other thing."

"Your training and mentoring?"

"Exactly," he said with a smile.

"Harry, you'd do that? Train me?"

"Yes."

"I thought you didn't mentor people at the level where I'm going to start."

"I never have."

"Then why make the exception for me?"

"Your training starts now, and here's your first problem to solve: Tell me why I'm making an exception in your case. I hope you don't mind, but I took the liberty of ordering lunch to be delivered here. Turkey breast sandwiches and Caesar salad, if that's okay."

"Sure, Harry."

"Good. I'll go see where our lunch is while you think about the question I just asked you."

This guy makes me think of what Ray's probably like, Ann thought. And then it hit her. *Harry is trying to help Ray, and thinks I would be a good choice as a wife and partner for him. Harry is trying to help me meet my goal of being with Ray because he thinks I'm the wife and partner Ray needs in life, or could be after Harry trains me.*

"Well?" Harry asked as he brought their lunches into his office.

"You matchmaker," she replied with a coy smile.

"I told you that you were smart and perceptive."

"But why the interest in helping Ray find a wife and partner?"

"Ann... you, me, Ray, my wife, Arlene, and a very small percentage of other people I know have much higher intellects than most other people. For us, finding a spouse that we are truly compatible with is a monumental task. It's tough enough for the typical person, where there are hundreds or thousands of potential compatible mates. But for people like us, it's almost impossible to find that 'right person' because there are so fewer potential mates to choose from in the first place. We find ourselves bored with virtually everyone we go out with. So we end up settling for a marriage or a situation that's not ideal. We men bury ourselves in our work to avoid a bad relationship at home, and many professional women like yourself opt not to get married in the first place.

"When Arlene and I first met, we had both been through bad marriages and divorced, but neither of us had children. She was a student working on her PhD in economics at Harvard and I was vice-president of business development for GSDC and going through Harvard's advanced management program. Allen Bloom, a friend of mine who Ray also knows, introduced Arlene and me and it was incredible, the closest thing to love at first sight that either of us had ever experienced. We were powerfully attracted to one another, and we still are. I remember I wanted to leave my job at GSDC and move to Boston just so I could be with her, and she was ready to drop out of Harvard and move to Memphis to be near me. Fortunately, she soon finished her coursework for her doctorate and was admitted to candidacy, and Harvard agreed for her to write her dissertation from Memphis so we could get married.

"I'm fifty-seven years old now, Ann. And although I've enjoyed my career at GSDC, selecting and training some of the world's best business minds will be my true accomplishment in this life and my legacy at this company. But now I have the rare opportunity to help Ray find his partner in life, and at the same time, create a husband and wife partnership that will create a professional team the business world has never seen before. Together the two of you will either be extremely valuable business consultants or run a large corporation, maybe even GSDC. And being able to be part of the creation of that is really appealing and special to me." Ann was awestruck, but what he said made sense.

As they started their lunches, Harry outlined his plan. "You take this commodity analyst position, which will essentially be implementing Ray's ideas that switch GSDC from sugar to HFCS. Successfully manage such a critical project, and not only will you develop important management skills, but there will also be a large promotion in it for you. We'll find a way to keep up with what's going on in Ray's life. At this point, I'd say he's likely headed to Tropical Citrus in Tampa, Florida to be their vice-president of procurement and operations planning."

"Isn't Tropical Citrus a subsidiary of the food conglomerate National Foods?"

"Yeah, they are based in Chicago. Anyway, once Ray's marriage breaks up, you'll probably be ready to go to him, and the rest will be up to you and Ray. However when that happens, at some point, I'd like to think that both of you would consider coming back to GSDC as a husband - wife team. What do you think?"

"Oh, Harry, I don't know what to say. Thank you for your willingness to help. And I can't wait to get started."

"Want me to introduce you to Ray? Because if you do, I can probably set up dinner tonight for just the three of us and let him meet my choice for the analyst who will implement his ideas."

"Harry, I want to meet Ray more than you know. But after listening to what you've just told me, I don't think it's the right time yet. I know now that the first time I meet Ray needs to happen when he is single and free of his marriage commitments. I don't want him ever blaming me for being a factor in the break-up of his marriage. And if he feels about me as I instantly felt about him when I first saw him present that paper at Clemson, or if our chemistry is like it was when you and Arlene first met, he'll be troubled by his desire to be with me even though he's married. And I don't want that."

"I understand, and I agree with your decision."

"When do you want to start your job here?"

"How about on Monday, September 24? That gives me time to wrap up my work as a research associate at Davis and move to Memphis."

"Great, I'll have Terry Bower, our HR guy, draft an offer that you can take with you when you leave today. Let's get Jack Lovelace in here and make him feel good about selecting the right candidate for this job. Then you and Jack can go back to his office and spend some time discussing what you'll be doing during your first few weeks on the job while Terry works on your offer letter."

"Thanks, Harry," Ann said softly, touching his arm in an effort to express how much she appreciated what he was doing.

"You're very welcome, and very deserving."

Chapter Eight

Ann stayed busy during her first few weeks at GSDC learning the soft drink business. She also traveled to various locations to meet with GSDC's sweetener suppliers. By the beginning of December, she was up to speed and ready to begin her project of implementing Ray's plan to switch GSDC to high fructose corn syrup. Jack Lovelace, Ann's boss, had told her that GSDC made films of all their board meetings and that she might find it helpful to get the film of Ray presenting his strategy for switching from sugar to HFCS to the GSDC board. However, she would need to see Harry Davis to get access to it. When she called to ask Harry about the film, he told her to meet him in the boardroom at three p.m. so they could view and discuss it, then he would give her a copy.

The room was darker than normal when Ann entered, and Harry was fiddling with the projector. "Have a seat, Ann. I think this thing's adjusted and ready to go."

And then Ann caught her breath as Ray Collins seemed to come to life on the screen in front of her. *God he was handsome!* But this wasn't the film of Ray's HFCS strategy; it was of his farewell to the board. As she watched and listened to Ray talk about why he was leaving GSDC, about his commitment to his family and what he was giving up for them, it again dawned on her what a rare person he was. Here was this special, beautiful man, telling the board and the company he'd served so faithfully and profitably why he now had to leave the career he loved behind. It was more than just his words; his expressions, and especially his eyes, told of the depth of his feelings and commitments, and of the sadness over abandoning his career that he couldn't hide. It moved Ann like nothing else she'd experienced. When it was over, she just sat, unable to speak, trying to hold back tears. She could tell that Harry was affected by it, too, although he'd been at the board meeting when Ray had made this farewell presentation. Harry cleared his throat and said, "I thought you would like to see that, to better know what he's all about."

"Harry, I had no idea."

"He's one of a kind, Ann. You know, come to think of it, I've now known Ray for over two years, and I've talked to a lot of people who he's worked with. I've never met anyone who doesn't admire him. I never thought of it before, but that's certainly very rare. Several of our senior executives came to me when they heard Ray was resigning, to say they were concerned. It seems as if Ray had been helping them solve business problems in their area in his spare time and nobody knew about it because he wanted them to get the credit. Now they're worried about what they'll do in his absence. I asked Ray what he'd do with his creative energies in a dead-end job many levels below his capability, like the one he's gone to, and you know what Ray told me?"

"What?" Ann asked, her voice breaking with emotion.

"That he would teach and train others so they could have a chance at the professional rewards that he was choosing to forgo."

"Harry, I - I'm so in love with him - even though I've never actually met him."

"I know, Ann. And that makes me happy, because Ray deserves someone like you." He then handed her a stack of film spools. "Here are all five of Ray's presentations to the board, including that last one we just watched. They are yours to keep."

It was September 14, 1956, and Ann was nervous as she headed to her meeting with Jack Lovelace, George Martin, and Harry Davis. Since joining GSDC a year ago, she had assumed the responsibility of developing the futures hedging strategies and the procurement processes that enabled the company to implement Ray's ideas for switching GSDC from sugar to high fructose corn syrup for its sweetener needs. By August of this year, the project was largely completed and GSDC was now one of the largest HFCS users in the world. But she hadn't heard what her next project would be, which she viewed as a bad sign. Moreover, Harry seemed to be preoccupied with something over the past few weeks, and she had not had the chance to have her monthly meeting with him. Ann had come to really look forward to those monthly meetings, where she and Harry had reviewed her work and managerial activities as part of her training. Maybe George and Jack had heard about the interest two of the HFCS suppliers had in hiring her and thought she should have told them about that. But those suppliers had asked her to keep their hiring attempts confidential, and she had told them she wasn't interested in leaving GSDC. One of them had made her a verbal offer anyway, which she'd declined. Maybe Harry had heard about that job offer and was upset that she hadn't told him about it. These were, after all, GSDC suppliers, and with her knowledge of the economics of HFCS procurement, whatever company that hired her could use that knowledge to its advantage.

"Ann, we've called this meeting to inform you that you are being relieved of your responsibilities as senior commodity analyst for GSDC," Harry began with a somber look on his face. *Oh, no! What went wrong?* Ann thought. *I bet they heard about that job offer.*

"Gentlemen, listen, I..."

"You are being promoted to chief economist of GSDC," Harry said with a big grin on his face. "And for the outstanding job you've done on the HFCS project, Ann, we have a special bonus check of ten thousand dollars[7] cash and another fifty thousand dollars[8] in GSDC stock for you," he said proudly. Ann was in shock.

"Ann, as chief economist, you will be reporting directly to me," George said. "You will have responsibility for all of GSDC's commodity futures trading, for estimating the costs of new ingredients and changes in ingredient formulas in our soft drinks, and for analyzing the costs and benefits of new procurement strategies. Your new annual base salary will be twenty thousand dollars, you will have a performance bonus of up to thirty percent of your base salary, plus stock options. The total package comes to about twenty-nine thousand dollars[9] a year. Sherry in HR will go over all the details of it with you.

"Oh, and you'll also have your own secretary," George told her. "You won't have to share one any longer. Her name is Donna Casper. She has a degree in economics from the University of Tennessee, and she's very bright."

Ann was still in shock. She'd hoped for a promotion, but had not expected anything like this! "I believe she's speechless," Harry said.

Ann regained her composure and said, "This was a lot more than I expected! Without your help, leadership and guidance, I couldn't have managed such a large project, so thanks to each of you. And I can't wait to start the new job!" They talked for a while longer, with everyone congratulating her on the job she'd done and on her promotion.

"Ann, this is Steve Hogan, director of marketing for processed products at Sun Ripe Citrus. Steve, Ann Robinson, our

---

[7] The same as $87,592 in 2014.

[8] The same as $437,960 in 2014.

[9] The same as $254,017 in 2014.

chief economist," George Martin said as he introduced the two of them. Sun Ripe was the largest packer and marketer of fresh citrus in the United States, and they were also GSDC's largest lemon oil supplier. It was January of 1957, and George Martin had brought them together because of a new soft drink that was being formulated that had lemon oil and orange essences as critical, and costly, flavor components.

"It's good to finally meet you, Steve," Ann said. Steve was tall, about six foot two, and slender, with sandy hair, gray eyes, and a well-kept beard.

"Same here," Steve replied, trying to hide his obvious astonishment at Ann's beauty.

"I hear that Sun Ripe is now selling orange juice to Tropical Citrus," George commented.

"Well, we couldn't get Bright Sun to buy our navel juice, so it's good that someone wanted it," Steve said jokingly.

"If we still had Ray Collins, Bright Sun would probably be buying your juice instead of Tropical Citrus," George kidded. At the mention of Ray's name, Ann felt a slight twinge.

"All kidding aside, George, Ray was able to get the Tropical Citrus research and development team to develop a cost-effective essence formula that enables Tropical Citrus to use navel orange juice in their products, which expanded our market and reduced their cost of goods," Steve continued.

"That guy is amazing, isn't he?" George observed.

"He sure is," Steve replied. "Ann, I understand that you implemented Ray's strategy to switch GSDC to HFCS. What's your opinion of him?"

"I've never met Ray Collins, but there's no doubt that he's a very talented business man," Ann said, trying to calm the butterflies she was feeling.

"What? You've never met Ray?"

"No."

"I think I'll get to my operations meeting and leave you two to solve the world's business problems," George said as he left the room.

"So you know Ray Collins pretty well, huh?" Ann asked Steve.

"Yes. We've been friends ever since Ray got responsibility for purchasing at GSDC several years ago. And he's someone I'm proud to have as a friend."

They talked for a while longer. They made plans for Ann to travel to Sun Ripe's facilities in Riverside, California so she could work with Steve and his colleagues on the lemon oil formulation for the new soft drink.

"How was your trip?" Steve Hogan asked Ann when he greeted her in the lobby of Sun Ripe's offices on Monday, February 4.

"Smooth flight, schedule was on time, and I've learned not to expect better than that."

"I've got you scheduled for a general tour of our processing plant, then the research and development labs. After that, we'll meet in my office with Eileen Rossi, our head of R and D. If you have no other plans, my wife, Sandy, and I would like to have you over to our house for dinner tonight."

"Sounds like a good schedule, and I would love to join you and Sandy for dinner. Thanks for inviting me."

"Sandy, Ann Robinson, Ann, my wife, Sandy," Steve said as he introduced the two women.

"Welcome to our home, Ann," Sandy said. Sandy was about five foot six and slender, with brown, medium-length hair, and wide-set, inquisitive brown eyes. She spoke with an accent that suggested she was raised in the northeast, maybe Massachusetts or Vermont, and her poise suggested a refined upbringing.

THE WINE QUEEN

During dinner that night, Steve said, "Sandy, Ann led the project that implemented Ray Collins's strategy to switch GSDC to HFCS."

"Really?"

"Yes," Ann replied.

"What do you think of Ray Collins?" Sandy asked.

"She's never met him," Steve offered.

"That's right. He left GSDC about the same time that I joined the company. Apparently he had some sort of family problems to deal with," Ann said, trying to act only casually interested and only partly aware of the circumstances surrounding Ray's resignation.

"HIs wife tried to commit suicide and he left his career to get more time to spend with her and his family, hopefully to help her," Sandy explained. "I think that was so sad. He had such a brilliant career ahead of him. Most men wouldn't have done that, but then Ray's one of a kind."

"You know the tragedy of it all is that his sacrifice did nothing to help his marriage," Steve said. "Ray and I are very close friends, and he shares things with me that he doesn't normally talk about. I guess it helps for him to have a friend to talk to. I don't think it would hurt to talk about it here, since you don't even know him, Ann. Anyway, when I was talking to him a few weeks ago, he said that his wife, Connie, had moved in with another man, a biker who refuses to work. She was threatening to take Ray's boys, Tommy and Jesse, away from him unless he gives her everything he's got: stocks, bonds, cash, even their house, plus a large amount of alimony each month. She's just using those children to get money for her and her lover. She also told Ray she's been cheating on him with various lovers for years."

At this point, Ann was shaking with emotion, and angry at what Steve was telling them about how Connie was treating Ray and his sons, particularly after all that Ray had sacrificed for their marriage. Then she remembered Harry telling her that, at some point, Connie's true nature would show itself, and that would be that. Harry had been right about Connie. *Maybe things are finally turning in my favor!* "I guess that means the end of his marriage after all," Ann suggested, trying to act disinterested.

"Maybe, but actually things aren't quite that simple."

"What do you mean?" Sandy asked.

"When Connie and her lover found out that Ray was not going to just hand over everything he had to them, and that he was going to fight for custody of his boys, Connie's lover packed up and left. Then Connie apologized and begged for Ray to take her back," Steve explained.

"Don't tell me he took her back!" Ann exclaimed, a little too excitedly.

"Yes, but only at the advice of his divorce lawyer, who advised Ray that judges in Florida, as in most other states, lean heavily toward giving custody to the mother. He described a scenario to Ray where getting custody of their boys would enable Connie to get half of Ray's assets and a large amount of child support and alimony each month. Then she and her biker friends would party on Ray's money while Ray's sons would have to get along the best that they could, certainly without adequate adult supervision or parenting. So Ray has agreed to take her back, following his lawyer's advice, and is trying to get enough evidence of her irresponsible behavior to win custody of the boys. But he and Connie are sleeping in separate bedrooms so there's no more love there. Ray's lawyer thinks it will probably be only a matter of time before Connie finds another lover and threatens to take his boys in exchange for money again. They hope Ray will have enough evidence to win custody by then."

"Oh, I think that's awful!" Ann exclaimed, now obviously very concerned with the situation. "That poor man, and those poor little boys. How old are they, Steve?"

"Tommy's eight and Jesse's six."

"To have a mother like that must be terrible," Ann said, trying to hide her emotions over what she had just heard.

"But Ray makes up for it," Sandy offered. "He's a devoted father and spends most of his spare time with them: fishing, gardening, going on picnics, things like that. A lot of men in a situation like that would hire a sitter for the boys and be out chasing women. Particularly if they had women falling all over them, as they do over Ray. I know you understand where I'm coming from when I say this, Steve, but Ray is an incredibly handsome man."

"You're not saying anything I don't already know. When he comes out to our offices, the women go nuts. I think Eileen Rossi, our R and D director, is in love with him. Every time he came out to work with her on the navel orange project she got her hair done and bought a new outfit," Steve said.

"Oh, you don't know the half of it," Sandy said. "I'm friends with several of the women at Sun Ripe, and I hear all of the 'girl talk.' But Ray doesn't respond to any of their advances. He's polite, and tells them he's committed to his marriage vows."

"I know, and that's pretty rare for a guy, particularly one that has beautiful women throwing themselves at him the way Ray does. But Ray believes that marriage vows are to God and to the children, and just because his wife doesn't honor them doesn't mean that he shouldn't."

"I'm sorry, Ann. Here we are going on and on about someone you don't even know." Sandy said.

"Oh, that's okay. I am intrigued about this whole story," Ann replied, thinking how awful life must be for Ray and his little boys now.

The phone then rang, and Steve got up to answer it. A few minutes later, he came back and said, "I'm sorry. There's a problem at the plant with some shipments, and Mike, who usually deals with that, is away on vacation. I'll need to run down there, but I should be back soon."

113

"That's okay, Steve. It will give Ann and I some time to get to know each other better."

After Steve left, Ann and Sandy exchanged backgrounds. "Steve and I actually met in London," Sandy explained. "He was working on his PhD at the London School of Economics, and I was taking a sabbatical from my teaching position at Wellesley College, actually trying to get over a divorce.

"I also went to Wellesley."

"Really? It's a small world. When were you there?"

"From 1946 to 1950," Ann replied.

"I was there from 1950 to 1953. Anyway, as you know, it's a great school. For Steve and me, it was practically love at first sight. I resigned my position at Wellesley, got a teaching position at Middlesex University in London, where I was on sabbatical, and moved in with Steve. We were married about four months later and have never looked back. Our marriage is a true partnership. I'm now a professor of humanities at the University of Southern California, and after six years of marriage, we're still very much in love."

"No children yet?" Ann asked.

"No, I can't have children, but we're on the waiting list to adopt." Sandy then changed the subject.

"What about you, Ann.?   You never found that right someone?"

"I was engaged to a doctor when I was a junior at Wellesley, but it didn't last. I wasn't willing to share him with his nurse. I've dated since, but no serious relationships."

"I bet most of the men you've dated either bore you or just want to get you into bed," Sandy speculated.

"How did you know?"

"Because that's the way it was for me until I met Steve. The right man will come along someday. You just have to be patient."

THE WINE QUEEN

They talked a while longer, then Ann got up to leave for her hotel. "Please tell Steve I really enjoyed dinner and your hospitality," Ann said as she walked to the door.

"I will, and let's not be strangers. You have an open invitation to visit anytime you are in town," Sandy said.

"You have my home phone number. Give me a call," Ann said as she left.

It was about eleven thirty when Steve returned home, and Sandy was waiting up for him. "Sorry to be so late, love," he apologized. "But we were out of spec on a customer's product, and the manufacturing guys didn't have the customer's blending protocols to correct the problem."

"That's okay, honey."

"Do you think Ann minded that I left that way?"

"No, in fact it gave her and me time to get to know each other better. I like her, Steve. She's smart and beautiful, but not hung up on herself about it. And unless I miss my guess, she's in love with Ray Collins."

"What? Sandy, she's never even met Ray. How in the world could you conclude that she's in love with him?"

"The way she looked and acted when we were talking about him. She may have never met him, but I bet she's seen him and knows a lot about him."

"No way, Sandy. You're way off base on this one."

"I'd like to get to know Ann better. Maybe go see her sometime when I'm in Little Rock visiting my parents. You know I can't help being a matchmaker. Would you humor me on this one?"

"Okay. Who knows? You might make a new friend. In fact, I'm scheduled to travel to Memphis to visit with George Martin at GSDC, then to Atlanta to meet with Don Lindsey at Coca-Cola, and finally to Tampa to see Ray. This customer trip is scheduled for the week of March eleventh. Why don't you fly with me to Memphis, then while I'm traveling to Atlanta and Tampa, you can visit with Ann, then go visit your parents for the rest of the time. I'll meet up with you in Little Rock on Saturday, March sixteenth, and spend that night at your parents' house. Then we can fly back to California on Sunday."

"If I can get someone to teach my classes that week, and if Ann's schedule will enable me to visit her then, you're on!"

The plans and schedules worked out, with a few changes. Sandy planned to fly to Little Rock on Saturday, March ninth, and visit with her parents until Thursday. Steve would fly into Memphis on Sunday and meet with GSDC on Monday and Tuesday. Then he would meet with Tropical Juices in Tampa, and finally with Coca-Cola in Atlanta. Ann planned to take off that Friday, March fifteenth, to show Sandy the sights around Memphis. Since Steve planned to play golf with Don Lindsey in Atlanta on Saturday morning, March sixteenth, he would get to Memphis in the afternoon, and Steve, Sandy, and Ann would all go to dinner in Memphis that night. Then Steve and Sandy would fly back to California on Sunday.

Ann was excited about the new friends she was making and Sandy's upcoming visit. She was also excited about being friends with a woman whom Ray considered a friend.

"Hi, Sandy. Come on in," Ann said when she answered the door at her condo and greeted her new friend.

"Hi, Ann. Gee, you really have a nice place," Sandy said as she came in and sat down to have a cup of coffee.

"Thanks. I've planned for us to see the Dixon Art Gallery and Gardens, have lunch at a great little bistro, and then tour the Memphis Music Hall of Fame. I just got a new charcoal grill, and yesterday I bought a pound-and-a-half of jumbo shrimp. So I and thought we'd prepare grilled lemon pepper shrimp Caesar salad, and have dinner here if that's okay with you." Ann explained.

"Great. I brought a bottle of Napa Valley Chardonnay and sour dough bread that we can have with it."

Tomorrow we can go shopping, or do something else if you'd like."

"That all sounds like fun to me," Sandy replied.

During their day, as Ann and Sandy got to know each other better, it became obvious that the two women had a lot in common and were fast becoming close friends.

They returned to Ann's condo at six p.m. While Ann soaked the shrimp in lemon pepper marinade and prepared and lit the charcoal grill on her back porch, following Ann's recipe, Sandy prepared the Caesar salad dressing.

"Here, try one," Ann suggested as she handed Sandy a shrimp hot off the grill.

"*Wow! That's phenomenal!*" Sandy exclaimed as she bit into the succulent Jumbo shrimp. "Will you share your recipe with me?"

"Of course," Ann replied as she was slicing Vermont cheddar cheese to melt over the sourdough bread.

"Here's to our new friendship," Ann said as she raised her glass of Chardonnay after they'd sat down to have dinner.

"To our new friendship," Sandy replied, touching her glass of wine to Ann's.

"So how long have you known Ray Collins?" Ann asked as she heaped grilled lemon pepper shrimp on top of her Caesar salad.

"Since early 1954, just after he got responsibility for purchasing at GSDC," Sandy replied, ladling parmesan-packed Caesar dressing over the fresh, crisp, romaine lettuce and crunchy garlic croutons on her plate, followed by a generous portion of the juicy shrimp. "He came to visit Sun Ripe and I went to dinner with him and Steve," Sandy explained as she took a bite of the steaming sourdough bread with melted cheddar cheese on it. "Ann, Ray's one of the most unique men I've ever met. Forget the fact that he's drop-dead handsome and a talented business executive with a very promising future. He's one of the kindest, most giving people I've ever met. In business transactions, there's no one more honest and ethical. When they were working on that new essence formula for navel oranges, one of Sun Ripe's accountants made an error that nobody at the company caught. It would have cost Sun Ripe several million dollars and probably have gotten the accountant and Steve fired. But Ray caught it when he was reviewing the contract. He contacted Steve and let him take the credit for catching the error and correcting it. Ray said that starting a new supply relationship with an agreement that made the supplier lose money was no way to build a capable, effective supplier relationship. Another time, one of the women at Sun Ripe lost her husband in an accident. She didn't make enough money to make it on her own, pay for a babysitter, and continue working on her college degree at night. So Ray gave Steve a cashier's check made out to her for fifteen hundred dollars, asking only that the gift be anonymous, and to tell her that it was from people who cared."

"I've only heard good things about Ray from people who know him," Ann observed, her voice starting to break with emotion.

"The sad thing is how terribly way his wife treats him. Steve says Ray's personal life is a nightmare, but somehow he bears up and doesn't let it affect his work. He always has a smile and a kind word to say, no matter what kind of pain his wife is inflicting on him and his two boys."

At this point, Ann could no longer hold back the tears welling up in her eyes, and she got up and said, "Excuse me please, Sandy." Then she went to the restroom to regain her composure.

When she returned, Sandy asked, "Ann, you're in love with Ray, aren't you?"

"Is it that obvious?"

"It is to me, but not to Steve, and probably not to anyone else."

Ann was glad to be able to share her feelings about Ray with someone other than Harry Davis, particularly with a woman who knew Ray. She told Sandy the whole story about how she'd first encountered him at Clemson and how she'd changed the entire course of her life because of her love for him. "I've never heard anything so special, Ann. It's such a beautiful love story," Sandy observed, her eyes becoming glassy with emotion.

"It's only that at this point: a story," Ann said. "But if his marriage breaks up, I'm planning to try to finally meet him in person and see where that leads."

"Oh, Ann. Would you let Steve and I set up your first meeting with Ray at our house in California? It would be perfect, because Ray comes to Sun Ripe on business, and so do you!"

"Sure, I suppose. But he isn't divorced yet."

"Oh, I think he will be. It's just a matter of time. And Steve can keep us apprised of what's happening in that arena, since he frequently talks with Ray about his personal life. You don't mind if I share this with Steve, do you?"

"I guess not, as long as he keeps it in strictest confidence," Ann said, recognizing that she trusted her new friend and that Sandy and Steve's input would be important in helping her plan her first meeting with Ray.

"You have both our words on that," Sandy affirmed.

Chapter Nine

"Hi, Ann it's Sandy Hogan," she said when Ann answered the phone. It was October of 1957.

"It's good to hear from you, Sandy. How have you been?"

"Fine. I've got a present for you Ann."

"What is it?"

"Let me give you its background first.

"Okay," Ann said, intrigued.

"Tropical Citrus and Sun Ripe recently signed a multi-year contract for Sun Ripe to supply the orange juice for Tropical Citrus's new West Coast packaging facility in Corona, California. Ray invited Steve and me to come to Tampa to celebrate the new supply relationship between Tropical Juices and Sun Ripe. It was to be a weekend for just us two couples, and the plans were to have dinner at Bern's Steak House in Tampa on Friday night and go fishing on Tropical Citrus's boat on Saturday. However, for some reason, Connie was unable to go. But Ray didn't change a thing, other than apologize for her and ask if we minded him bringing his sons along instead of Connie. We agreed, then I asked if Ray would mind if I took a home movie of the weekend's activities since he was bringing the boys along. He thought that was a great idea. So that's your present. A two-hour home movie of Ray Collins and his sons having a wonderful time together."

"Really? Oh, Sandy, I can't begin to tell you how much that means to me. I'll be glad to pay for the shipping if you'll send it by airmail."

"It's already on its way and you should have it day after tomorrow."

"Sandy, you're such a good friend."

"Ray's two sons, Tommy and Jesse, are little darlings. Tommy's nine and Jesse's seven. When Ray met us at our hotel to take us to dinner on Friday night, Jesse gave me a rose he'd picked from a bush in their yard and Tommy pinned it to my jacket. Then, when we were having dinner, I excused myself to go to the restroom. Tommy got up and pulled my chair out for me, and when I came back, he pulled it out again for me to sit down. Ray's raised those boys to treat women with admiration and respect, and they really do."

"They sound so special. I can't wait to get the film."

Two days later when Ann got home from work, the package with the film was waiting on her doorstep. She put the film in her projector, and once again gasped at the sight of Ray. He and his boys were walking toward the fishing boat carrying an ice chest and two duffel bags. Ray was talking to his boys, probably about what type of fish they were going to try to catch. Now she'd be able to see him in a more relaxed casual family setting with his two sons. *Thank you, Sandy*, she said silently.

As she watched Sandy's film of the fishing trip, her eyes became glassy with emotion. Ray was so kind and considerate to everyone, always helping with little things, making a genuine effort so that everyone had a good time. And his boys! Sandy sure was right. They were little darlings.

After the fishing trip, the next part of the film was shot the next day when they all went on a picnic to the beach. When she saw Ray take his shirt off to go swimming, she became dizzy at the sight of him. He was so muscular! He had a body like a

Greek god, the muscles in his chest, shoulders, and legs rippling as he threw a football back and forth with Tommy, Jesse, and Steve after their swim. He was the most beautiful, sexy man she'd ever seen, and watching him made her long to be with him in a way that she never had before.

Watching this film, it became obvious what a wonderful father Ray must be. The relationship he had with Tommy and Jesse was different from any she'd ever seen between a parent and his or her children. There was a bond, a connection between the three of them that was unique. It was obvious that they were all best buddies as well as father and sons, and it was almost like they could read one another's thoughts. No arguing between brothers, or scolding for misbehavior by the parent. They just had fun together. She could tell that Tommy and Jesse absolutely adored their father, and that he felt the same about them. And Ray's boys were so kind, so well-mannered, so well-behaved and giving - unlike any children she'd ever seen.

When the film finished, she just sat, awestruck by what she'd seen. *Every time I see or learn something new about Ray, I'm even more impressed and I fall deeper in love with him,* she thought. And then the tears came – those of desperation at not being able to be with Ray, not being able to be a part of his wonderful family and enjoy times with them like she'd just seen. After what she'd seen, she not only longed for Ray more than ever, but now she also wanted to be the loving, caring mother to Jesse and Tommy that they'd never had, but deserved so much.

Ann didn't know how long she had been sitting, engrossed in her thoughts, when the phone rang. It was Sandy Hogan. "Well, did you get the film?"

"I sure did, and I've already watched it. I can't thank you enough for shooting it and sending it to me, Sandy."

"You're more than welcome, I'm glad that you enjoyed it."

"I know what heaven is now."

"What?"

"Heaven for me is being married to Ray Collins and being a mother to those wonderful little boys."

"They really are something, aren't they? So kind and considerate, just like Ray."

"Watching Ray at the beach with his shirt off, I couldn't believe how muscular he is."

"That's because he stays in shape lifting weights and jogging. Steve says Ray's in the same shape now as he was when he played football in college."

"Ray played football in college?"

"I thought you knew. Ray was a college football star. In fact, he had opportunities to go to the pros, but turned them down to get married and go to graduate school."

"Really? I didn't know that!" Ann exclaimed.

"Let me put Steve on. He can give you more details about Ray's college football accomplishments, if you're interested."

"Are you kidding? I'm interested in everything about Ray."

"I thought you didn't like jocks," Steve kidded when he picked up the phone.

"I usually don't. Most of the ones I've met are stuck on themselves and boring to be around. But obviously that doesn't characterize Ray."

"Okay. I'll tell you what I know. But Ray doesn't talk much about his football years, so all I really know is what I learned from one of our employees, who is a member of the local University of Florida Alumni Association and Gator Fan Club, and was intrigued that Ray was a business associate and close friend of mine. Ray played quarterback for the University of Florida Gators and helped lead the Gators to an SEC championship in his junior year and their first national championship in his senior year. That national championship game also finished the season where he was the NCAA Division 1-A top quarterback, leading the nation in passing yardage, touchdown passes, yardage and touchdowns ran, and yards of total offense, and set several NCAA records that remained unbroken for years. He also won the Heisman trophy. That was also the year that GQ magazine did a cover article on Ray about his football accomplishments and his turning down the pros." There was silence on the line for a moment. "Ann, are you still there?"

"I'm in love with a football star and celebrity, and you didn't tell me?" she finally replied.

"Ann, that was twelve years ago, and Ray never talks about it. I doubt if he even cares about it anymore."

"But I care about it! I want to know everything about him. By the way, did either of you get a feel for how things are going with Connie when you went on the fishing trip?"

"That's Sandy's department, so I'll get off and let you two talk."

"Okay, and thanks for telling me about Ray's football accomplishments, Steve."

Then Sandy got back on the line. "Ann, Ray didn't talk about Connie, but I didn't think he would with the boys around. However, when I asked him why she couldn't join us, he didn't have an answer, and his manner suggested that maybe they'd had a fight or something."

"Have you ever met her?"

"No, and after hearing how she's been treating Ray and those wonderful boys, I don't want to."

When they got off the phone, Ann just sat, again engrossed in her thoughts. *So Ray was a national college football star! Is there no end to the many impressive things about him?* Then she got an idea. *Why not start a scrapbook about Ray?* She already had the paper he presented at Clemson, films of his presentations to the GSDC board, and this recent family movie. If she could get some old newspaper clippings about Ray's football successes, a copy of that GQ magazine article about him, and maybe some films of his championship football games, she'd have a pretty good inventory of memorabilia about him.

She remembered that someone at the University of Florida had a citrus essence cost model, but didn't know who. Maybe if she could find out who he was, he could help her get the films of Ray playing football.

She decided she'd call Ron White to see if he knew the economist at the University of Florida who had the essence cost model. "Why, Ann Robinson. How have you been doing?" he asked when she called.

"Great. Life at GSDC is good. I was wondering if you knew someone in the agricultural economics department at the University of Florida. I understand that they have a cost model for citrus essences that might be helpful to us."

"Let me see... I believe Tom Taylor specializes in citrus costs. Give me a minute and I'll get his phone number for you."

"Tom, this is Ann Robinson from the Global Soft Drink Company," Ann said when she phoned Tom. "I got your number from Ron White."

"How's Ron doing these days?"

"Fine. He told me you have developed a cost of production model for oil and water-phased citrus essences."

"That's correct."

"I'd like to come to Gainesville and discuss it with you."

"Great. I'd be honored if GSDC wanted to use my model."

A few days later, Ann flew to Jacksonville, then rented a car and drove to Gainesville, where the University of Florida is located for her meeting with Tom Taylor. "Just enter the fruit volume processed and the price of the fruit into the formula, and it will give the cost of the essence per pound and per gallon," he explained as he went over his cost model with Ann.

"That's great. We can use this at GSDC for our contract negotiations." She then changed the subject. "Tom, a friend of mine is in the Memphis Gator fan club and she wants some films of when Florida won that national championship."

"Yeah. If I remember correctly, Ray Collins was the quarterback who led us to the championship that year. I believe it was 1945. The athletic department has those films and other memorabilia, but they're only available to faculty, students, and alumni. Here, take my faculty ID card," he said as he handed her the card. "They'll let you see the films with that, and I believe for a fee, you can buy copies of the ones you want. Just remember to return my card before you leave."

"Oh, thanks, Tom. I really appreciate this."

Ann was able to get copies of the films of Ray's SEC and National championship football games, a film clip of Ray accepting the Heisman Trophy, and a copy of his *GQ* article from the athletic department. She also got a number of newspaper stories from the *Gainesville Sun* about Ray's football games and his other successes. The university's newspaper, the *Florida Alligator,* also had some interesting articles about Ray's football years, but the ones she found most interesting were the ones about Ray being voted *"Most Handsome Man on Campus"* by one of the campus sororities during his sophomore, junior and senior years. *I bet every eligible coed on campus was after Ray,* she thought.

Ray's athletic accomplishments and college years were a part of Ray's life Ann hadn't known about for the six years she had been interested in him, and getting all of this was very special for her. When she returned home, she organized all of the newspaper stories and the *GQ* article and its cover page into a scrapbook. Then she labeled all the films she had about Ray and put everything into a special fireproof wall safe for storage.

Whenever she longed to be with Ray so much that it was almost unbearable, she'd watch some of the films she had of him, like when he won a championship football game, or made a presentation to the GSDC board, or was having fun with his boys at the beach. She'd also read the articles about his athletic successes. These were all parts of Ray's life, part of who he was, and they gave her a connection to him that kept her going.

"Ann Robinson," she said as she answered her phone. It was July 15, 1958.

"Hi, Ann. Steve Hogan"

"Hi, Steve. What's going on?"

"Guess what happened last Tuesday to Connie Collins?"

"What?"

"She was caught dealing drugs in a large sting operation and was arrested. She's in jail awaiting a hearing."

"Oh my God! Really?" Ann asked, hardly able to believe what she was hearing. Those butterflies started up again as what this could mean sank in. "Are Ray and his boys okay?"

"I just got off the phone with Ray, and he's fine. I think he's glad to see everything finally come to a head. Ray and his lawyer think they have the evidence they need for him to get custody of Tommy and Jesse and a divorce from Connie."

"Steve, I'm in shock. Can I call you back a little later?"

"Sure, Ann. I'll be in my office for the rest of the day."

Ann got up and closed her office door so nobody could see that she was shaking. Finally, after almost seven years, she would have her chance to meet Ray on her terms. To see if he was as attracted to her as she was to him. To see if they could have a future together. Before she knew it, she was calling Harry Davis's office. He was in a meeting, and Lisa said she'd have him return the call. Then she called Steve Hogan back.

"A penny for your thoughts right now," Steve said teasingly.

"What's the situation, Steve?"

"Let's see. The economy is..."

"Not that, silly! You know what I'm asking about!"

"Oh, *that* situation," Steve replied with a comical tone in his voice. He then gave her the details of the situation and told her that Ray's attorney had said it would probably be a couple of months before the divorce was final. She and Steve talked for a while, and then Ann's secretary buzzed in to say that Harry was returning her call. Ann ended her conversation with Steve and took the call.

"Harry, Ray and Connie are separated, and he's getting a divorce and custody of his sons!"

"I've got to go into another meeting now, but if you could come to my house and have dinner with Arlene and I tonight, we'll discuss this further."

"What time should I be there?"

"Seven thirty."

That night Ann, Harry, and Arlene were sitting in the Davis' living room, having a drink before dinner. "I take it you found out about Ray's separation from Connie from Steve Hogan?" Harry asked.

"Yes. Steve and Ray are good friends, and they talk frequently." Then Ann went into the details.

"My God, what a horrible situation!" Arlene said once Ann was finished.

"Well, one thing's for sure. Ray will get the divorce and custody, and on his terms," Harry observed. "What do you plan to do, Ann?"

"Obviously I want to meet Ray more than anything. But I think that I shouldn't rush it. I want to give him time to get over this ordeal, and maybe even date some, before I approach him about a serious relationship."

"I agree," Arlene said. "Let him sow some of his wild oats first."

"Both of you are wrong," Harry said. "I know Ray, because he's just like me. The best thing you can do, Ann, is to let me get him up here as soon as we can schedule a weekend visit. He can stay with us and you can meet him at a dinner party here at our house."

"Before his divorce is final?" Ann asked in disbelief.

"Absolutely. All he needs to do is meet you, and I know he'll be very attracted to you. When he asks me about you - and he will - and I tell him more about you - you know, the stuff you can't tell him without bragging - he'll call you. Then things will be up to the two of you. But I think Ray will fall in love with you because the two of you are so much alike, and you embody the type of woman he probably dreams about. You know he'll never break his marriage vows, but as soon as that divorce is final... well, it doesn't take rocket science to know where his heart will be."

"I'm not sure I agree," Arlene interjected. "You remember when Tony got his divorce four years ago? He chased women for over a year, even lived with one, before he was willing to settle into a serious relationship that led to marriage. Things have changed since we dated, Harry."

"Things may have changed, but I know Ray Collins. And he's not like other men in that regard. Tell me one thing either of you know or have heard about Ray that's negative." There was silence. "Well?"

"He's about as perfect a man or person as I've ever met," Arlene said.

"I've never heard anything bad about him," Ann reflected.

"Oh, but there is one major problem with Ray. He may be a business genius, one of the kindest, most honest people you've ever met or heard of, and an incredibly faithful husband and responsible father, but when it comes to judging women in a romantic relationship, he's extremely naïve. Ignorant may even be a more accurate term. Otherwise, he wouldn't have married Connie in the first place.

"The last thing you want, Ann, is for Ray to start dating, because here is what may happen. Ray's not the type of guy who goes from woman to woman satisfying his sexual urges. He will start looking for the right woman to be a partner with him and a mother to his sons as soon as he starts dating. And when he thinks he has found her, he'll ask her to marry him. The problem is that Ray is so kind and giving, and also such a bad a judge of romantic relationships with women.

"Some sexy, manipulative opportunist will focus on his major vulnerability, his boys. She'll appear to bond with them, and before Ray knows it, he'll think he's in love and that he's found his partner in life. Next thing you know, you'll find out he's remarried. Even though that marriage will probably turn bad, this time he will be even more determined to make it work. The result will be Ray caught in a miserable marriage for the rest of his life, and you'll either be alone or with someone you'll never love as much as Ray. I know what you and Ray could have together, because I know both of you very well."

"Harry, since you're such a good a judge of people and you know Ray so well, I'm going to take your advice, but with one difference. I want to wait until his divorce is final. Considering the circumstances with Connie that Steve Hogan described, that shouldn't take long."

"I think that will work just fine, Ann," Harry said.

"What would be the best way for me to meet him?"

"Either let me invite him to our home for a weekend visit and have you over for dinner, or we'll put together some kind of business conference and you can meet him there."

"I like the conference idea better. It can be of benefit to the participants, and it also enables me to meet Ray in a situation that doesn't look like match making."

"I agree," Arlene added.

Later that night Ann called the Hogans'. "Steve, this is Ann. Is Sandy there?" Ann asked when Steve answered their phone.

"Sure, let me get her."

"Actually, I want to talk to both of you. Can you could get her on the other line, Steve?"

"Certainly. She's picking up now."

"Hi, Ann," Sandy said cheerfully. "I bet you're happy with the recent news from Florida."

"I sure am. In fact, that's what I'm calling about. At first I thought I should let Ray get past his divorce and date some before I met him."

"I agree. Let him work some things out first," Sandy replied.

"Well, Harry disagreed with that," Ann said. "Since he knows Ray so well, I agree with him."

"What did he say to change your mind?" Sandy asked.

After Ann related what Harry had told her, Steve said, "One thing's for sure. Harry knows Ray and what he's all about."

"I would like to organize a business conference for Ray and I to meet rather than meet him at Harry's or your house at dinner, so it doesn't look like matchmaking. Plus, it will be of benefit to those who attend," Ann explained.

"That's a good idea," Sandy agreed.

"How about a citrus conference?" Steve suggested.

"I think I should be a speaker," Ann said, "But I'm not involved with citrus."

"Yes you are. You buy citrus essences for GSDC," Steve reminded her. "You could give a talk about the situation and outlook for the citrus essence market."

"I like that. That would work fine," Ann replied. "What other topics could be addressed?"

"Critical issues facing the world citrus industry, such as citrus supply, markets, international trade, and so on."

"Steve, it could be you and Ray who organize it, with Sun Ripe, the largest marketer of fresh citrus, and Tropical Citrus, a major marketer of citrus juices, as organizing sponsors. When do you think we should have the conference?"

"Well, I don't want to bother Ray about it now. He's got enough on his mind going through this divorce and all, hiring a nanny, and consoling his boys about all the disruption in their lives. Let's give him a few weeks after the divorce is final to get settled before I mention this conference."

"I understand all of that, Steve, but I want to meet him as soon as is practical," Ann said.

"How about if we give Ray three or four weeks after his divorce is final, then I'll call him and begin talking about the conference. At that point, we just need to plan it far enough in advance that invitees can fit it in their schedules to attend, probably two or three months."

"I think that works just fine," Ann agreed.

Chapter Ten

In August of 1958, Ray and Steve began to discuss having an international citrus conference that would cover issues and topics of interest faced by the world citrus industry. "Steve, I think a conference like that would be of significant value. At the least, it will get everyone communicating about the common problems and opportunities we face as an industry," Ray observed.

"What topics do you think the conference should cover?" Steve asked.

"Off the top of my head, I would say changes in world fruit production in Florida, California, and Mexico; costs to grow oranges for juice versus the fresh market; the impact of last year's Florida freeze on fruit prices and the juice market; the growing importance of orange concentrate in export markets; and the growth potential of the United States orange juice market."

"I would add demand for fresh citrus in the US, European, and Japanese markets, and the situation and outlook for citrus oils and essences," Steve suggested.

"Ray, if it's okay with you, I would like to have the conference at the Harbor Island Palms Resort in San Diego, California. It's an elegant resort with great conference facilities. We held our national sales meeting there two years age and were very pleased. The San Diego Municipal Airport is not far from the resort, and there are excellent restaurants nearby as well."

"That sounds perfect to me."

Ray and Steve then agreed on which speakers would be ideal to address each of the topics, and who each of them would call to extend an invitation, based on how well each knew the proposed speaker. When they came to the last topic about citrus oils and essences, Ray said, "Steve, I assume that someone from Sun Ripe would be ideal to address that one?"

"Actually I'd like us to invite Ann Robinson, chief economist for GSDC. She manages GSDC's essence procurement program and knows the topic very well."

"Chief economist for GSDC?"

"Yeah. She's real bright, too. Summa Cum Laude graduate of Wellesley, Phi Beta Kappa, and Harry Davis is her mentor at GSDC."

"Harry is her mentor?"

"He sure is. Not only that, she's only thirty, single, and gorgeous. In fact she worked as a fashion model when she was in college at Wellesley."

Ray was intrigued, but he said, "Even if a woman like that would go out with me, I've sworn off dating for now after my bad marriage. In fact, I might not date again until the boys are teenagers. The last thing they need to deal with is another bad or failed marriage."

"Well, at least you'll get to meet her at the conference. In fact, why don't you invite her to be a speaker? It will give you a chance to meet her over the phone. Her number is LE-29894."

"Okay."

After Ray got off the phone with Steve, he called Harry Davis. "Mr. Davis's office," Lisa answered.

"This is Ray Collins. I'd like to speak to Harry."

"Sure, Mr. Collins. I'll connect you."

"So how does it feel to be a single man again, Ray?" Harry asked when he answered the phone.

"I'm not sure I know yet."

"What's on your mind?"

"Steve Hogan with Sun Ripe and I have agreed to hold a citrus conference in October, and he suggested Ann Robinson as a speaker. He said you were her mentor."

"That's right, even though she reports to George Martin. Ray, she's brilliant. In fact, she reminds me of you more than anyone else I know. When I interviewed her, she explained everything about how to switch GSDC to high fructose corn syrup, except for your concept of exchanges for physicals. Her implementation of that project has been flawless. She's also one of the most beautiful women I've ever met."

Ray was moved by Harry's description. "Steve suggested I call and invite her to be a speaker at the conference. Plus I'll get to meet her there."

"Do you need her phone number?" Harry asked.

"No, Steve gave it to me."

"I know you'll be very impressed with her. In fact, I'd like to take both of you to dinner the first night of the conference."

"Great, I accept."

"When you talk to Ann, tell her I'll be taking both of you to dinner."

After talking to Harry, Ray's mind was racing with a million thoughts. He was both curious about and incredibly interested in Ann, and so was dying to meet her. But he kept reminding himself of the promise he had made himself for the sake of his sons, that he would not date until the boys were teenagers. *The last thing they need is another failed marriage to get over as young children,* Ray reminded himself. *Don't worry,* he reasoned. *A woman like Ann, as she's been described to me, could have just about any man she wants. There's no way she's going to be romantically attracted to me. Besides, she probably has a boyfriend, or if not, doesn't want one at this time.*

Ray then called the number Steve had given him. "Ann, this is Ray Collins at Tropical Citrus."

Ann almost dropped the phone as she thought, *Oh my God! It's Ray Collins!!* She quickly regained her composure and said, "Hello, Mr. Collins. It's good to meet you over the phone. I've heard a lot about you."

"I've also heard a lot about you. And please call me Ray."

"Okay, Ray."

"I'm calling to invite you to be a speaker at the International Citrus Conference."

"Great. What topic?"

"The market situation and outlook for citrus oils and essences."

"I accept. I've heard about the conference, and think you and Steve are putting on an excellent one."

"Thanks. Oh, Harry Davis is going also, and he's invited both of us to have dinner with him on the first night of the conference."

Thank you Harry, Ann thought.

"Great, I'll see you there, and I look forward to dinner."

When she got off the phone, Ann was dizzy with emotion and shaking. *I've actually just spoken to Ray Collins for the first time! I think he's looking forward to meeting me! And I'm going to dinner with him!*

Her phone then rang. "Ann, this is Steve Hogan."

"Hi, Steve. Ray called and invited me to speak at the conference as well as invited me to dinner with him and Harry Davis."

"Yeah, I know. I suggested that he invite you to be a speaker so you two could meet over the phone."

"Thanks. Did Ray call you back after I talked to him?"

"He sure did. Boy, is he fascinated with you. He says he's not going to date anyone until his boys are teenagers because he doesn't want to risk putting them into another bad marriage."

"Oh, no!" Ann replied.

"Calm down. That might be what he's telling himself, but that will change once he meets you."

"How do you know that?"

"Because, he wanted to know all about you, and when I told him, he was even more intrigued - infatuated actually. You definitely have his attention. Ray said when he asked Harry about you, Harry said that he was mentoring you, even though you didn't report to him, because he thought you were brilliant."

"Harry told Ray that I was brilliant?"

"Yeah, and also one of the most beautiful women he's ever seen."

"Steve, I'm so excited! Things are off to a better start than I could have ever imagined!"

As the date of the citrus conference approached, Ann was on an ever-increasing emotional roller coaster. On the one hand, she didn't know how she could stand to wait almost another entire month to finally meet Ray in person. But on the other, she also worried about what she'd do if he wasn't attracted to her or if he stuck to his plan to not get into another relationship until his boys were much older. So, one day she would be happy and excited, then moody and worried the next. She also couldn't decide what to wear for the first time they met and for their dinner together. She'd been shopping a dozen times, and even bought a few outfits, but kept changing her mind because nothing seemed just right, and she wanted it to be perfect. Finally, in desperation, she called Sandy Hogan.

"Sandy, this is Ann."

"The conference is only about two weeks away. Are you excited?"

"Yes, excited. And worried. And confused. I just don't know what I'll do if Ray decides to stick to his plan to not get into a relationship his boys are older - and I can't stop worrying about it. I also can't seem to find the right outfit to wear for when we first meet."

"Ann, you've got to stop acting this way or it will affect how you are when you meet Ray at the conference. Remember, this needs to look like Ray's the one who's initially attracted to you, or he just might decide he doesn't want to get into another relationship now. You shouldn't look nervous, or like you dressed specifically for this occasion. Pretend Ray's not even going to be at the conference, and that your dinner is with Steve and your boss, not Ray, then dress accordingly."

"But Sandy, I don't want to look like every other woman there. I want to look special for Ray."

"Ann, with your looks and figure, combined with Steve's observation that Ray's intrigued with you and dying to meet you, you'll look plenty special in whatever you decide to wear. You can save the fancy clothes and hairdos for when the two of you begin a romantic relationship. Just remember, when you first meet him, you're not a woman who has been in love with him for years. You're simply a professional colleague whom he's taking to a business dinner, and your manner needs to reflect that."

"What you say makes sense, Sandy. I'm just so emotionally charged about meeting Ray, I can't think straight these days."

"By the way, before I forget, Steve is having breakfast with Ray and Ray's boss, George Baker, on the first day of the conference at Chatham's, one of the resort's restaurants and he asked me to tell you that you are also invited. I guess that's when you'll formally meet Ray for the first time."

"That's great. I just hope I'm not an emotional wreck by then."

THE WINE QUEEN

It seemed like the date of the citrus conference was years away rather than only two weeks. Ray kept trying to reason with himself over his excitement about meeting Ann, but his thoughts would not respond. Finally, on Wednesday afternoon, October 22, he and George flew to San Diego and took a cab to the Harbor Island Palms Resort where the conference was to be held. They arrived just in time for their scheduled dinner with Tropical Citrus' orange juice suppliers from Spain.

When Ray and George returned to the resort after dinner, George asked, "Are you feeling okay?"

"Yeah, probably just jet lag," Ray lied.

"Yeah it's after midnight Florida time. I understand there is a breakfast meeting at Chatham's at seven thirty in the morning, so I will see you then."

Ann arrived at Chatham's early on the first day of the conference and went into the ladies' room for a final check of her hair and makeup. Then she went out and sat on a sofa that was just down the hall from the front door to the restaurant, affording her a view of its entrance where nobody would particularly notice her. It had been seven years since she had first encountered Ray Collins. Then she had been a wide-eyed young woman just starting out in life. Now, at thirty years old, she was a very successful and respected professional woman, the chief economist of one of the largest corporations in the world. But three things hadn't changed: her breathtaking beauty, her incredibly deep love for Ray, and her determined commitment to be with him.

Then she saw Ray and an older man head into the Chatham's. Although it had more than three years since she'd seen him in person, those same butterflies came back as she was once again amazed at his unbelievable good looks and how strongly she was attracted to him. *It's time*, she thought. *After seven years it's finally time.* Then she stood up, gathered her courage, and headed through the doors into the dining room, and into the rest of her life.

As George and Ray walked into the dining room, Steve Hogan came up and asked them, "Did you have a good flight?"

"Yes," George answered.

Then Ray saw this incredibly beautiful woman dressed in a black skirt and red blouse who walked up, smiling, and Steve said, "George Baker, Ray Collins, this is Ann Robinson." Ray's knees grew weak and he almost stumbled. He couldn't speak, but managed to gently press her hand and smile in greeting. Ray was captivated by her beauty and couldn't take his eyes off of her while he took in every detail about her. As Ray looked at her, he realized that she was the most beautiful woman he'd ever seen. Her magnetism was irresistible. All he could do was stare.

"It's a pleasure to finally meet you, Ms. Robinson," George said, trying to hide his own obvious astonishment at her beauty.

"That's Ann," she corrected.

Her voice sounds so beautiful and melodic, Ray thought, still speechless.

This is it! I'm finally meeting Ray Collins in person! Ann thought, feeling giddy with excitement. Then she reminded herself, *Calm down and act business-like.*

"I have a table reserved, so let's all go sit down," Steve suggested.

"Ann, how long have you been at GSDC?" Ray asked, finally able to speak.

"So you can talk?" Ann joked, as she thought, *Thank God, he's finally talking to me!*

"I think Ray must be sick, because this is the longest time I've ever known him to be silent," George kidded.

"I've been at GSDC ever since I finished my master's degree in agricultural economics at the University of California at Davis."

A lump formed in Ray's throat as he thought, *She has a master's degree in agricultural economics from UC Davis, the same as me?* "I never remember talking with you," Ray said.

"My graduate committee chairman, Ron White, called you. It was back in May of 1955. You were instrumental in getting me an interview for that job in the sweetener procurement department."

"Before I forget," Steve Interrupted, "Harry Davis called and said he would not be able to make it to the conference."

"Gee, Ann. I guess it's just you and me for dinner tonight," Ray said.

"I guess," Ann replied.

Was that a twinkle I just saw in her eye? Ray wondered.

After breakfast, George and Ray visited with a number of suppliers, customers, and old friends as they made their way to the conference room. In front of about one hundred and fifty conference participants from nine different countries, Steve and Ray took turns making the remarks that opened the conference. As Ray sat through the different presentations, he couldn't keep his eyes off of Ann. And every time he stole a glance at her, she smiled, captivating his thoughts and making him feel as he had never felt before. When it was time for his first presentation, on the market potential for frozen concentrated orange juice, it was as if Ray was making the presentation only to Ann and nobody else was in the room.

Later, Ann was nervous as she dressed for her upcoming dinner with Ray. *Okay, here it is! The most important date of my life!* Ann thought. *He's been stealing glances at me all day, so I think he's attracted to me. I need to let him know that I'm also attracted to him without seeming too obvious. Please, God, don't let me screw this up.*

Ray was also nervous as he prepared for his night out with Ann. Finally logic took over after he reminded himself of the numerous reasons that she would never be interested in him romantically.

They met in the lobby of the resort where they were staying, and Ann looked incredible. "I've called a taxi, which should be here any minute," Ray said.

"I rented a convertible, if you would like me to drive," Ann suggested.

"That's fine," Ray agreed, and he asked the concierge to cancel the cab.

Steve had made dinner reservations for them at The Breakers, a very elegant restaurant and nightclub that served some of the best gourmet food in California. They soon arrived, and when they entered, Ray gave the woman behind the desk Ann's shawl. As they were seated, Ray took off his blazer, then they ordered drinks. The waiter soon returned with the drinks, and asked, "May I take your order now?"

"I'll have the guava-glazed pheasant breast with wild rice and steamed broccoli," Ann replied.

"I'd like the New York Strip, medium rare, baked potato with butter and sour cream, and mixed vegetables," Ray said.

Ray sipped his martini and tried to relax. The presentations had seemed endless today. And ever since breakfast, he could only think of Ann. She had begun the day looking fresh and beautiful in a light skirt and blouse. Now, after hours of business talks in a stuffy conference room, she was still gorgeous. She sat across from him, sipping a glass of white wine. He tried not to stare, to be casual, as if being near her didn't fill him with inexplicable heat. Her hair, which had been pulled back during the day, now hung soft and loose around her shoulders. She'd swapped the skirt and blouse for a silky summer dress with spaghetti straps that left her ivory shoulders bare. Irrationally, he wanted to place a kiss on that soft spot between the strap and her throat.

Ray took a long sip of his drink and reminded himself that Ann was just here with him to be courteous. They were two acquaintances at a conference where they hardly knew anyone else. It was natural that they should go out for drinks and make polite conversation. Nothing more.

The evening flew by as they talked and talked, and described their backgrounds to each other.

Ray marveled at the incredible interpersonal skills that it must have taken when she was first starting out with National Farm Equipment, to go into dealerships in places like Clewiston, Florida, or Valdosta, Georgia, as a very attractive young woman in her twenties, telling the "good ol' boys" at the tractor place what they had to do or change to meet company objectives. "How did you manage to get Ron White as your major professor when you were working on your master's in agricultural economics?" Ray asked.

"The same way you did," Ann replied. "With good enough grades and test scores to bring graduate research grant money to the table before I selected my thesis topic."

"How did you know that Ron was my major professor?"

"Oh, I know a lot about you," she teased. "Did you serve in the military?"

"No. I had a draft deferment when I was in college from 1941 to 1945, and the war was over about the time I graduated. Plus, I went straight from my undergraduate program to graduate school, so I didn't finish college until 1947."

"Where did you grow up?"

"In Lake City, Florida, about sixty miles west of Jacksonville. I was adopted when I was seven months old. My adoptive father was a real estate developer and my mom was a high school teacher. My dad was killed in an automobile accident when I was ten years old, and my mom died of cancer the year after I graduated from college."

"I'm so sorry," Ann said.

When Ray described to her the mess his personal life was in, he was surprised at her interest in how he was dealing with everything, as well as her many questions about the boys, the relationship he had with them, and how they were handling all the turmoil. Ray could tell she was genuinely concerned and not just making conversation.

"Where do Tommy and Jesse stay when you're at work or away on business?" Ann asked.

"We have a live-in nanny and housekeeper, Norma Wright, who is a retired nurse, with a daughter and two grandchildren living in Tampa.

The band then started playing a mix of oldies and dance hits. Just as Ray was wondering if he should ask Ann to dance, a burly man in a suit strode up to them with purpose.

"Do you mind if I ask the lady to dance?" He spoke to Ray, not Ann. This alone was enough to embarrass him, as he suspected that Ann would not thank him for allowing a strange man to proposition her. But this wasn't a date. Not really. So he couldn't claim any dance rights.

"Sorry," Ann said, as she laid a hand on Ray's sleeve. "I've promised all my dances this evening to him." The stranger frowned, but nodded. After the man had walked away, Ann took the last sip of her wine before placing the glass back on the table.

"You're not going to make a liar of me, are you, Ray?" Her smile prompted a twinkle in her eyes, and Ray knew he was lost.

"Certainly not," he assured her. Ray then took her hand and they walked to the dance floor. While earlier he'd been sure Ann considered him as nothing more than a colleague, as soon as he took her in his arms and twirled her around the floor, he knew this was something more. They fit. Her hand rested on his arm like it was meant to be there. His palm cupped the lower part of her back with perfect poise. Their feet moved in synchronicity.

The music changed and the band bellowed out a doo-wop hit. Ann laughed as Ray sang along, and her laughter was the sweetest music he'd heard all night. The next song was a hot salsa number.

"Want to try something I learned in dance class?" Ray asked.

"You took dance classes?" Ann's arms were loose around his neck and she leaned back to see if he was teasing.

"Ballroom, tap, and salsa," he said with a wink.

"Show me," she instructed.

Ray dipped her once and pulled her into a simple salsa rhythm. Ann picked up the steps quickly. She was a natural. Her long legs matched his stride for stride. The band warmed to their fun and played a mambo. Ann twirled and Ray caught her tight against his chest, before she whirled away again. Suddenly, they were the only ones on the dance floor. Other couples watched, scattered among the tables. Ann moved like an angel, following his every cue. Their bodies flowed along the same lines as if they had been dancing together all their lives. On the last beat of the song, he clasped her to him and they dipped. Their eyes met and their chests heaved from the adrenaline pumping through them. For a brief, silent second their lips were poised for the perfect kiss. Then the crowd burst into applause. Ann stood and smoothed down her dress, her face bright from exertion and a touch of shyness. Ray raised her hand to his lips and kissed her soft fingers.

"Thank you," he said. "You're a wonderful dancer." He started to lead Ann back to their seats as "Earth Angel" began to play.

"Oh, no," said Ann. "You're not getting off that easy." She wrapped her arms around his neck and swayed her hips to the music the damp curls of her black hair stuck to her cheeks.

She smells so good, Ray thought. He placed his hands on her hips, wanting only to pull her up against his chest and bury his face in those curls.

She's just being friendly to a lonely guy at a business conference, he reminded himself. *Don't read anything more into it.* But he wanted to kiss her. He'd never wanted anything more in his life. She seemed determined to tantalize him. Completely unaware of her effect on him, Ann laid her head on his shoulder.

"This is much better," she said. Ray wished the music would never end. And it didn't. Song after song, they swayed together. Her hip pressed against his thigh. Her breasts nudged his chest. Every place her body touched his, he burned with desire. They didn't speak. They didn't need to. The night's magic had all the answers.

When the DJ announced last call, Ray reluctantly pulled away. He and Ann retrieved her shawl where they'd left it what seemed to be a lifetime ago.

On the drive back to the resort neither of them spoke, preferring instead to ride in silence, lost in their thoughts. *I can tell he's very attracted to me, but he won't act on it,* Ann thought sadly. *Maybe he's sticking to his plan not to get romantically involved until his boys are older.* The idea depressed her and she struggled to hold back tears.

Meanwhile, Ray was suddenly feeling awkward again. He'd begun the day thinking he and Ann were simply colleagues, but this night had shown him that they had a chance for something much deeper - a chance for the happiness that had been missing from his life for so long. Did she feel it, too? Or were these feelings all his? He couldn't believe that. His emotions had been feeding on her desire for him all night. The way she looked at him, the way she licked her full lips as if contemplating a kiss. Her hands on his back, claiming their right to hold him. He hadn't imagined any of that.

They soon got back to the resort and Ray walked her to her villa. Standing outside the door, a sweet-scented fall breeze tugged at her hair. Ann shivered.

"Well, I guess this is goodnight," she said. "I had a wonderful time."

This is the moment of no return, Ray thought. If I'm making a mistake, so be it. I have to have her. She made a soft gasp as he took her in his arms and his lips brushed across hers in the gentlest kiss.

"Ray," her voice was full of emotion.

"Shhh." He touched her lips with the tip of a finger. She closed her eyes and he kissed each eyelid. More kisses ran down the side of her face. He tilted her chin up and claimed her mouth again, this time with an unspoken challenge. She accepted and sank into his arms. Her lips were soft and giving, just as he had imagined. She opened up to him and his tongue explored her mouth with light strokes, each one fine-tuning the desire that was strumming through him. Her hands moved under his jacket, blazing fire along his chest.

"I've wanted to do that since the first moment you danced with me. Probably a lot longer than that," he laughed harshly, "if I'm being honest."

"Me, too." She smiled.

His lips found hers again before they could speak more. He didn't want words tonight. Words would ruin this incredible moment. He deepened the kiss, plunging his tongue into her mouth, seeking the succor only Ann could provide. He gripped her back, even as her hands sunk into his hair crushing him against her. Then their lips parted, their breath warm and erratic on each other's faces.

The words that he wanted to ignore crept back into his mind. *Will I wake up and find that this has all been a dream? Am I falling in love for the first time in my life? There are so many things I want to say to her, to know about her, to share with her. Where do I begin?* And then he realized that he'd been holding her and gazing into her eyes.

She was achingly beautiful.

"I guess we'd better get some sleep, he said reluctantly. "Your presentation is tomorrow."

"And so is your second one," she reminded him, a touch of reluctance in her sweet voice too.

After going inside her villa, Ann leaned her back against the closed door and wondered if Ray still stood outside pondering their kiss. Or had he already shrugged it off and gone back to his room. No, she couldn't believe that. He wanted her as much as she did him.

When they'd first headed to the dance floor, she'd told herself that the energy between them was all in her imagination. After all, she'd been thinking about this night for so long. Surely, her anticipation was bathing a simple dance in a more meaningful light than it deserved. Then Ray had touched her. His hands seemed to find every sensitive spot on her body. His eyes found hers after every turn. And she'd had no idea he could dance like that!

Or kiss like that either. *Oh my God! I had no idea it would be like this!*

She sat on the edge of her bed and touched her swollen lips. She could still taste him, sweet and musky. His hands were still shadows on her back and, if she closed her eyes, she could feel him beside her.

Harry Davis had told her they would be perfect together. *Oh, God, Harry,* she thought. *You were right. I thought I loved him before, but I didn't have a clue.*

She wanted to forget about her presentation tomorrow, and about all her other obligations. All she wanted was to go to Ray's room and spend the rest of the night in his arms. But Ray had obligations, too. Two small boys. A job back in Florida. She wished none of that mattered. She wished there was no one else in the world but her and Ray.

Tomorrow they'd be leaving. Ray would go home to Florida. Ann would return to her empty condo in Tennessee and continue to dream about a time when she could be with Ray. Only now she would know exactly what she was missing. It was an unbearable thought. Before she could talk herself out of it a second time, she dialed Ray's room number.

THE WINE QUEEN

From the time Ray left Ann's villa, he felt an infinite happiness that he had never felt. Once he got to his room, he realized he wasn't going be able to sleep after what he had experienced. He wanted desperately to call her and talk, but restrained himself from doing it because he knew she needed her sleep. When he could resist no longer, and was reaching for the phone, it rang. It was Ann. "Were you asleep?" she asked.

"No, I was just getting ready to call you. Ann, I don't know what's happening, but I know I want to see you again. Tonight."

"Oh, Ray, I feel the same way. I don't care about sleeping. I just know I have to see you, to talk to you. Could we meet in that all-night coffee shop?"

"I'll see you there."

And so they met there, and sat across the table from each other holding hands, alone in the empty coffee shop where the lone waiter was dozing. "Ann, I've never felt like this before."

"Neither have I, Ray."

"I was concerned that it was inappropriate to treat tonight as a date, but I'm sure glad I was wrong about that."

"Oh, Ray, I was praying that you would want it to become a date."

"I'm scheduled to fly back to Tampa after the conference is over at noon tomorrow, and should get home about eleven to eleven thirty p.m. What are your plans?"

"I'm headed to the Sweetener Users Association meetings in New Orleans after the conference is over, but I don't remember where I'm staying. One of my colleagues is meeting me at the airport and she has our hotel information. I will call you on Saturday after you get back home."

"Good. Here is my home phone number," Ray said as he wrote it on his business card.

"And here is my home number in Memphis," Ann said as she borrowed Ray's pen after he was done.

They talked a while longer about little insignificant things, discovering more they had in common and things that were important to each of them, holding hands and gazing into each other's eyes. Neither of them wanted to leave the other's company, but both recognized that they had professional responsibilities as speakers at the conference and needed to get some sleep.

They walked to her villa in the crisp, night air. Standing at her door, she paused and looked up. The moon shone like a jewel.

"Look at that," she said. "The moon is so full. It makes everything glow silver. Even your hair." She ran her fingers along the tips of Ray's usually black curls, now highlighted by the moon's silver luminescence.

"God you're beautiful," he said. He was looking intently at her. His eyes were hooded in shadow and the light carved out his strong features. Lightly, he brushed a stray lock of hair from her face. His fingers trailed across her cheek and she rested against his touch. His hand cupped her head. He leaned in to kiss her, gently at first. A brief brush of his lips against hers. An inquisitive dart of his tongue. And then passion overcame them. His mouth carved across hers. She pressed her body against his. Her trembling hands skimmed over his face and into his hair. She shook with a fervor she'd never imagined. Ray deepened his claim on her mouth, their kiss growing urgent, hungry, and feral.

Ann forgot about the past and the future. Only the now mattered with her need pounding in her chest. Ray's desire strained against his pants and she dug her fingers under his waistband, pulling him even closer. She opened her eyes to find him staring at her. His irises were large and black in the dim light and he seemed dazed with passion. She wanted him so badly, she shook with desire and his body reacted in kind.

He did not want to let her go, but he did, so they could get at least a few hours of sleep before the conference was to begin its second day.

THE WINE QUEEN

The next morning, Ray skipped breakfast in favor of another hour of sleep, and George called his room to see if he was okay.

Because of their professional affiliations, Ray and Ann were seated in different areas of the conference room, but frequently during the conference as well as while each was giving their presentation, they couldn't avoid smiling at each other. The conference adjourned at noon and most attendees left for the airport, including Ann for the sweetener conference. Ray felt a stabbing pain as he waved good-bye to her and her colleagues, as he and George had later flights. George was headed to Los Angeles for a Saturday morning budget meeting with Tropical Citrus's west coast sales organization, rather than flying back to Florida with Ray.

"Want to grab lunch?" George suggested. At lunch, George asked, "What's going on with this Ann Robinson?"

"What do you mean?" Ray asked innocently.

"Every time I look at you, you're smiling at her and she's smiling back. What happened last night at dinner?" Then when Ray had nothing to say for himself, "Not Ann Robinson?" George guessed. "It's too soon for you to get romantically involved with someone."

"I felt the same way, George, until I met Ann. I'm completely in awe of her, and I can't stop thinking about her. I've got to pursue this and see where it leads."

"Ray, she's nothing like Connie."

"I know, George, she's me in female form - or at least what I think I would want to be like if I were a female."

"Does she know about the boys and the ex-wife?"

"Yes, and she seems fine about it."

"Really? But how will you see her, with you living in Ruskin and her in Memphis?"

"I don't know, George. At this point I don't even know if she will want to have a romantic relationship with me. But if she does, I guess we will fly back and forth."

"You really are taken with this woman, aren't you?"

"Yes, George. More than I have been with anyone ever before in my lifetime."

George's eyes moistened as he said, "You've certainly paid your dues, Ray. God knows you and your boys deserve someone like her in your lives. I hope it works out for you. You know I'm always here to listen if you need someone to talk to."

"Thanks, George."

On the flight back to Florida, Ray's mind was racing. *Why would a woman like Ann be romantically interested in me, considering all my emotional baggage?* Then a terrible thought hit him. *Could this be a joke that Steve Hogan put Ann up to? No,* he assured himself. *Ann's got too much character for that. Besides, that special look I saw in her eyes was genuine.* Then reason and logic began to take over. *Once Ann has time to think about this she will decide that a romantic relationship with me - what with the boys, divorce as proof of my failure in a relationship, and all that, is not a good idea. I probably won't hear from her again, unless it's in a professional capacity.* Then he started to imagine not seeing her again and the idea was so painful he couldn't stand to think about it anymore.

As Ray's plane flew into Tampa, he was very sad, as he'd convinced himself that he would probably never get that call from Ann. And although he would call her after she returned home to Memphis, he could imagine her words as she tried to respectfully tell him that what happened in San Diego had been a mistake and that she wasn't ready to commit to a romantic relationship with him.

Although it was late, before he left the airport, Ray stopped at a pay phone and called Brent, the captain of Tropical Citrus' 48'offshore fishing boat. While its primary use was by the sales, marketing and procurement departments to entertain customers and suppliers, officers of the company could use it personally if it wasn't scheduled by noon on Friday, for one or both weekend days. However, since many of them already had boats of their own, the Tropical Citrus boat was often available on weekends if it had not been scheduled for business purposes.

"Boat's available if you want it Mr. Collins," Brent said. "Fishing's been good but the water's a little choppy. Are your boys coming with you?"

"You bet they are."

"Good, I think I know a spot for some nice red snapper." *A day of fishing with the boys is just what I need,* Ray thought. *They're so special. Being with them always reminds me just how lucky I am. Besides, the last thing I want to do is sit around and think of all the reasons that Ann will probably not call.* It was after eleven p.m. when he got home.

Chapter Eleven

Ann got to her hotel in New Orleans a little after eight p.m., and she was still unable to concentrate on anything but what she'd experienced with Ray. She didn't want to go out again, so she ordered a salad and sandwich from room service. She wanted to call Ray and talk to him so badly that she could hardly stand it, but she knew it would be almost midnight before he got home and she didn't want the phone to wake his household. While she was waiting on dinner to be brought to her room, she decided to call Steve and Sandy Hogan.

"Steve? This is Ann."

"Ann! Let me get Sandy on the other line because I know she will want to know how dinner went with Ray."

"Well, how did the date go?" Sandy asked after she picked up.

"I'm in heaven," Ann said in a dreamy tone.

"I take it that means it went well," Steve observed.

"'Well' doesn't even begin to describe it! It was the most incredible experience of my life!" And then Ann went on to describe her date with Ray.

"I told you he wouldn't stick to his plan to not become romantically involved with anyone once he met you," Steve reminded her.

"I've never felt like this before. I'm in a constant state of euphoria!"

"We're so happy for you, Ann. You've certainly paid your dues. You deserve to be this happy," Sandy said.

"Thanks, you guys, for all the help you've been to me."

"You're more than welcome, Ann," Steve said. "Have you talked to Ray since the conference?"

"No. He said he probably wouldn't get home until almost midnight and I didn't want to call his house so late."

"I can't wait to hear what Ray has to say about all of this," Sandy said.

"Norma, we have a cooler full of fish fillets," Ray shouted as he, Tommy and Jesse came into the house after their Saturday offshore fishing trip. "Why don't you invite your daughter and her family to come over tomorrow for a seafood cookout?"

"That would be fun," Norma replied. "Oh, you had a phone call at about nine this morning."

Ray's heart skipped a beat but he tried to act calm.

"Who was it from?"

"Ann Robinson. She said you knew her, and she asked if I was Norma. Of course I said yes. She left this number and said to call her. She handed Ray a slip of paper with the information written on it. If you don't need me, I'm going to spend the night at my daughter's house. I'll call you from there and we can decide what time to have the cook out."

"Okay, have a good time."

Ray's hands were shaking as he and the boys unpacked from the fishing trip. Ann's *call doesn't change anything*, he thought. *She's had time to think, and is calling now rather than later to say that what happened in San Diego was a mistake.* Ray's hands were still shaking as, in the privacy of his bedroom, he dialed the number Ann had given Kelly. But when the front desk at her hotel rang Ann's room, there was no answer. So he left her a message saying he had returned her call. After looking at his watch, Ray realized it was only about four in New Orleans, so she was probably still at the conference. *I'll try her again at about five thirty her time and see if I can catch her,* he thought. But when he called back, she was still not there. "Want to go to Ben's barbecue for ribs and beans?" he asked.

"Yeah, let's go," Tommy said excitedly.

At ten thirty that night Ray was just dozing off and jumped when the phone rang. It was Ann! "Did you have a good flight home?" she asked.

"Yes. How is New Orleans?"

"Not as good as it would be if you were here with me."

Ray was dizzy with emotion. *Maybe this is for real!* "I wish I were."

"You mean now that you've had time to think about it you still want to date someone who lives a thousand miles away?"

"If it's you, I do. What about you? You want to date a guy with two young children and a failed marriage?"

"If it's you, I do."

"I figured once you had time to think about it, reason would prevail and you wouldn't want to get involved in my life."

"Reason did, but so did emotion, and both are in agreement. I definitely want to get involved in your life if you want me to."

"Boy, do I!"

"You don't remember it, but actually the first time I met you was in August of 1951."

"What?"

"It was at the American Farm Economics Association's annual meetings at Clemson University. You presented a paper that I believe was titled 'Optimal Asset Replacement Under Conditions of Technological Change.'"

159

"That was when I was still at the National Agribusiness Company. Were you that beautiful young woman who got up and left just as I was finishing my talk?"

"That was me."

"I remember thinking, either she must not have liked my talk, or she has a tight schedule and somewhere else to be."

"One of our agricultural engineers at National Farm Equipment was working on a problem similar to the one your paper was about. When he was reviewing the literature and saw that your paper was selected for presentation at the annual Farm Economics meetings, he asked that I go hear it and get a copy since Clemson was in my region. I was very impressed by your paper. Using integral calculus to introduce the continuous effects of technology into discrete time financial periods, then simultaneously solving for the cost-minimizing results was brilliant. Your paper was also the only one with just you as the author. All the others that were selected had two, three, or four authors. I think I developed a crush on you then. Listening to your presentation of that paper helped me decide to go back to school and get a master's degree in Agricultural Economics. I was disappointed when I didn't get the chance to train with you at GSDC."

"I think you've done just fine on your own."

They talked for a while longer, then as they got sleepier they said good night. "When should I call you again?" Ray asked.

"How about first thing in the morning?"

"What time?"

"How about whenever you wake up?"

"Sounds like a good idea to me." Ray noticed that it was one a.m. as he turned out the lights to go to sleep. His last thought was, *How could something this wonderful really be happening to me?*

The next morning, Tommy woke up Ray at seven thirty a.m. "Daddy, can you come outside with Jesse and me so we can shoot our BB guns?" Since it was six thirty Ann's time, Ray decided to let her get some more sleep.

"Okay, Tommy, just give me a minute to get some clothes on."

At about eight thirty, while Ray was making breakfast, the phone rang. It was Ann, who said, "Time to get up sleepy head."

"I've been up, shooting BB guns with the boys. Now I'm making breakfast. I didn't call because I wanted to let you sleep."

"Call me back after breakfast."

About nine a.m., Ray called her back. "Don't your neighbors complain about shooting BB guns?" she asked.

"No, we live out in the country on five acres."

"Really?" They talked for about half an hour. Then she said, "I need to get breakfast and get over to GSDC's booth. What are your plans for today?"

"The boys and I went fishing yesterday and brought home a cooler full of fish fillets. We've invited our nanny, her daughter, and her family over for a cookout this afternoon."

"Sounds like a lot more fun than my day's going to be."

Recalling their brief discussion about the BB guns, Ray hoped she wasn't against guns and hunting like so many women. Shooting and hunting had been his favorite hobby before the boys were born. After they came along, he got busy with work and spending time with them while they were still too young to shoot and hunt. Then his guns were stolen, and because the boys were young he hadn't replaced them. He had just started hunting and shooting again, taking the boys rabbit hunting with his .410 shotgun, which had not been stolen with the other guns, and teaching them to shoot with BB guns. Ray planned to buy some hunting rifles and shotguns and slowly start this hobby again, this time introducing the boys to this wonderful sport. *However, if Ann is negative about it, it would be a small price to pay not to start this hobby again,* he reasoned. There were many other things he and the boys could do together.

Norma called and said that three p.m. would work for them for the cookout, and Ray agreed. Ray and the boys went to the supermarket to get sweet corn, baked beans, and bread to go with the fish. As they came into the house the phone was ringing. "Ray Collins," he said as he answered the phone.

"Hi Ray, it's Steve and Sandy Hogan," Steve said.

"Steve and I are just dying to know how dinner with Ann went!" Sandy chimed in.

"Super! Thanks for recommending that gourmet restaurant, it was great."

"What do you think of Ann?" Sandy asked.

"She's the woman of my dreams and I can't stop thinking about her."

"Now that I'm no longer sworn to secrecy, I can tell you the international citrus conference was actually Ann's idea," Steve admitted.

"What?"

"She wanted to meet you but didn't want to make it obvious. The conference made it easier."

"You mean all those people came to our conference just so Ann and I could meet?"

"Sort of. As you and I discussed when we were planning it, the conference made good sense in its own right. After it was over, a number of the participants told me how they were glad to have been able to attend."

"Yeah, a number of them told me the same thing," Ray remembered.

"Ann just happened to be the one who thought of it. Her using it to meet you didn't change its value to the citrus industry."

"Now I know why you wanted her to be a speaker."

"Not really. You've got to admit she was well-qualified to speak on her topic and she did a great job."

"That she did. So what's your opinion about all of this, Steve?"

"That she's attracted to you and wants to see if there is any long-term potential for both of you on a personal level."

"Oh, quit being so logical, Steve," Sandy said. "Ann's been in love with Ray for years and is just now getting the courage to pursue it."

After his conversation with the Hogans', Ray was in a state of shock. *This beautiful, smart, successful woman is going to all these lengths just to meet and be with me,* he thought. *I just can't believe it.*

That afternoon, Ann decided to call Sandy and talk about Ray. "Hello, Sandy? This is Ann."

"Hi Ann."

"Have you talked to Ray yet?"

"Yes. Steve and I called him this morning. I asked him what he thought of you, and you know what he said?"

"What?"

"'She's the woman of my dreams and I can't stop thinking about her.'"

"Oh, Sandy, I'm so excited and deliriously happy. I can't describe how I feel! I just want to forget about everything and go to him."

"I understand, but you know that would be irresponsible."

"Yes, but I don't care. I just want to be with him more than anything."

"Have you and Ray decided when you will see each other again?"

"Not yet, but I plan to discuss it with him tonight. I was thinking that maybe I'd cancel my session next Saturday to work on GSDC's upcoming sweetener suppliers' meeting, and go spend that weekend with Ray."

"I think that would be a mistake, Ann."

"What? Why?"

"You've been in love with Ray for years, and you know a lot about him from the many discussions you've had with Steve, myself, Harry Davis, and others. In fact you've even got a scrapbook and film library about him. But he's just met you and is only beginning to learn about you. You know when you two spend a weekend together, you'll make love. And I think that's too soon for Ray. As Harry has told you, Ray's not like most other men when it comes to sex. He treats it much more seriously. Even though you know him well enough, I think he needs to have more time to get to know you better before you complicate the relationship with sex."

"I guess I'm too mesmerized about everything to have thought about it like that, but I think you're right. Waiting at least past beyond weekend would give Ray a chance for his feelings about me to develop further before we make love."

"It's too bad that you and Ray can't date like normal people. But living a thousand miles apart prevents that."

"Yeah, I guess nightly discussions over the phone will have to do. Thanks, Sandy. You're really a special friend."

The cookout seemed to drag on and on. The boys played horseshoes with Marie's granddaughter, Laurie, who was seven years old. But Ray couldn't get his mind off Ann. He was glad when the cookout was over at seven thirty and started counting the minutes until his call to Ann at ten.

"So, how was your day?" Ann asked when Ray called her.

"Boring. I wish you had been here."

"Same for me. We've got to do better than this over the phone stuff."

"I agree. When are you free for us to see each other again?"

"I've got a three-day weekend on Veteran's Day, which is the weekend after next, from Saturday, November 8 through Monday, November 10. Veteran's Day is on Tuesday, November 11, but GSDC honors it on Monday to give us a long weekend."

"Tropical Citrus also honors that holiday on Monday, but I don't want to wait that long before I see you again."

"Neither do I. But the annual GSDC supplier meetings are coming up in a few weeks and my colleagues and I have scheduled next Saturday as a group work session to wrap up our contributions to it, so I think we will just have to wait until Veteran's Day weekend."

"Well, okay. Where would you like to go that weekend? The Bahamas? New York to see a play? Where?"

"I think I would like to come to Ruskin and meet your boys."

"That sounds great to me!" Ray said excitedly, thinking, *she really does want to get to know my boys!* "When do you return to Memphis?"

"Tomorrow night. I should get home about nine. Did you call Steve?"

"Yes, I did, and we had a long talk."

"About what?"

"You, of course."

"What did Steve tell you?"

"That I'm incredibly lucky to have a smart, beautiful woman like you interested in me, which I already knew."

"Good, then my bribe worked, she teased."

"You know, Ann, you can do much better than me, a man who already has children and a failed marriage."

"Does that mean you want to call this off?" Ray could sense her panic, even through the phone.

"Absolutely not", he reassured her. "I'm just trying to understand what you see in me."

"At this point, my understanding of you is based mostly on what Steve and Harry have told me. But I know how we all share our most private thoughts and opinions with our best friends, so I think they really know you, and I don't think they would lie to me. So here goes...

"Ray, in you I see a man who is very smart and competitive, and who is also kind and compassionate. Someone who had to grow up without the guidance of a father, in a place where even going to college was a major challenge, but who met those challenges and excelled more than others who did not have to overcome the same obstacles you did. You're someone with the highest of principles, who is loyal to them in all circumstances, not just when it is convenient. I believe that you are a man who made some bad choices in marriage, but who still remained faithful to his marriage vows even when his wife no longer honored hers. A man who, despite the most painful personal life imaginable, remained focused and productive in his work, a leader to his employees, and a responsible father to his children. Someone who by now would be CEO of a large corporation, but instead turned down numerous professional opportunities because his unfaithful wife was not a responsible parent and he wanted to be there for his sons. Someone who, despite getting a raw deal in life, never complained or laid blame on others. Who was able to teach and train other professionals so they might someday gain the professional successes that he was choosing to forego. But most important, you, Ray Collins, are a man I want to spend time with and get to know much better."

Ray was speechless. "I want to take you in my arms and hold you," he finally said.

"I feel the same way, but our other responsibilities require that we wait."

"It seems like November eighth is forever away, rather than thirteen days from now." It was after midnight when Ray finally hung up the phone and turned off the light to go to sleep.

On Monday, the time seemed to drag by. Ray returned a number of phone calls, conducted his regular plant managers meeting, then a fruit buyers meeting, and finally a financial analysts meeting. Then he called Stanley Bedford, one of Tropical Citrus's sales representatives who covered the Memphis area, and asked him to recommend a good florist near GSDC's offices. When Ray explained to Stanley that this needed to be a very special flower arrangement for a very special lady,

Stanley said, "That's out of my area of expertise, but my wife knows a florist who is really talented and creative, although she's expensive."

"Do you have the florist's number?"

"No, but I will have my wife call you with it."

"I need it this afternoon."

About forty-five minutes later, Stanley's wife, Melanie called with the florist's name and number. "The best way to get a really exquisite arrangement is to let Joan do her thing," Melanie explained.

Joan, who owned Artistic Floral Designs, was expecting Ray's call. He then explained to her, "I am not financially constrained and I want a special floral arrangement for a very special lady who I am romantically interested in. It needs to be delivered to her office at GSDC by or before four thirty p.m. tomorrow." Ray gave Joan Ann's office address and phone number. "The card should say, 'Ann, a very special lady deserves very special flowers. I'm so happy that you are in my life, and so looking forward to getting to know you better and spending time with you. Love, Ray.'" Then Ray gave Joan his credit card number.

"No problem. And thanks for doing business with us." Just as Ray was getting ready to leave at six p.m., John Edwards, Tropical Citrus's CEO, came by. "Ray, Ellen and I are having a small get-together on our new yacht on Saturday at two p.m. and we would like to invite you. Dress is casual, and we're going to take her for a short cruise. Richard Dawson is returning from Venezuela on National Foods' plane and will be there also. Then on Monday, I want you and George to fly to New York on the National Foods plane with Richard and go to our new packaging facility in New Jersey. George needs to review the final operating budget, and I want you to get familiar with the facility, since it will be part of your operations planning responsibilities when it starts up in December. You and George can fly back on the National Foods plane on Tuesday afternoon with Sam Kehoe, who will be headed to Argentina to meet with National Foods' beef suppliers."

"That's fine. Thanks for the social invitation, John. I've never been on a one hundred-ten-foot yacht before, or on any yacht for that matter. So I'm really looking forward to it." In reality, the only thing Ray was looking forward to was seeing Ann.

At three thirty p.m. the next afternoon, Ray's secretary, Gerry, came into Ray's office and said, "There's an Ann Robinson on the line for you."

"Ray, the flowers are gorgeous!" Ann exclaimed when Ray picked up the phone. "I've never seen such an exquisite and lovely arrangement! All the women in the office are so envious. The card's also very special."

"An exceptional lady requires exceptional flowers! I'll call you at nine thirty tonight if that's okay."

"I'll be counting the minutes," she said teasingly.

The rest of the week seemed to drag by, and the only thing Ray looked forward to each day was his nightly telephone conversations with Ann. During one of his calls, he told her about John Edwards's yacht party and his upcoming trip to New York. "What type of plane does National Foods have?" she asked.

"A Gulf Stream."

"Have you ever flown in it?"

"Yeah, and it's nice. When you board the plane, the aroma of leather is very evident. That's because the seats, sofas, and headrests are all expensive leather. The wood trim is mahogany, and the light fixtures and control knobs are gold-plated. The cabin is spacious, more like a living room than the cabin of an airplane, and it also has a private office. Then there are a kitchen and bar, and usually a cook on board who prepares and serves meals, and they serve drinks and hors d'oeuvres between meals."

THE WINE QUEEN

"I sometimes fly in GSDC's Gulf Stream and you're right, they are really nice. Like flying in a luxury hotel suite."

John Edwards's yacht was elegant. The main deck was long and spacious with chairs, tables, benches, and a fully stocked bar. The captain's galley had a mahogany-paneled dining room with original paintings on the walls. The formal dining room had a large cherry-wood table that seated ten people, above which was a gold and crystal chandelier. There were four teakwood-lined staterooms, each with its own private bathroom. The master bedroom was spacious, with a king-sized bed and hot tub.

It should have been a thrill to cruise along Florida's coastline on a beautiful fall day, sipping wine and munching on lobster and oysters Rockefeller while engaging in light conversation with National Foods and Tropical Citrus senior management and their wives. But Ray just couldn't get Ann off his mind. Finally George's wife, Judy, came up and asked, "Ray, what's got you in such deep thought?"

"Nothing I care to discuss."

"Well, if you need someone to talk to, you know George and I are always here."

"Thanks, Judy."

Ray asked Lee Hansen, Tropical Citrus's director of engineering to fly with them to New Jersey. The construction of this packaging facility had been a project managed by Lee and his staff, and Ray wanted Lee to personally guide him through an understanding of its packaging and inventory capacities, line speeds, downtime for size changes, and blending capabilities. Lee was also a personal friend.

On Monday night, George went to dinner with Don Hoffman, National Foods' controller, who was also in New Jersey to get information about the new packaging facility.

So Lee and Ray had dinner at a restaurant in their hotel and Ray told Lee briefly about Ann.

"Jill is going to have you shot, Ray! You know it's too soon for you to get into another relationship!" Jill, Lee's wife and an attorney and partner in a Tampa law firm, had taken a mother-hen approach to advising Ray about romantic relationships. Ray's family and Lee's family frequently had cookouts at each other's houses, and Lee's son and daughter enjoyed playing with Tommy and Jesse.

"Lee, it's different with Ann."

"I don't believe you can rationally make that decision at this time."

"Ann's coming to visit this coming weekend, and if it's okay, I would like to bring her over to your place for dinner Sunday night along with the boys."

"Ann is flying down from Memphis to see you this weekend?"

"She sure is."

"I need to clear it with Jill, but when she knows that Ann is coming to see you, I'm sure you couldn't keep her from missing an opportunity to meet this woman."

That night, during their phone conversation, Ray told Ann about the plans to have dinner with Lee and Jill, and gave her the background on the relationship he had with them. "Going to see if I pass muster with another smart female, aren't you?" Ann kidded.

"No, I want to show you off."

"That's fine. If they're your friends, I'm sure I'll enjoy meeting them."

"Also, Tropical Citrus has a fishing boat that is mostly used to entertain customers and suppliers, but officers can use it if it isn't scheduled. In fact, that's the boat the boys and I took out for a fishing trip the Saturday after I returned from San Diego. Would you like to go fishing on it with the boys and I this weekend? Because if you would, I'll try to reserve it."

"Yeah! Boy, a deep-sea fishing trip, too! What are you trying to do, sweep me off my feet?"

"A guy like me has to use everything he's got," Ray joked.

On the flight back to Tampa, Ray asked George if he knew whether Bud Holt, Tropical Citrus's head of sales, or Roy Ashley, Tropical Citrus's head of marketing, were going to entertain on the fishing boat on Sunday. "I'm not sure, why?"

"Ann's coming to visit this weekend, and I want to take the boys and her out on it."

"Ann's coming to visit?"

"Yes."

"How is it going with her?"

"Better than I could ever have imagined, George."

Lee interrupted, "Has this guy gone crazy, George?"

"I don't think so. Ann is one special lady."

"I agree," Sam Kehoe, the executive vice-president of National Foods, interjected. "I remember meeting her at the Sweetener Users Association Conference a couple of years ago and she was one smart, impressive lady."

"Why don't you just call Brent and schedule the boat?"

"I tried to but it's already reserved."

"Let me see if I can help out here," Sam offered. "What's Captain Brent's phone number?" Ray dialed the number and handed the phone to Sam. "Brent, this is Sam Kehoe."

"Yes, sir," Brent answered nervously. "I'm looking forward to taking you fishing."

"Good. Brent if something happens and I can't come, I will have Ray Collins call and cancel, okay?"

"Sure thing Mr. Kehoe," Brent replied.

Sam then hung up the phone.

"Ray, I think I will be calling you on Friday afternoon to cancel," he said with a smile.

"Thanks!" Ray looked at Lee, who was still speechless.

They got back to the Tampa airport at 5:20 p.m. and as Ray was getting in his car to leave, Lee motioned Ray over to his car. "Ann's in her fifties and weighs two hundred pounds, right?" Lee joked.

"Lee, you're crass. You know that?"

"Come on. Level with me, Ray. What does she look like?"

"You'll just have to wait and see."

When Ray got home, Norma said that Jill Hansen had called and wanted him to call her as soon as he got in. *Lee must have called and told her about Ann,* Ray thought. He decided to wait and see how long it would take Jill to call again, and so went into the family room to visit with the boys. After about fifteen minutes she called again. "Tell me about Ann!"

"Why not wait until you meet her on Sunday evening?"

"Because I'm a curious female who likes to meddle in your personal life. Lee said she's an economist for the Global Soft Drink Company and knows Sam Kehoe."

"That's partly correct."

"Well, tell me about her then. Don't you think it's too soon for you to be getting back into a relationship? Where did you meet her? How long have you known her? Where is she from? What type of education does she have? Where did she meet Sam Kehoe?"

"Okay, okay, Jill, slow down. Since you and Lee are being nice enough to have us over for dinner on Sunday, I'll give you a quick overview about Ann - but that's all. Beyond that, you'll have to meet her and form your own impression.

After Ray finished describing Ann's education and experience, Jill said, "That's an impressive background. But with all her accomplishments, how old is she? Ray, I know that physical appearance doesn't enter into your judgment of women, and I admire that. But anyone that has accomplished all that must be at least in her fifties. Do you really think there is any long-term potential with a woman who is probably fifteen to twenty years older than you?"

Ray refrained from telling her that Ann was five years younger than he was. "You'll just have to wait until you meet her to see. What time should we be at your house for dinner?"

"How about six?" Jill suggested.

"Sounds fine to me."

During that night's regular phone conversation with Ann, Ray shared with her the discussions he'd had with Lee and Jill. "It sounds like Lee is a typical American male, and Jill just wants to help. She probably has a crush on you."

"What makes you think that?"

"Her interest in your personal life. She's married and can't have you, but if one of her friends gets in a relationship with you, she can experience it second-hand."

"Boy, I sure don't understand women."

"You don't have to, now that you have me to explain them to you, Ann teased. "By the way, my plane gets into Tampa at 9:05 p.m. on Friday night and leaves for Memphis at 4:10 p.m. on Tuesday. I will already have had dinner on Friday night."

"I plan for us to spend that night at a hotel in Tampa, if that's okay," Ray said cautiously.

"In the same hotel room, I hope," she said nervously.

"Are you kidding? Of course."

"I'm nervous about it."

"So am I, but I am also looking forward to being with you, holding you, and making love to you more than anything I have ever anticipated."

"I feel the same way, and I wish it were tonight rather than three days away. I want you so badly I can hardly stand it."

"My reoccurring dream each night is about holding you, touching you softly and intimately, kissing you, and making passionate love to you," Ray said, his voice filled with emotion.

"We'd better stop this or we'll drive each other crazy," Ann said breathlessly.

The next day, Wednesday, Ray called the Sheraton hotel and reserved an executive suite for Friday night and requested they put a bottle of Dom Perignon Champagne on ice in the suite at eight p.m. Then he called the limo service that Tropical Citrus used and requested that a stretch limousine meet them at his house at five thirty p.m. on Saturday, present Ann with a rose on a velvet pillow, then take the two of them to the Gulf Sands Restaurant on Longboat Key for dinner and bring them back home after. The weekend was set. Meet Ann's plane at nine on Friday night in Tampa; a romantic evening at the Sheraton hotel; off to Ray's house in Ruskin on Saturday morning to spend time with the boys; limo to the Gulf Sands on Longboat Key for dinner; a deep-sea fishing trip on Sunday; dinner with Lee and Jill that night. Then relax on Monday until they left for the Tampa airport about two thirty p.m. so Ann could catch her 4:10 flight back home to Memphis. Ray could barely contain his excitement and anticipation. He decided to leave the limo date as a surprise for Ann, since she already knew about the rest of the weekend's plans.

Friday finally came, and Ray was worthless at the office. At about three p.m. he told Gerry that he was going home. She said she could tell that something was occupying his thoughts. The boys were home from school when Ray got there, and Norma was surprised to see him. "I didn't think you had to leave for Tampa until about six thirty," Norma said.

"That's right, but things are slow at the office and I thought I would spend some time with the boys." They played fliers and rollers with the softball and Ray explained that he would be in Tampa that night, but bringing home a special woman friend for them to meet in the morning.

"She's not someone like Mom is she?" Tommy asked.

"No, she's very special."

"Do you like her, Dad?" Jesse asked.

"Yes I do. Very much."

"Then we'll like her, too," Jesse assured his father.

"I want to meet her before I decide," Tommy said.

"And you will get a chance to do that tomorrow."

"Are you going to marry her?" Jesse asked.

"I don't know. We are just getting to know each other."

At five p.m. Ray called Brent and canceled Sam Kehoe's fishing reservation, then reserved the boat for Sunday. "We'll be there at nine a.m. and need to be back at the dock no later than three p.m. if that's okay."

"That's fine," Brent said.

Ray then left for the Tampa airport and was inside the terminal at just after seven. He grabbed a sandwich and was at the gate that Ann's plane would arrive at by eight, and then sat down to wait.

A mixture of thoughts and emotions were churning through him. *I want to make love to her with an incredible longing and desire that's more intense than any I've ever felt. But is it wise to plan to sleep together on only our second date? But during the thirteen nights that we've talked on the phone, we've gotten to know each other even better than I knew my ex-wife - most likely because Ann and I communicate so well and are totally honest with each other. Our long-distance relationship definitely makes things different for us,* he reasoned. *What if I'm a disappointment to her in bed? What if we aren't sexually compatible? Stop it!* he thought. *I'm crazy about Ann. She's everything I've ever dreamed of and nothing else matters.*

Chapter Twelve

When Friday finally arrived, Ann had scheduled back-to-back meetings on purpose so that the day wouldn't seem a million years long. She left her last meeting at two thirty, went home and took a shower, did her hair and makeup, dressed, and made it to the airport just in time for her flight. As the plane got off the ground and she settled into her seat, she began to think about her upcoming weekend with Ray. She'd dreamed about and planned this weekend down to its smallest detail for years. She had bought the dress she was wearing in Rome when she'd been at a meeting of the Food and Agriculture Organization of the United Nations about a year ago. The purse and shoes were from a trendy shop she'd been to with Sandy Hogan in Beverly Hills. And her diamond earrings were a present from her uncle when she'd graduated from Wellesley.

She was nervous about tonight, about making love with Ray. She thought about how exciting it had been when he'd held her and kissed her in California, and then she tried to imagine him holding her and kissing her when they were joined as one, and the idea excited and overwhelmed her until she couldn't think at all.

After what seemed like an eternity, Ray heard the announcement of the arrival of Ann's flight. As Ray stood and waited at the gate, he tried to calm down, but couldn't. Then he saw her walking toward him and he gasped at how unbelievably beautiful and sexy she was. Ann had on a clinging black silk dress, with dangling diamond earrings that sparkled. Her light makeup was just enough to bring out her young, innocent beauty, and her long, black hair was shimmering. She took his breath away.

Every man in the room was staring at Ann when she walked up to Ray and said, "Hi Ray!" Then she put her arms around him and gave him a long, lingering kiss. He was again weak in the knees, the way he'd felt when he'd met her for the first time in San Diego. He'd forgotten how gorgeous she was, and had a difficult time realizing that this ravishing, sexy creature was the woman he had been talking with nightly since their first and only date two weeks ago in California. He again realized that she was the most beautiful woman that he'd ever seen.

"Are you okay?" she asked.

"Yes, I just forgot how gorgeous you are."

"Thank you. Just remember, it's me - Ann, the person you've been talking to nightly for the last two weeks." And then Ray calmed down, some.

Holding hands, they went to get her luggage, and then were off to the Sheraton hotel.

Ray closed the door to the suite and leaned against it. He raised Ann's hand to his lips, like he had after their amazing dance at the citrus conference. But this time he swiveled her wrist and pressed a kiss to the center of her palm. A jolt fired from his touch right to her core.

"Your hands are so elegant," he said, kissing her fingers one by one. "Like a princess's hands. You should be living in a castle tower."

"And would you be the handsome prince who comes to rescue me?" she laughed.

"Always."

He took her face in his hands and gently opened her lips with his own. Then, as if a dam broke, he clasped her to him, devouring her with his kiss, hands tangling in her hair, body pressing against her with overwhelming need.

Ann let go. Time spun out, drifted, stopped. There was only his mouth against hers.

Ray broke off the kiss to taste more of her. His lips blazed a line down her throat. Ann clung to him weakly, letting the sensations wash over her.

"I wake up shaking after I dream of you." His voice was thick with desire.

"I'm shaking, but I'm not dreaming now," said Ann. "Please tell me I'm not dreaming." His only answer was to claim her lips again before picking her up in his arms and carrying her to the bedroom. With careful gestures, he unbuttoned her dress and slid her dress straps below her shoulders, down her arms, and past her hips. His mouth trailed after the material, planting whisper kisses in its wake. His hands massaged the soft skin of her waist and she groaned. Next he slid her panties down her so she could step out of them.

"Now it's my turn," she said, her voice hoarse with desire. She was trembling as she unbuttoned Ray's shirt and removed it, unbuckled his belt, unfastened his pants and slid them down, then slid his shorts down. He looked ruggedly masculine and powerful, and the naked sight of him made her feel weak at the knees. His heavily muscled chest and shoulders rippled when he moved, making her catch her breath. He aroused something in her she'd never felt, and she wanted him more than she'd ever imagined that she could want any man.

"I've wanted you for so long." His voice was husky and shushed by his lips against her throat, her chest, her stomach.

So have I, thought Ann. *Oh, God, so have I.* But she could no longer speak the words. Passion had caught her in its crushing grip, and she knew only that she had to have this man right now or go insane from the wanting. Ray lifted her in his arms and laid her gently in the bed, then slipped in beside her. Never in her wildest dreams had she thought something could feel so good.

Finally, they were together, with nothing between them.

She shivered, and tiny cries rippled out of her as they made passionate love, desperately, then gently, and finally fell into exhausted satisfaction.

Ray let his lips take a slow, lazy journey down her face and neck. Her hair was a mess on the pillow and he rubbed its softness against his cheek. The look of pure joy had faded from Ann's face and now she watched him sleepily. Ray didn't know which expression he would cherish most. He realized that this was the first time he had ever really made love. Nothing before come close. Everything else had just been sex.

"I love you, Ann," he blurted, and then worried that it was too much, too soon. But her smile and the glistening tears in her eyes reassured him.

"I love you too, Ray. I have for years." Her words warmed away all the lonely nights he'd spent wondering if he deserved real love in his life and if he would ever find it. He touched her again. It didn't matter where. He needed the solid sensuality of her skin on his. He knew that there would never be another moment exactly like this one, but he planned to make many others just as good.

And then, quietly, patiently, she told him the entire story of how she'd changed the course of her life because of her love for him, beginning with seeing him present his paper at Clemson, why she decided to get her master's even though she was on a fast-track career, her interview with Harry and the real reason he became her mentor, the films of Ray, and the scrapbook of him she'd assembled and cherished, and how she'd decided that if she couldn't have Ray, then she'd have no one.

Tears welled up in Ray's eyes as he listened to her special story and realized that he'd never been loved like this. "Oh, Ann, my beautiful, special darling… I never thought I'd find you, but I know now that you're God's answer to my prayers."

"Do you believe in soul mates?" she asked.

"I do now," he replied.

Then she playfully nibbled his ear as she teasingly said, "I think it's time to open that wonderful bottle of Champagne you bought and drink a toast to the first time we made love!"

There could be no heaven better than this moment, Ray thought. Later that night, they fell asleep in each other's arms.

When Ann woke up, at first couldn't remember where she was. Then she did, and looked over at Ray sleeping peacefully next to her. *He's in love with me! He said he's in love with me!* She knew that Ray would not have told her he was in love with her unless he really meant it, and just thinking about his words again made her giddy with happiness. Making love with Ray had been the most incredible experience she'd ever had. *What a special, giving man.* She had dreamed about this night, this weekend, for years. *He'll never know how much I love him,* she thought as she gazed at him, *because there's no way to express such a deep love as I have for him.* Then her mind drifted back to the seven long years she had waited for him, changing her life to be a partner for him. All the nights and weekends she had been alone, wanting to be with him. *Had it been worth the price? Without a doubt,* she thought, realizing what this weekend meant, and what it represented. Then she carefully snuggled up to the man of her dreams and quietly fell back to sleep.

On the drive to Ruskin later that morning Ann said, "I can certainly tell that you lift weights. You look like you are still a football hero."

"Weightlifting has been a hobby of mine for almost twenty years. That and jogging are part of a health and fitness lifestyle that I am committed to."

"I have only lifted weights for about a year, but I would really like some advice about barbell squats."

"I have a pretty complete gym in my garage, so why don't we just plan to work out on Monday and I can handle your questions then."

"That sounds great to me. I also read those articles in the *Florida Alligator* about how you were voted the most handsome man on the University of Florida campus, and I definitely agree with that sorority's vote," she said teasingly. When they came to a stop at a traffic light, Ray playfully pulled her to him and kissed her.

They got to Ruskin about eleven a.m., and it was a beautiful, sunny autumn day. As they drove onto Ray's property, Ann remarked, "This is a beautiful place." The driveway was about seventy-five yards long, and lined with a mix of pine and palm trees. Ray's house was nestled in a small grove of shady oak trees and the three-and-a-half acre backyard had pine, oak, and palm trees, grown in a park-like setting.

After they pulled up to the house, Ray introduced Ann to the rest of his household. "Tommy, Jesse, Norma, this is Ann Robinson."

"Hi, Miss. Robinson," Jesse said nervously. He then he handed her a bouquet of wild flowers that he and Tommy had picked for her.

"That's Ann," she corrected. "And thank you for the flowers, Jesse. They're beautiful."

"You're welcome, Ann. Tommy and I picked them for you."

"Thank you too, Tommy. That's so thoughtful."

Tommy was silent.

"It's good to meet you, Ann," Norma said.

"Norma, it's obvious that you are an important part of this family."

"Thank you, Ann. There are cold cuts and sandwich makings in the refrigerator. I'm headed to my daughter's until Monday afternoon, unless you need me."

"Have a good time," Ray said as Norma left.

Ray was bringing Ann's luggage into the house when he heard her say, "Where are those BB guns you boys like to shoot?" The next thing he knew, she was out in the backyard getting ready to shoot the BB guns with Tommy and Jesse.

"Boys, go set those cans up against that bale of hay," she instructed. "I'm sure your dad put it there to use as a backstop for your shooting. Remember when you are target shooting with a rifle or pistol to always have something behind the target to stop your bullets." She handed one of the rifles to Tommy.

"Now let's see you shoot." He hit the can on the right all three times.

"Okay, Jesse, now your turn," Ann said

But Jesse missed the can.

"Get your cheek down against the stock so you can see through the sights better," she instructed Jesse with a smile. "Now try again." This time Jesse hit the can all three times in a row.

As Ray walked up and lovingly put his hand on her shoulder, he asked, "Ann, where did you learn about shooting?"

"You done found you a ver-sa-tile gal," she joked in a Texas drawl. "Actually, I spent a good bit of time shooting and hunting with my grandfather when I visited my grandparents. I have a Colt .38 Special revolver that I shoot regularly, sometimes in competition matches. I also like to hunt quail and shoot skeet and trap with my twenty-gauge Browning shotgun."

Once again Ray was totally in awe of this amazing woman, remembering his earlier fear that she may not like hunting and shooting, which were his favorite hobbies. Tommy and Jesse continued to shoot their BB guns as Ray and Ann talked.

"I also grew up hunting in the woods around Columbia County," Ray said.

"I continue to be amazed at the many things we have in common."

"So do I. All of my guns but my .410 shotgun and .357 magnum revolver were stolen several years ago, but I haven't replaced them yet. With the boys now eight and ten, I want to start hunting and shooting again, and introduce them to these great sports. So far we've been small game hunting with the shotgun and shooting the BB guns."

"Anybody ready for lunch?" Ann asked.

"I am!" Jesse said.

"We are, too," Tommy and Ray answered. While Ray and the boys continued to shoot the BB guns, Ann prepared a lunch of sandwiches, chips, and fruit, then laid a table cloth over their picnic table that was under an oak tree, and served the meal with soft drinks for the boys and, for her and Ray, a bottle of Chardonnay that had been chilling in a container of ice and water. When Ray tried to help Ann with the preparations, she had refused, suggesting that he go back outside and shoot with the boys.

After lunch, time seemed to float lazily along as they all played horseshoes, and then piled on the garden tractor to go to the back of their property where there was a giant old Duncan grapefruit tree. It had ripe grapefruit they could pick so they could make fresh-squeezed juice. Ann climbed the tree alongside both boys, and the three of them tossed down grapefruit for Ray to put in a mesh bag he had brought. As Ray took in the scene before him, he thought how special it was. *Here is this beautiful, sexy woman, a woman who is chief economist for one of the largest corporations in the world, up in a grapefruit tree with Tommy and Jesse, picking fruit and having a ball. I wish I had a camera.*

THE WINE QUEEN

They eventually went back to the house and squeezed the grapefruit into a gallon of juice. As Ann was unpacking her bags later in the master bedroom, Ray heard her ask, "What's this? A hot tub?"

"Yes," he answered as he joined her in the spacious bedroom. "It was Connie's idea, to help us work on our marriage. What it really did was help her work on Tommy's Little League coach. I came home earlier than expected from a business trip, and here they were."

"You've really been through a lot, haven't you?" Ann said, her voice breaking with sympathy.

"So have you," Ray said, not wanting to bring up any more painful memories.

They then went back outside to a very large porch swing suspended from the limb of an oak tree in the backyard. While the boys played in their tree house, Ray lay on the swing with his head in Ann's lap. As the swing gently rocked back and forth with a creaking sound, she tenderly twisted her fingers in his hair.

"Ann, I had many lonely times: weekends and holidays while Connie was away with her boyfriends. I finally believed that I was destined to spend my life alone, with no partner, and that saddened me so. Now that you've come into my life, you've changed my world. And for the first time, I know how it feels to truly be in love. I've never been this happy before."

"Oh, Ray darling, those times you were alone, wondering why you didn't have a partner in life, I was also alone. In love with you, but unable to have you. At least I was able to go on dates."

"I'm glad you were able to find companionship and have some fun. But I'm sure glad those relationships didn't last, or we wouldn't be together now."

"You know who those dates were with?"

"No."

"They were with you, Ray."

"Huh? I don't understand."

"I buried myself in my work most weekends. But sometimes, on Saturday nights, I would watch those films I have of you playing in those championship football games and being interviewed after the games, or the ones of your presentations to the GSDC Board, or the home movie Sandy gave me of you and the boys at the beach after fishing. Then I'd dream about what it would be like when we were finally together. Other than my talks about you with Harry and Steve, those films were the only connection I had to you, and they kept me going, believing that someday we'd be together. They were my version of going on a date with you, and I cherished them. And I always will."

"Oh Ann," Ray said, taking her hand and looking into her eyes. "We really are together now and nothing can make one of us ever be without the other again."

"This weekend is the culmination of more dreams and wishes than you'll ever know, Ray."

"For both of us. But it's not just the culmination of our dreams and wishes. It's the beginning of a beautiful future together."

As she bent down to kiss Ray, Tommy ran up and said, "Come on, Ann! We want you to throw the ball to us. Please?"

She looked at Ray, who nodded, then she said, "Okay, Tommy." And off she went to play with the boys.

Ray continued to sit on the porch swing, and sipped fresh grapefruit juice as Ann and the boys threw the soft-ball back and forth. Watching her play ball with his sons and listening to their joyous laughter reminded him that this was the first time a woman had paid this much attention to Jesse and Tommy, and that this was the happiest he'd ever seen them. Ann was capturing their hearts the same way as she had captured his. He looked at his watch and realized the limo should be arriving at any time, so he walked to the front of the house to check. Just as he did, the long white limousine pulled up the drive to the house.

"Ann, boys, there's something in the front yard you need to see."

Once she and the boys had all walked around to the front yard, Ann said excitedly, "Ray! A limousine?"

"For our date tonight."

Then the driver got out and presented Ann with a rose on a velvet pillow, saying, "For you, miss."

"Oh, this is too much, Ray!" she gushed.

"Dinner tonight is at the Gulf Sands restaurant on Longboat Key. So let's go get dressed. Boys, Paula is coming to stay with you, and I think she is bringing you a pizza from Tony's."

"Oh, Dad... can't we go with you and Ann?" Tommy begged.

"Now, Tommy..." Ray started.

"Now, Dad, Ann interrupted, "we can't leave these wonderful guys behind. Can't they come, too?"

"But I thought —"And then she winked, silently mouthing out of sight of the boys, "Is it okay with you?"

He nodded his head and then said, "Well, boys, since Ann insists, you can come if you want to!"

"OH BOY!" Tommy shouted.

Jesse went up to Ann and gave her a hug. "Thanks, Ann."

"Now, boys, we have the Tropical Citrus boat reserved for fishing tomorrow, but we're going only if you are well-behaved tonight at dinner."

"A limo tonight and fishing tomorrow, too! WOW!" Tommy exclaimed.

"Well, let's go get dressed!" Ray suggested.

Ray then called and cancelled the babysitter, and they put a bottle of Champagne on ice in the limo and brought soft drinks for the boys.

The Gulf Sands restaurant sat on the beach overlooking New Pass, and was luxurious as always. They had a window-side table, and although it was dark outside, they could see the lights of sailboats anchored in the bay with a beautiful moon in the background. "This place is exquisite," Ann remarked.

They ordered, and then talked for a while. Ray then excused himself to go to the restroom, but upon returning toward their table, he saw two tuxedoed waiters trying to decide whether to serve dinner to an empty table. *Where are Ann and the boys?* he wondered. Then Ray heard giggles behind him.

There they were, with Ann giving Tommy and Jesse dimes so they could call their friends on the restaurant's pay phones and describe their limo ride. She was totally focused on them, and it was obvious that at this moment they were the center of her universe, and they were really responding to her kindness and attention. This was the first time that they had truly experienced the loving attentiveness of a woman. Their mother had never been there for them and although Connie's mother had tried to be close to the two boys, she was just too old for them to relate to her. A lump formed in Ray's throat when he saw how happy Ann was making his sons. "Y'all want to eat or just spend the evening on the telephone," Ray joked when he finally interrupted the moment.

"Now, Dad," Ann said, "we were just taking care of some important business."

"I believe the waiters also have some important business with us." They went back to their table, where they were served a wonderful meal.

They got back to the house at about ten, where the boys begged Ann to read them a bedtime story. It had been over a year since they had wanted bedtime stories, saying they were too grown up for that now, so Ray knew that this was just their way of spending more time with her.

"She will read to you for thirty minutes, and that's all," Ray said. "We have to get up early for our fishing trip tomorrow."

While Ann read them the story of a dog named Big Red, Ray went down to the master bedroom and began to fill the hot tub. As it was filling, he lit half a dozen scented candles and placed them around the sides of the tub, placed two towels next to the tub, and put a record of soft romantic music on the phonograph. When he went back to the boys' room, Jesse was already asleep and Tommy was beginning to nod his head. Ray motioned Ann to come out of their room, which, after turning off their light, she did. As he led her to the master bedroom, she teased, "What are you trying to do? Seduce me?"

"You better believe it," Ray joked. He'd barely been able to resist taking her into his arms so he could make love to her again all day, and now that they were finally alone, he was overflowing with passion and desire, and so was she.

Ann took in the bath, the scented candles, and the music. Ray had done this for her. Standing on tiptoe, she trailed kisses up his neck. His two-day old beard tickled her lips. He felt her shiver and caught her mouth beneath his. Their tongues met with the ferocious need that was now always simmering just beneath the surface. Clothing fell to the floor, forgotten. Ray swept her into his arms and stepped into the tub. The water was only marginally hotter than the kiss that consumed them. They sank into the warm depths and Ann settled on his lap with her head nestled against his chiseled chest, which was solid and strong against her yielding breasts. The roughness of his unshaven face scratched her skin and doubled her heartbeat.

"I never knew how amazing this would be," she said.

"What? This?" He nipped her neck, then kissed her passionately.

She squealed and squirmed, teasing him beneath her as he groaned.

"That, yes." She grinned. "But also being in love." She looked up at him. His eyes were dark and shimmering in the candlelight. His lips were full and needed kissing. "I'm yours, Ray. Now and for always."

He sucked in his breath as if her words were a caress on his bare flesh.

"I love you more than you'll ever know, Ann."

Afterwards, she clung to him weakly, desperately. He wrapped her in a towel, and then in one motion he swept her into his arms and carried her to the bed. They held each other, exhausted. She was still shaking, and then she began to cry softly. "Ann, what's the matter, I didn't hurt you did I?"

"No, no, darling. I'm fine. That was just such an incredibly intense emotional experience that it made me cry, but these are tears of euphoric happiness." Ray held her while she cried, whispering softly into her ear how much he loved her, how beautiful and sensual he thought she was, and how gloriously happy she made him.

Finally, she stopped shivering, the tears subsided, and she gazed at him, the most beautiful look of love in her eyes that he'd ever seen. "Oh, darling," she said softly, her voice breaking with emotion. "Oh, darling." No more words would come, only a special glow about her that told him how intensely she must love him.

Then holding her close, he spoke softly into her ear, "My beautiful, special lady, I love you. I love you so much more than I can express." She fell asleep peacefully in his arms. Ray silently thanked God again for bringing her into his life, and also fell asleep.

Ann woke up and looked at the alarm clock. It was five forty-five in the morning, forty-five minutes before the alarm was set to go off. She turned it off and looked lovingly at Ray, who was sleeping soundly. *You're more wonderful than I ever imagined and I feel like I'm in paradise*, she thought as she gazed at Ray. Then she went to the bathroom to get ready for what she knew was going to be another fun and exciting day: a family off-shore fishing trip, and dinner with Ray's friends.

She heard the boys in the kitchen and decided to let Ray sleep a while longer. "Good morning, boys," Ann said in hushed tones as she walked into the kitchen.

"Hi, Ann," Jesse greeted her.

"We're making breakfast," Tommy said.

"Yeah, when we go fishing we like to surprise Dad with breakfast - 'cause that's when we get to eat the good stuff," Jesse explained.

"Dad doesn't like bacon and eggs for breakfast too often because he says they're not good for us," Tommy explained. "But it's okay every now and then. Jesse, where's that can of biscuits?"

"Norma fixed them for dinner Friday night and that's all we had," Jesse replied.

"Darn. I guess we'll just have toast," Tommy said.

"Mind if I help, boys?" Ann asked.

"Not at all," Tommy said.

"Let's see, do you have any flour?"

"Everything like that is in there," Jesse said, pointing to the cabinet where flour, sugar, coffee, and other essentials were kept.

Ann was able to find not only flour, but also baking powder and shortening, and there was milk in the refrigerator. She then got a bread board and began to make biscuits. As she, Tommy, and Jesse were making the family's breakfast together, Ann realized how much fun she was having. *They're such wonderful boys*, she thought. *It feels so special to be here with them, fixing breakfast for all of us, looking forward to spending the day together.*

Ray awakened to the smell of bacon frying, biscuits baking, and freshly ground coffee brewing - and to the laughter of Ann and the boys. He looked at the clock and it was seven a.m., thirty minutes past the time he had set for the alarm. *Ann must have gotten up early and turned it off so I could get more sleep*, he thought. As he listened to the happy sounds coming from the kitchen, he couldn't remember how long it had been since the house had been filled with so much joy.

Ray got up and walked into the kitchen, where Ann and the boys were making breakfast, and she said, "Good morning sleepy head."

"Good morning, beautiful," Ray said sleepily. "Boy, something sure smells delicious."

As he walked up behind Ann so he could put his arms around her waist and give her a good morning hug, Tommy said, "Dad, Ann's making homemade biscuits for breakfast!"

"Homemade biscuits! That must be what smells so good!" Ray said.

"I've never had homemade biscuits before," Jesse said.

During breakfast, Ray and the boys discussed whether to fish the reefs for grouper and snapper or to troll for tuna, but Ann only partially participated in the discussion. In her thoughts, she was pretending that she was married to Ray and this was her family, getting ready for an exciting day together. It made her realize again that being part of this wonderful family was something she wanted more than she'd ever wanted anything.

After breakfast, they packed some extra clothes, hats, and sunscreen. Then they filled a cooler with soft drinks, beer, sandwiches, and fresh fruit. They decided they would release anything they caught because they didn't want to have a fish fry and preferred to eat fish when freshly caught rather than freeze them. They arrived at the dock at 8:55.

"Brent, this is Ann Robinson," Ray said as they loaded their gear onto the boat.

"Hello, Ms. Robinson," Brent said, trying to hide his obvious astonishment at her beauty.

"Good to meet you, Brent. Ray says you're the best fishing guide on the west coast of Florida and I'm really looking forward to today's trip."

"He ought to know. He sure brings these boys out a lot. By the way, Mr. Baker sent this for you." Brent pointed at a large basket of fruit and cheese in the main cabin. There was a note that said, "Ann, welcome to Florida. Hope you and Ray are having a wonderful time. Best Regards, George and Judy Baker."

THE WINE QUEEN

The forty-eight foot Sea Boots was powered by two 480 horsepower Cummins diesel engines. On the bottom deck were three carpeted staterooms. The master bedroom had a queen size bed flanked by cherry-wood nightstands, two cedar-lined wardrobes, a hot tub, and private bathroom with a shower. The other two staterooms shared a bathroom. The middle deck consisted of a full kitchen with a stove, oven, refrigerator, dining table, and a living area with reclining chairs, a couch, television, and wet bar. The rear fishing deck had two swivel fishing chairs, two stationary chairs, live bait wells, and a bait preparation table. Two thirty-foot outriggers graced the sides of the vessel, and there was a swim platform that enabled getting off the boat and into and out of the water easily. The flying bridge, located on the top deck, was where the captain navigated the boat. It contained a couch and chairs, a small bar, and is where passengers could get the best view.

"This is a very nice cabin cruiser," Ann observed.

"I chartered it to go to the Abaco Islands of the Bahamas once as a surprise to Connie when we were married," Ray explained. "I thought a week away together cruising around tropical islands and eating in rustic waterside cafes would help our marriage. Her mother was coming to stay with Tommy and Jesse. But she went off with two of her boyfriends instead, so I canceled the trip."

"Well, that's all in the past now," Ann reassured him, thinking, *how could any woman refuse a trip like that with this wonderful man.*

Although it was a sunny day, a late night rainstorm had churned up the water and it was murky and still fairly choppy offshore. When Brent said he didn't think the fishing would be very good, they decided to go back in and cruise slowly along the Intracoastal Waterway, where they could admire the beautiful homes and scenery and find an ocean-side restaurant for lunch.

They enjoyed a nice lunch at an outside table that overlooked the Sarasota bay. On the way back to the boat's dock, they were all up on the flying bridge. Ray put his arm around Ann and she laid her head on his shoulder as the two of them admired the beautiful scenery, while Brent let Tommy and Jesse take turns steering the boat. It seemed like they were in another world as they cruised along; the aroma of a light mist of seawater in the air mingled with the sounds of seagulls, the landscape a beautiful scene of sailboats, palm trees, and crystal-blue water.

Ann looked at the beautiful tropical scenery as she snuggled against Ray and thought dreamily, *I never knew I could be this happy.*

They arrived back at the dock at about two thirty and everyone thanked Brent as they unloaded their stuff. "That's some lady there, Mr. Collins," Brent observed as Ann and the boys were headed to the car.

"I agree, Brent," Ray replied.

They got back to the house at three fifteen, and did not have to leave for Lee and Jill's until about five thirty. Ann asked if Ray would take her through a workout in his home gym as they'd discussed earlier while the boys went outside to play. "Wow, you really are serious about weight training," she said as he showed her his gym. They enjoyed their workout together, and when it was time to work their legs, he helped her with barbell squats, as she'd wanted. They'd just finished taking a shower and Ray was dressing when Jesse knocked on the door. "Dad, can you help me find my new shoes?"

"Okay, son," Ray said as he tucked in his shirt.

Just as Ray finished helping Jesse with his shoes, Ann walked into the boys' room and said, "I'm ready."

"You look fantastic," Ray said.

"Thanks, so do you."

"I'm ready, too," Tommy said, and then they were off to see Lee and Jill Hansen.

THE WINE QUEEN

They got to Lee and Jill's house just after six p.m. and Ray rang the front doorbell. Jill and Lee both answered the door, and Ray said, "Lee, Jill, this is Ann Robinson." Both of them just stared at Ann, looks of shock and surprise on their faces.

"Welcome to our home, Ann," Jill said, finally managing to break the silence as she regained her composure, still somewhat in shock at how different Ann looked from what she'd expected.

Lee continued to stare at Ann in an awkward silence, then recovered as he tried to flirt with her, saying, "Ray, you son of a gun, why didn't you tell us Ann was so young and beautiful?" Tommy and Jesse had already gone outside to play with Chris and Barbara, the Hansen's two children.

"Ann, Lee designed this house and Jill built it. Jill, why don't you give Ann the grand tour?"

After the ladies had walked away, Lee exclaimed, "My god, Ray, she's one of the most beautiful women I've ever seen! How did you find a woman that smart who's also that beautiful, and then get her romantically interested in you?"

"It's a long story, Lee, and personal."

"I figured that."

Lee and Ray were fixing drinks when Ann and Jill came back into the living room. Ann was saying: "Organizational politics is not about power and intimidation. It's about building valuable job skills, getting those recognized by the right people, and creating strategic alliances and teamwork among coworkers. That's where many women go wrong, because they think of men as competitive and adversarial to one another, and believe they also have to be that way to advance. Actually, men are natural team players and have been that way since the beginning of time." It was evident that Jill was fascinated with Ann.

They all had a nice visit and dinner, and Ann and Jill exchanged phone numbers when it came time to leave.

Ann, Ray and the boys got back home about eight forty five p.m. and the boys wanted Ann to continue reading the story of Big Red the dog. "Twenty minutes," Ray said, "because tomorrow's a school day."

After they had retired to the master bedroom, they made love until almost midnight. Then, exhausted, Ray and Ann fell asleep in each other's arms.

The next morning Ray woke up at about five thirty unable to sleep. Actually, he had a dream where none of what had happened over the past two weeks was true, and that Ann had never called him or returned his calls after San Diego. It was that nightmare which woke him up. He calmed down when he saw Ann sleeping next to him.

As he gazed at her sleeping peacefully, he thought, *She looks like an angel.* Then he added, *If there are angels in human form, she is one. My life has changed so much since I met her in San Diego, and now Tommy and Jesse's lives are changing too.*

Ray's poor brave little boys had had to endure so much turmoil, and had been treated rudely, abandoned, and lied to by so many nannies as well as by his ex-wife that Ray had been worried about them. At a time in a young boy's life when his mother is an important source of security and loving support, in ways that a father can't be, Tommy and Jesse had been without. They had repeatedly trusted and opened up to the various women that Ray had brought into their lives, only to be hurt or left with false promises. Tommy had begun to withdraw into an emotionless silence, and Ray was the only person in the world he trusted. Jesse had started to cling harder to Ray, worried that something might take his dad away from him, too.

Watching how loving and focused Ann was with the boys this weekend, and how they opened up to her and enjoyed being with her so much, filled Ray's heart with indescribable joy. At first, when he saw how close she and the boys were quickly becoming, he was worried, because by now they adored her so much that he didn't know how they would deal with it if he and Ann broke up. But then he thought, *I must trust Ann. As smart as she is, she understands the situation and would not bond with them this way unless she is certain about our feelings toward each other.*

For Ray, there was no doubt that Ann was the love of his life, the only person he was ever intended to be with. He never knew how powerful a feeling this type of love could be. And he now understood what pure love must really be - the heavenly type of love. No jealously, no feelings of possessiveness, just unlimited love and trust with no demands. He knew that his feelings for Ann had grown to such a depth that neither she nor anyone else could do anything to make him not love her for the rest of his life and he believed that she felt the same way about him. After experiencing the past eighteen days and hearing Ann's story about how she'd changed the course of her life to be with him, Ray would never wonder if there was a God in heaven again, because he now knew Ann was surely God's answer to his desperate prayers.

Ray decided to turn off the alarm and let Ann sleep in. At six thirty, he quietly got up and woke the boys. Then he fixed their breakfast as they got ready for school. As Ray sat with them while they were having their breakfast, Tommy said, "Dad, I like Ann a lot."

"I like her, too," Jesse said. "Will she be here when we get home from school?"

"No. Her plane leaves for Memphis, where she lives, this afternoon. I am taking her to the airport, but Norma will be here when you get home from school."

"Dad, why does Ann have to live so far away?" Tommy asked.

"That's where her job is located."

"Can you find her a job here so we can see her more?" Jesse asked.

"Maybe sometime in the future. Now we plan to spend time together so we can get to know each other better. But she'll be coming back to visit us, and maybe sometime you boys can go to see her in Memphis."

"We'd like that," Tommy said.

"Yeah," Jesse agreed.

Tommy and Jesse were just going out the front door to wait for their school bus when Ann, who had overheard the boys getting ready to leave when she woke up, walked into the living room, wearing a robe, and called to them. "Boys?"

They turned and ran to her, and both of them began to hug her tightly. "We don't want you to leave," Jesse said.

"Can't you call your boss and get him to let you stay a few more days?" Tommy asked.

"I really wish I didn't have to leave today, boys, but I do. But I'll be coming back to see you again, and you'll be coming to Memphis to visit me, too."

"Okay," Jesse said, a touch of sadness in his voice.

And then Tommy said, "You make Dad very happy. I'm glad you like him."

"Oh, Tommy, Jesse, your dad is very special to me, and so are each of you."

She then hugged both of them and the boys left to catch their school bus, which picked them up at the front of their property at 7:55 a.m.

Ray was standing in the hallway, watching her say good-bye to the boys, and it moved him. Ann had captured their hearts and it was evident that they adored her. "Good morning, beautiful," he said as he walked over to give her a good morning kiss.

"Good morning, handsome. I'm sorry I overslept."

"I wanted to let you sleep in so I turned off the alarm. By the way, you were quite the topic of discussion while Tommy and Jesse were having their breakfast this morning."

"What did they say?"

"They really like you a lot, and want you to live closer so they can see you more."

"They have my vote on that," she joked.

"Mine, too. Ann, thank you for spending time with them and treating them the way you did. You're the first woman they can remember, other than Connie's mother, who has ever really enjoyed their company, and they're fascinated with you."

"Oh, Ray, they're wonderful boys. And I love them because they're a part of you."

"Now go back to bed and maybe put the TV on the morning news while I fix you breakfast in bed," Ray suggested.

"Going to pamper me, huh?"

"Yep."

Ray fixed her eggs Benedict and oatmeal with sliced bananas and milk. He also brewed some freshly ground coffee and poured two glasses of the fresh grapefruit juice they'd squeezed on Saturday.

"He can cook too! You've captured my heart," Ann joked as Ray brought their breakfast into the bedroom on serving trays.

While they were having their breakfast, the morning news on the TV was about the Cold War, and Ray and Ann got into an interesting technical discussion about its impact on the nation's economic productivity and the likelihood of accelerated inflation and higher interest rates as a result.

"God, I enjoy being with you," Ann said.

"I enjoy being with you, too. We think so much alike and enjoy each other's company so much that we're becoming best friends as well as lovers."

"I know, Ray. And that's very rare."

"You're very rare," Ray said softly as he looked deeply into her eyes before he kissed her. They made love and held each other for the rest of the morning, trying to enjoy as much as they could of the last day of their first weekend together.

At noon, the doorbell rang; it was Singleton's seafood market. They were delivering the two-and-a half-pound live

Maine lobsters Ray had ordered for their lunch. "Lobster for lunch?" Ann asked.

"Yes, I hope you like them. It's one of my favorite foods."

"Are you kidding? Lobster is one of my favorites too!" They steamed the lobsters in a large pot, and had sweet corn, Caesar salad, and sourdough bread along with a bottle of white wine out on the picnic table in the backyard.

The most emotionally difficult thing Ray had ever done was to put Ann on the plane back to Memphis that afternoon. On their drive to the airport they were like two high school kids experiencing their first crush. She practically sat on his lap and they kissed at every traffic light they stopped at, clinging to their last chance to be affectionate with each other for a while. Actually, Ray planned to fly up to see her in Memphis on Thursday night for a three-day weekend, but even though Thursday was only three days away, to them it seemed like an eternity to be apart.

Once they were inside the airport terminal, Ann said, "Oh Ray, I don't want to leave you."

"I know. I don't want you to, but we'll be together again in only three days."

"To me that sounds like three years, " she said, her voice breaking with sadness.

As they held each other and waited for the flight to depart, Ray said, "Ann, this weekend was the most special and magical time I've ever spent. You have redefined my life. I know now that you are the only person I was ever intended to be with. I love you more than any words can describe."

"Oh, Ray, with you I've found a joy and happiness I never knew I could experience. I love you so much. You're the most important thing that's ever happened to me. During all those years when I was in love with you but couldn't have you, I imagined what it would be like when we were finally together. But I never imagined it would be anything as wonderful as this." Ray held her until the last possible minute, and then he kissed her and said good-bye. "Good-bye, darling," Ann replied, her voice breaking with emotion, and then she hurried onto the plane, tears streaming down her cheeks.

She boarded the plane and found her seat. "Is everything okay, miss?" a stewardess asked.

"Yes, I'm fine," Ann replied. She soon regained her composure. The plane then took off and reached its cruising altitude.

"Ladies and gentlemen, we expect a smooth flight, and should be arriving on time at Memphis International," the pilot announced.

Ann reclined her chair and sat in a glow of infatuation that transcended reason or any reality she'd ever known. *How could any mortal experience be this overpowering, this exciting, this...?* She couldn't think of words to express how she felt. It was as if she had been one person, with one reality and life when she arrived last Friday. But once she came off the plane and met Ray, she had been transformed by an experience so phenomenal, so enchanting, that she was now in another life. She felt as if she'd spent the last three days in a heavenly paradise with a man who couldn't be real. But he was real, and so was their intense, indescribable love for each other. Now her future would be more beautiful, exciting, and more fulfilling than anything she'd ever imagined.

Three days later Ray came off the partially filled plane at 7:23 p.m. and into the terminal at Memphis International. He smiled broadly when he saw Ann. She ran to him and they flung their arms around each other in an embrace and passionate kiss. "Oh, darling, darling, I've missed you so," she said in a voice that broke with emotion.

Ann lived in a tastefully decorated two-bedroom condo located in an upscale section of Memphis. She had planned for them to spend their days alone together, running errands and just being with each other. Then they were scheduled to have dinner with Harry and Arlene on Friday night, and attend a party with some of Ann's friends and colleagues on Saturday night. On Sunday morning they would go to brunch, and Ray's plane left at 3:47 p.m. that afternoon.

On Friday night, Arlene Davis greeted the couple at the door of her home. "Hey, Ann, Ray."

"Arlene, it's good to see you again," Ray said as he greeted her back.

"Ray, how have you been?" Harry said as they came into the family room. A large fire was crackling in the fireplace, and Cedrica, their maid, was bringing hors d'oeuvres into the room on a large platter.

"Better than ever, Harry, now that I've found Ann."

"We're so happy for you both," Arlene added.

"How are Tommy and Jesse?" Harry asked.

"Great," Ray replied. "They really adore Ann."

"And I adore them, too. They're wonderful boys," Ann said.

"Ray, before I forget, Ed Bardwell and I are going fishing in Canada from November thirtieth to December sixth. You're welcome to join us if you'd like."

"Thanks, Harry, but I've scheduled a meeting with about two hundred of our citrus growers that week to review Tropical Citrus's performance in the orange juice market. There will be presentations from our sales and marketing people, as well as a preview of our new advertisement from Benton and Bowles, our ad agency. We view our growers as partners and want to share our success in the marketplace with them."

"That's a novel idea. I take it you came up with it?" Harry asked.

"Yeah. I want to make our relationship with our growers and other suppliers one where both sides work together as team, rather than as adversaries."

"I like that concept," Harry replied.

"So, Ann, what are you and Ray up to for the rest of the weekend?" Arlene asked.

THE WINE QUEEN

"Running errands tomorrow and a party tomorrow night. Ray goes back to Florida on Sunday."

The two couples had an enjoyable visit and dinner. Harry was very glad that Ray and Ann were finally together.

After lunch on Saturday as Ray and Ann were unloading groceries to take into Ann's condo, a football rolled up and stopped in front of them. Some guys who looked to be in their thirties were playing a game of flag football on a field that was part of the condo's park about fifty yards away. One of them had punted the ball into the parking lot. Ray picked up the ball and yelled, "Heads-up, guys." He then threw the football back to one of them.

When they returned to Ann's car for the final load of groceries, the guy Ray had thrown the ball trotted up. "Man, where did you learn to throw a football like that? I'm Jerry Cain."

"Ray Collins," he said, shaking Jerry's hand.

"I thought you looked familiar, you're the Ray Collins that played quarterback for the Florida Gators in the early 1940s, aren't you?"

"That's me."

"Wow, it's great to finally meet you, Ray! I was a sophomore at Florida the year you led the Gators to their first national championship. I was one of your fans. Hey, guys, come meet the football legend and Heisman Trophy winner that led Florida to its first national championship in 1945," he yelled to his friends.

"Jerry, I don't think..."

And then Ann interrupted, saying, "Why don't you play some ball with the guys while I put the groceries away."

"Oh, man, it would be a real honor if you'd play ball with us," Jerry said as four other guys came up. It was an unusually warm afternoon for Memphis in November, and a beautiful sunny day.

"Yeah, sure. It might be fun," Ray agreed.

Although Ray had stayed in shape from lifting weights and jogging, other than throwing the ball around with Tommy and Jesse, it had been some time since he'd played football. It felt good and he was enjoying himself, even if it was only back-lot ball. "Go long, Nick. No, longer," Ray yelled as he ran and dodged players trying to pull the flag off him; he was waiting for his teammate to get clear so the other team wouldn't block or intercept the pass. Suddenly, he was in the clear and Ray threw the ball. Nick caught it just in front of the goal line, making the touch down. "Great catch, Nick," Ray yelled.

Jerry whistled. "Wow! Did you see that pass?"

"Yeah," Mike said. "It was almost seventy yards!"

Ray looked up and Ann was standing there, looking incredibly beautiful in her blue slacks, white sweatshirt, and tennis shoes, a smile on her face as she watched. "We're done," Jerry said. "Unless you want to switch sides, Ray, so we can catch up."

"Sorry, guys. I really enjoyed it, but Ann and I have plans."

"Next time you're in town, give me a call," Jerry said as he gave Ray a business card. "Maybe we can play again, or just have a beer."

"Yeah," Mike said. "I'd love to hear the war stories about when you played for the Gators."

"We all would," another team member suggested.

After Jerry and the others had left, Ann asked, "Is there anyone who doesn't admire you?"

"What?"

"Never mind," she said with a giggle as she grabbed the football they'd left behind and ran down the field. "Tackle me before I make a touchdown, Mr. Football Legend," she teased.

"Miss. Top of Her Class at Wellesley," Ray shouted as he ran after her.

"Mr. Most Handsome Man on Campus," she added as she laughed. Ray soon caught her and gently rolled her onto the soft grass and into his arms, a maple leaf catching in her beautiful hair. He held her and looked into her eyes, which were dancing with excitement. After he said softly, "Beautiful lady, woman of my dreams," he then planted kisses all over her face and neck.

"Oh, Ray, I'm so deliriously happy. Is this really happening or am I dreaming?" Then she said, "I know it's real, because I've never even dreamed about feeling like this!"

That night they went to the party, which was at Bill Porter's house – who was one of Ann's colleagues - and Ray met a number of Ann's friends and colleagues.

"Well, aren't you going to introduce me to this handsome man?" one of Ann's close friends, Betty Clayton, said as she walked up."

"Ray Collins, Betty Clayton," Ann said.

"It's a pleasure to meet you, Betty," Ray said as he gently squeezed her hand. Betty was about five foot six, with blonde hair, blue eyes, and an hour glass figure that usually made most of the male heads turn when she entered a room.

"A pleasure for me to," Betty replied. "Ann's told me a lot about you."

Later, when Ray was getting drinks for Ann, Betty, and himself, Betty rolled her eyes at Ann and said, "God, Ann! He's dashingly handsome! I think he's sexier than Elvis Presley! And he's so sweet!"

"He's also off-limits because I'm in love with him, not that it would matter. Ray's never been unfaithful to a relationship."

When Ray and Ann were driving back to her condo, Ray asked jokingly, "Well, did I pass muster with your friend, Betty?"

"Are you kidding? If you weren't strictly off-limits to her because I'm a close friend and she knows I'm in love with you, she'd have been all over you."

"What? What makes you think that?"

"We women just know these things about each other," Ann replied in a joking tone.

Chapter Thirteen

On the night of Sunday, December 7, Ann's phone rang at about seven. It was her boss, George Martin. "Ann, I have some horrible news. Harry Davis and Ed Bardwell were killed yesterday morning when their plane crashed in Canada. They were coming back from a fishing trip." The words hit Ann like a sledgehammer, and suddenly she was weak in the knees. "Ann, are you there?"

"Yes, George," she said, her voice breaking as she began to cry.

"There will be more details about the funeral arrangements tomorrow. I just wanted to let you know as soon as I heard. Are you okay?"

"Yeah, and thanks for calling me." She went into her bedroom, sat on the bed, and cried as she thought about how special Harry had been and what their relationship had meant to her. *I just can't believe he's gone,* she thought. She considered calling Arlene, then decided against it, reasoning that Arlene would probably be surrounded by family and absorbed in her grief. Instead, she called Ray.

"Hello, Ray?" Ann said as he answered the phone.

"Hi, Ann, I was just getting ready to call you. Harry's been killed in a plane crash."

"I know. George Martin just called and told me."

"I assume the funeral will be in a few days, so I'm going to fly to Memphis tomorrow night."

"Okay, I'll pick you up at the airport. Just give me your flight schedule when you know it."

"Okay."

Visitations for Harry and Ed were scheduled for Tuesday and Wednesday nights, and the funerals were to be on Thursday; Ed's in the morning and Harry's that afternoon. Late Monday morning, Ann got a call from Derrick Mobley. "Ann, there's going to be a get-together of the people Harry mentored at Arlene's house after the funeral on Thursday. Can we expect you to come?"

"Certainly, Derrick. Ray Collins will be staying with me and he will also come."

The people Harry had mentored met at Arlene's house as planned, and twelve of the nineteen people were there; their spouses did not come with them. Amazingly, Arlene looked composed as she tapped on her wineglass to get everyone's attention. "The people in this room, and the others Harry mentored who were unable to come today, were the most special people in Harry's professional life. I thought it would be appropriate if I invited all of you to get together and share your thoughts and feelings with one another on this tragic occasion. I appreciate you honoring my request for letters describing how you felt about Harry. They will all go in a book to preserve the memories of what he meant to each of you. I would like to begin by reading some of those letters." Arlene read five of the eighteen letters she had received. They were brief but meaningful notes about how important Harry had been in their lives, his contributions, and how much he would be missed.

When she came to the last one, a somewhat longer letter, it became evident that she was beginning to lose control of her emotions. "Many of you may know that Ray Collins and Harry had a special connection with each other. Ray, you remind me more of Harry than anyone I ever knew." Then she began reading his letter.

Ed Bardwell introduced me to Harry Davis and to the Global Soft Drink Company, and was always a special friend and colleague. Moreover, Ed was a member of an elite and special group. He was one of "Harry's People," and because of Ed, I got the opportunity to become one of Harry's People, too, something I consider the finest privilege anyone can have.

Harry Davis was certainly one of a kind. He was, in my opinion, the embodiment of the American dream: Work hard, take smart risks, treat others ethically, be responsible in your dealings, and you will succeed. Harry helped each of us to achieve our own American dream. He brought out the best in each of us, and helped us conquer our worst. He gave us courage when we needed it, and self-confidence when we had doubt. When things seemed impossible, Harry was always on the scene, his booming voice, gregarious presence, and unwavering optimism and support making any problem or situation look trivial and manageable. And when you were on top, achieving successes beyond your dreams, he was always there to cheer you on and be proud. You could depend on Harry to always be in your corner, no matter what. With Harry as a mentor, there was only one way not to succeed, only one way to make a mistake, and that was to ignore his advice. Harry's advice was always right, because if he wasn't sure that it was, he wouldn't give it.

Harry's talents and abilities were numerous, and without a doubt the Global Soft Drink Company wouldn't be what it is today without the contributions that he made. But Harry's true genius was in knowing and understanding people. Many of us were always astounded at how he often interpreted our innermost thoughts, knew our fears, and understood our motivations, better than we did. I lost a father when Harry died.

Today we mourn the passing of a great man. But he isn't really gone. His philosophies live on in each of us, because as he mentored us, so we will do the same for others, and they in turn, will mentor still others. That's Harry Davis's legacy, and it's a profound one. So let's drink a toast to a unique and gifted man, and to the rare opportunity each of us had to know and learn from him. Harry, you will always be loved, and your memory cherished.

Ray Collins

When Arlene finished Ray's letter, there was silence, eyes reddening with emotion as each person remembered Harry in his or her own special way. Arlene became so emotional that she left the room. Tears began to stream down Ann's cheeks as she remembered how special Harry had been to her, and finally understood what Harry and Ray had meant to each other.

Ray and Ann decided to spend Christmas Eve and Christmas Day with each of their families. Then she would fly to Tampa on December 26. They were both taking enough vacation days so that they would not have to return to work until Monday, January 12. Ray let Norma have off from Saturday, December 20 until Wednesday, December 31 as paid holiday and vacation time, then he and Ann were going to be away from Wednesday, December 31 until Thursday, January 8, so Norma would stay with the boys then. That gave Ray and Ann time with Tommy and Jesse, then the two of them would be alone for just over a week, and back to Ruskin for three days before Ann had to fly home on Sunday.

Ray planned to propose to Ann on New Year's Eve in Coconut Grove, Florida, and present her with the very fine diamond ring he had bought. He had made reservations at the Tropical Palace in Coconut Grove, an exquisite resort where, as guests checked in, a waiter dressed formally in top hat and tails would serve the guests Champagne while they sat in huge leather chairs. Ray reserved a condo for two nights. The condo had original paintings decorating the walls, a large chandelier in the living/dining room, a stocked wet bar, and a private terrace and garden with a Japanese hot tub. The spacious bathroom had a separate shower and Jacuzzi tub, as well as marble floor and tabletops and gold-plated fixtures. The posts and headboard on the king-size bed were hand-carved mahogany.

On Friday morning, January 2, Ray and Ann would leave Coconut Grove and fly to Puerto Rico to stay at the El Conquistador Resort, which was located in Fajardo, about a forty-five minute drive from the airport in San Juan. The National Juice Products Association had held its annual meetings there in April of the previous year, and Ray had stayed there when he attended those meetings. He had been impressed with the tropical beauty of that elegant resort and its many amenities. The El Conquistador Resort sat high on a cliff, on a point of the tropical beach where the Atlantic Ocean and The Caribbean Sea merged. The view from the open-air lobby was a panorama of turquoise ocean and distant islands.

A tempting variety of exceptional gourmet food selections including Northern Italian, French, Puerto Rican, Oriental, seafood, steaks, Latino and Mexican specialties could be found there in the resort's seven world-class gourmet restaurants. A casino, dancing at the Casablanca night club, snorkeling and scuba diving, deep sea fishing, surfing, a spa and fitness center, horseback riding, golf, tennis, relaxing at Drake's sports bar with a game of billiards, and enjoying refreshing tropical drinks at a swim-up pool bar in one of the seven swimming pools were some of the many things offered there.

For their first night at the resort, Ray made reservations for them at the Embers, one of the resort's world-class gourmet restaurants. There would be a popular comedian and a band and dancing until the wee hours of the morning. They would stay at the El Conquistador from Friday afternoon until the following Thursday morning, when they would return to Miami and drive back to Ruskin.

Then for Saturday, January 10, George and Ray had gotten John Edwards to agree to have a get-together with Tropical Citrus's five largest Florida citrus growers and their wives on his yacht. These growers were the owners or CEOs of some of the largest agribusiness firms in the United States, and included Gene Nelson, CEO of US Produce Corporation; Wayne Richardson from Richardson Enterprises; Jim Baron from the National Agribusiness Company; Pat Worden, CEO of National Ranchlands, Inc.; and Robert King, owner of the world's largest orange grove and also owner of the Orlando Panthers football team. This get-together with its largest growers was something Tropical Citrus had done every January for years, but this would be the first time it would be held on John's yacht, because he had only had it since last August. This would also give Ray an opportunity to show off his new fiancé, which only George and John Edwards knew about. In fact, George had kidded, "You'd better be there even if she says no."

Ray could barely contain his excitement about the approaching events and the time he and Ann would get to spend together. Ann knew about all the plans except for the two nights at the Tropical Palace Resort, which was when Ray planned to propose to her, and the week at the El Conquistador Resort. To keep the two nights at the Tropical Palace a secret and add to the effect of the surprise, Ray told Ann they were going to Miami (Coconut Grove is part of Miami) to meet two of Tropical Juices' smaller juice suppliers and their wives for two days of fishing in the Keys, rooming aboard the fishing boat both nights.

Ray could tell she was disappointed about having to spend two of their vacation days and their first New Year's Eve with people she did not know rather than alone together, but she hid it very well. Finally, Ray told her that after the fishing trip was over, where they were going and what they would be doing for a week was a surprise. "Oh, Ray, I love surprises, but can't you just give me a hint about where you'll be taking me?"

"Just bring your swimsuit and plan on dining, dancing and having fun." She would not need a passport to go to Puerto Rico, so there was no need even to tell her they would be leaving the continental United States, Ray reasoned.

Ann's plane arrived at nine p.m., and when she saw Ray standing in the waiting area, she ran to him and threw her arms around him saying, "Oh, darling, darling, I've missed you so!"

"I've really missed you, too," he said as they embraced and shared a passionate kiss.

"I'm alive again now that we're together," she said excitedly. They went straight to their hotel and into each other's arms.

The next four days with Tommy and Jesse were slow, lazy days of bike riding, soft ball, shooting the BB guns, picnics, and just the four of them being together. On Wednesday morning, Norma came at eleven to stay with the boys while Ray and Ann went to Coconut Grove in Miami, ostensibly to meet with two of Tropical Citrus's smaller juice suppliers and their wives for a fishing trip. Actually, Ray had something else in mind, but it was a surprise.

The trip to Coconut Grove took just over than four hours, and they arrived in Miami at about five thirty p.m. "We're supposed to meet them at this resort," Ray explained as they drove up to the Tropical Palace and the valet parked the car. Then they went inside.

"This is an unbelievably beautiful place!" Ann remarked as they walked through the exquisite lobby with its fountains, gardens, and art sculptures.

"You really like this place?"

"I sure do. Don't you?" she asked excitedly.

"Tell you what, then," Ray suggested with a grin, "why don't we ditch those old juice suppliers and stay here?"

"Really! Wait a minute... Ray Collins, we were never actually supposed to meet those juice suppliers, were we?"

"Guess not," he admitted, as his grin grew wider.

"What have you got planned?" The expression on Ann's face was a mix of excitement, anticipation and confusion.

"You'll just have to wait and see," Ray teased as the two of them were ushered into a plush office and sat in a pair of large leather chairs. Then they were served Champagne as Ray checked them into the luxurious resort.

Did he bring me to this incredibly romantic place because he's going to propose, or was the fishing trip just an excuse to make staying here on our first New Year's a surprise? Stop it, she then thought. *I shouldn't get my expectations up about Ray proposing, because if he doesn't I'll appear disappointed and I should be ecstatic just to spend our first New Year's in such a romantic and beautiful place. Still, imagine what it would be like if he was to propose to me while we're staying here,* she thought dreamily.

"A flower for the lady," a bellman said as he presented her with a beautiful red rose. Ann was the most excited and confused Ray had ever seen her. As they were escorted to their condo, he'd never seen Ann more surprised and excited. Ray dealt with tipping the bellman and moving their bags into the bedroom. Ann strolled wide-eyed through the sitting room that was decorated with priceless works of art, the kitchen nook with a fully stocked bar, and then onto the terrace, where she gasped in delight at the sight of the manicured garden. A small patio set with rattan chairs and a stone table gave way to a gravel path that wound through night blooming shrubs, past a hot tub, and ended at a fairytale gazebo.

THE WINE QUEEN

She then felt Ray's hands lift her hair and place a kiss on the back of her neck. Leaning against him, she said, "This is the most beautiful resort I've ever seen."

"Come on." Ray said as he tugged her down the path. "It's too nice to stay inside tonight."

They ambled along the path, hand in hand. The sweet, intoxicating scent of jasmine drifted on the night breeze. Ann dipped her fingers in the warm water of the hot tub as they passed by, thinking they would have an opportunity to make good use of that. They finally stopped at the gazebo. Inside, a padded love seat and table were the only decorations, but it needed no other. Hidden from the rest of the world by the garden and the shadows of the night, Ann felt like they were in their own paradise. Ray pulled her down to the love seat and kissed her - a long, languid kiss. Then he knelt on one knee and produced a black velvet box from his pocket. With a soft click, it opened to reveal a large, sparkling diamond set in a white gold band.

Oh my god! thought Ann. He's going to do it! Right now!
Since the beginning of this trip she both dared to hope he would propose, but also forced herself not to dwell on it. And now here he was on one knee, his rugged, earnest face gazing up at her with pure love shining in his eyes. She could barely breathe.

"I had planned this better," said Ray. "I left the Champagne chilling in the room and I meant to ask you after our walk. But I couldn't wait. Ann, you are so beautiful, the most beautiful soul I have ever met. I didn't think I would ever find someone like you, and now that we're together, I thank God every day for bringing you into my life. You are the woman I want to spend the rest of my life with. Will you marry me?"

Tears of happiness glittered in her eyes, making the whole world sparkle.

"Yes!" she said. "Yes, of course! I love you so much, darling!"

He slipped the ring on Ann's finger and crushed her to him in a kiss that promised deep passion and happiness for the rest of their years.

"I love you too, Ann," Ray said as he gazed into her eyes.

The night was filled with emotion and passion, gentle touching and tenderness, as the intensity of their lovemaking consumed them and joined their souls as one. They fell asleep in each other's arms.

Ann woke up and looked at the clock. It was just after nine a.m., and Ray was still asleep. She decided to let him sleep and went over to sit in the reclining chair next to their bed, engulfed in her thoughts. *I'm engaged to marry Ray Collins!* It still seemed too incredible to her to be true, but it was. And the romantic way he had proposed was such a sweet and special surprise! *What a wonderful, giving man,* she thought.

It was almost ten a.m. by the time Ray woke up and saw Ann sitting in the reclining chair studying her engagement ring. "Good morning, beautiful," he said.

"Good morning, my handsome darling. This is the most beautiful diamond I've ever seen, Ray. Where did you find it?"

"A jeweler George connected me with in New York City had it. It came from an estate sale in London. The jeweler said it was originally owned by eighteenth-century European Royalty. He also told me that its cut is rare, and hasn't been used on diamonds for more than a hundred years because of the craftsmanship it requires. If you'd like, the jeweler said he would research it and send us the papers that trace its history."

"Really? Of course I want those papers."

Then she went over and put her arms around Ray and said, "Ray, thank you for making this such a wonderful surprise. So many of my friends who are professionals discussed their marriages like they were a planned merger or something. Sometimes the proposal is just one of them saying that they should get married, and then the two of them discussing the reasons why and then going together to pick out a ring. You went to a great effort to make our proposal a surprise, and the incredibly romantic way you did it will remain my most special memory for the rest of my life."

Ray held and kissed her while he said, "It will be my most special memory, too. But I'm starved."

"Yeah. Me too. Guess we missed dinner last night," she said, teasingly. "Reckon we can find some grub in this here fancy joint you done hauled me off to?" Ann continued in a Texas drawl.

"I dunno, you purty thang, but we shore kin try," Ray replied using his own playful accent. And then they walked, holding hands, to the dining room to eat and discuss building the rest of their lives together.

After they'd finished their meal, they called family and close friends to tell them about their engagement. When they called Ann's Uncle Dave, Loretta answered the phone. "It's good to hear from you, Ann. Are you having a good holiday?"

"The best. I've got some wonderful news. Is Uncle Dave there?"

"Yeah. He's putting a new Webber barbecue grill together. I'll go get him."

"Hello, Ann," Dave said. Are you enjoying your New Years?"

"Yes I am, very much."

"I'm on the other phone," Loretta said. "What's the good news?"

"Last night I got engaged," Ann replied.

"To Ray Collins?" Dave asked.

"Yes, to me," Ray replied

"Hey, Ray, it's good to finally meet you over the phone. I've heard a lot about you. Welcome to the family, son," Dave said.

"I've heard a lot about you as well, Dave," and thanks."

"Uncle Dave, Would you give me away at our wedding?"

"I would be honored."

"Have you set the date yet?" Loretta asked.

"No, but we'll let you know as soon as we do," Ann replied.

"Ann when you get back home, give me a call. I want to hear all about Ray's proposal."

"Okay."

Judy Baker and George said, "Congratulations, you guys. Ann, I hope it will be okay with you if we try to put together a position for you here at Tropical Citrus, or maybe a position at National Foods based at Tropical Citrus's offices. We would love to get you on our team."

"Thanks, George. At this time Ray and I am keeping my options open, so I would be glad to discuss something at Tropical Citrus, or National Foods based in Tampa, when or if you have something."

"Let's call Ron White," Ann suggested.

Betty, Ron's wife, answered the phone, and said excitedly "Ann, let me go and get him."

"Ann, this is certainly a pleasant surprise, are you enjoying the holidays?"

"Yes, more than ever before, Ron. Ray Collins asked me to marry him last night and I accepted!" There was silence, and Ann asked, "Ron, are you there?"

"The Ray Collins I know that now works for Tropical Citrus?"

"Yes," Ann replied.

"Oh my! Ray Collins and Ann Robinson together as husband and wife! Only in my wildest dreams did I ever imagine such a partnership! Is Ray there?"

"Yes, Ron he's been on the line all along."

"Good afternoon, Ron."

"It sure is, now! Ray, you probably know how much I admire what you stand for, what you've accomplished, and how you've trained so many of our young professionals in agricultural economics. I always hoped the two of you, my best students, would end up together, but I didn't think there could be any chance of it. You can't begin to imagine how much this means to an old professor like me."

"She's the woman of my dreams, Ron. Thanks for the training, help and support that you've given to her and to me over the years."

Then Betty said, "Ann you must bring Ray and come visit us. We want to catch up with what's been going on in your life." After promising to make plans to visit Ron and Betty, they hung up and called Lee and Jill, but they weren't home.

"Ray, do you have Arlene Davis's phone number?" Ann asked.

"No, but Ron White might. He and Harry were friends, and Ron and Betty still visit Arlene sometimes." They called Ron back and he gave them Arlene's phone number.

"Arlene, this is Ann Robinson."

"Ann, it's been so long since we've talked, it's sure good to hear from you."

"I'm here with someone that I think you know."

"Happy holidays, Arlene, this is Ray Collins."

"Ray! It's so good to hear from you, how have you been?"

"Never better, Arlene, I proposed to Ann last night and she accepted."

"Really?"

"Yes, Arlene," Ann said.

"Harry admired both of you so much, I wish he were here now to know that you are together," Arlene said.

"We both miss Harry a lot," Ray said with emotion in his voice.

"Be sure to send me an invitation to your wedding," Arlene requested.

"Of course," Ann replied.

"Saving the most important until last, huh?" Ann asked.

"You realize that if it weren't for Steve and Sandy, we may never have gotten together?"

"I know." Ann said as she thought of the important role they had played in getting her and Ray together, from all the discussions she'd had with them, to organizing the citrus conference where she and Ray met, and many other things.

Steve answered when Ray dialed their number, and put Sandy on the line also. Guess what guys? Ray and I are engaged!" Ann exclaimed excitedly.

"Congratulations to both of you!" Steve and Sandy said at the same time.

"After all I've seen both of you go through, you certainly deserve to have each other," Steve said.

"We're so happy for you!" Sandy exclaimed.

"Steve, Sandy, I want to thank each of you from the bottom of my heart for what you did to help bring Ann and I together. She's the most wonderful partner that I could ever dream of. She's the love of my life, and I thank God every day for her. Both of you will always be the most special of friends to both of us," Ray said with a sincerity in his voice that made it evident how strongly he felt about what he was saying.

"In a voice breaking with emotion Ann said, "We love both of you guys."

"We're just so happy for both of you," Sandy replied. They talked awhile longer, and Ann described the romantic way that Ray had surprised her with his proposal.

After they finished talking with Steve and Sandy, they went out to the pool for a swim. "Ray, this is such a lovely and romantic place to spend our week, what do you want to do tomorrow?" Ann asked, obviously assuming that this was the surprise place he'd planned for them to spend their week together.

"We're leaving here tomorrow, Ann. There's still another surprise to come!"

"Another surprise! Oh please, Ray, give me a hint!"

"Okay, we're going someplace other than Miami."

"That's not much of a hint," she joked.

"Guess you'll just have to wait and see what's in store, then," he teased.

The next morning when it became evident to Ann that they were driving to the Miami International airport, she asked excitedly, "Ray, we're flying somewhere?"

"That's right."

"Where?"

"To Puerto Rico!"

"Puerto Rico! I've never been there, but I've heard it's a very beautiful, romantic island!"

"Well, you can soon judge it for yourself." The flight took about two hours, and their plane arrived in San Juan on time at 1:47 p.m. "El Conquistador Resort," Ray told the taxi driver as he was putting their luggage in the trunk. Just before three p.m. they pulled up to the entrance of the El Conquistador resort in Fajardo. As they entered the open-air lobby with its panoramic view of turquoise oceans and distant tropical islands, Ann gasped, "Ray, this is the most beautiful place I've ever seen!"

After they'd checked in, the bellman took them to their luxurious suite overlooking the ocean and showed them it's various rooms and amenities. He then explained the numerous things to do at the resort, described each of the gourmet restaurants, Ray thanked him, tipped him, and he left. As a result of the geography, their suite sat on a cliff hundreds of yards away from the beach and high above it, affording them a spectacular, yet very private view. While they could see the white beach, crystal blue waters and distant islands from the living room and bedroom, even with the ceiling-to-floor sliding glass windows open, no one could see inside their suite.

Ann stood, staring out the large window at the incredible view of beautiful, tropical oceans and distant islands, moved by the exquisite loveliness of this romantic place. She thought about all that Ray had done to make things very special, researching and buying such a rare diamond for her, making his proposal a surprise in such a romantic hotel, his sincere words of gratitude to Steve and Sandy as he tried to explain what helping him to find her had meant, and now flying her off to this beautiful exotic island paradise with him. She now more fully understood the depth of his love for her, and how much she really meant to him. It moved her like nothing else ever had.

Ray walked up to her, put his arms around her, and spoke softly in her ear, "Surprise, my love, for our first week together."

She gazed at him, her beautiful eyes glassy with emotion and deep love, and asked, "Oh, darling, how do you always know how to make me happier than I've ever dreamed I could be?"

"Because I feel a special connection to you. One that goes far beyond the time we've been together. And making you happy is the most wonderful, exciting thing I've ever experienced."

"It just keeps getting better, doesn't it?"

"Yes, that's because our love for each other continues to grow, and I believe it always will."

"Oh, darling..." she began.

And then his mouth closed over hers, stifling her words as she gasped with surprise, then desire. He lifted her in his arms and with a soft, eager sound, she melted against him as he carried her to the bedroom. They made passionate love for much of the afternoon, the spectacular romantic view of this tropical paradise before them, the realization that they were engaged to be husband and wife adding to their euphoria.

The remainder of their week was magical as Ray and Ann enjoyed the longest uninterrupted time they had ever had together. The days were spent swimming, snorkeling, relaxing on the beautiful beach, and enjoying the many things the resort offered. The nights were filled with intimacy and passion, and they made love as the large red sun burned its way into the tropical sea each night, their love for each other continuing to grow. They also made their future plans, and decided that May would be a good time for the wedding, and picked Saturday, May ninth. That date would give Ann time to wrap up her current commitments at GSDC and time for her to evaluate alternative employment, such as the potential at Tropical Citrus.

They got back to Ruskin at about four thirty on Thursday afternoon. Ray called Tommy and Jesse together and explained that he and Ann wanted to talk with them. When they were all seated in the living room, Ray said, "Boys, Ann and I are going to get married."

"Yippee!" Jesse yelled.

Tommy went over and hugged Ann, saying, "I'm glad you're marring my dad." Ray had never seen the boys happier.

Then they spoke to Norma, who congratulated them. They explained that they would like her to stay on because of the busy schedule they knew they both would probably have, but she explained that her other daughter, who lived in Orlando, was having her first baby in June and she had planned to go live with her and her husband to help out. They told her they had set May 9 as the date for their wedding, and that they would be on their honeymoon from May 10 until May 17. She agreed to stay on until after they returned from their honeymoon.

Ann was a hit at the get-together on John's yacht, which didn't surprise Ray. Tropical Citrus's growers really liked her and congratulated the two of them on their engagement. Pat Worden, in his usual gregarious manner, said, "Ann, I'm glad that Ray's finally met a woman that can keep him straight." Judy Baker and Ellen Edwards spent a lot of time talking to Ann, inviting her to call them to get together once Ann moved to Ruskin.

On Sunday afternoon Ray and Ann were at the airport, holding each other while they waited for her flight back to Memphis. "Ray, this was the most exciting, special, and wonderful thirteen days of my life. I'm so happy and excited about our engagement."

"I feel the same way, Ann. I can't wait for us to be married."

The price of the sixteen continuous days they'd just spent together was that it would be almost two weeks before they could see each other again, because both of them had to work the following weekend to catch up on things they had not been able to do while they were on vacation. This would be the longest time they would go without seeing each other since they spent that first weekend together back in November. "Oh, Ray, I don't know if I can stand to be away from you that long," she said as she began to cry softly.

Ray had a lump in his throat as he said, "I'll miss you so much, Ann. But I'll call you every night."

"I hate these awful good-byes at the airport," she sobbed.

"But just remember, we'll be married in a few months and then nothing can keep us apart."

"But that doesn't help now."

Then Ann's flight was announced. She continued to cry, holding him tighter as they kissed tenderly. Somehow, they tore themselves apart and said good-bye as she hurried onto the plane in tears.

On Friday, Ray was depressed at the thought of having to be away from Ann over the weekend, but at least he had their nightly phone conversations to look forward to. When he called Ann on Friday night she said, "Ray, I just can't stand being away from you this weekend. I'll manage to get my extra work done somehow, even if I have to stay up all night on Sunday and Monday. And if your workload is that demanding, then I'll just sit next to you and watch you work. I simply have to be with you."

"I feel the same way, Ann. I'll find some way to get my work done. I want to see you, too. Norma has already gone for the weekend, though. Can you fly here?"

"Of course."

"Let me see if I can find you a flight."

THE WINE QUEEN

Ray was able to book her a flight into Tampa at 12:05 Saturday afternoon, with the return leaving for Memphis at four p.m. on Sunday. He met Ann's plane at noon and they ran into each other's arms for a passionate kiss. Then she said, "Oh, darling, I just can't stand being away from you."

"I can't stand being away from you either."

"Where are Tommy and Jesse?"

"This morning a friend invited them to spend the night, which gives us some time alone."

They enjoyed a nice lunch at a sidewalk café overlooking the bay, and after that, went to Ray's house and into each other's arms. Later that afternoon, they drove out to the beach and walked along the shore as they watched the sunset, holding hands, and talking about the little things that were important to them, both excitedly looking forward to their future together. They made love and held each other for most of the night, not wanting to miss any of their limited time together by sleeping. After that, neither of them ever even considered spending a weekend apart again.

On Sunday night, March 8, Ray and his boys were riding home from church when Jesse asked, "Dad, will God mind if I love Ann like she's our real mom?"

"No, Jesse. I think that would make God happy, and I know it would make Ann very happy. And she will be your real stepmom after we are married."

"She told us she loves us like we were her own boys," Tommy said.

"I know she does," Ray observed.

"I wish we'd met her sooner," Tommy said.

"I do, too, Tommy. But she's a part of our lives now and that's what counts," Ray replied.

"Do you think she'd mind if we called her 'Mom' after you are married to her?" Tommy asked.

"Tell you what, Tommy, why don't you and Jesse call her and ask her?"

When they got home, Tommy dialed Ann's number, and then he and Jesse both got on the line. Ray was also on the other phone. "Hello, this is Ann Robinson."

"Ann, this is Tommy Collins."

"And this is Jesse."

"Hi boys. This is a great surprise!"

"I'm also on the other phone, Ann," Ray said.

"Boy, all you guys at once! What's up?"

"Ann, this is Tommy. Jesse and I want to know if it would be all right if we called you Mom after you marry our dad."

"Yeah, Dad said God wouldn't mind if we love you like you're our real mom, so we want to call you Mom," Jesse explained.

"Oh, Jesse, Tommy, that makes me so happy! Of course you can call me Mom. And I love each of you - bunches and bunches."

"Okay," Tommy said.

And then Jesse said, "Bye."

"I'll call you in a little while," Ray told her.

Then he tucked the boys in and said goodnight to them. About fifteen minutes later, he went quietly back to check on them and he heard Tommy praying: "...and thanks, God, for letting Dad meet Ann. He was so sad before, because our mom didn't love him, but now he's always happy because Ann loves him and he loves her. And God, Jesse and I love Ann, too. Oh, I almost forgot, God, after Dad and Ann get married, when we talk to you about our mom, we'll be talking about Ann."

When Ray called Ann again that night, he told her about Tommy's prayer and she was moved by it, as well as by her earlier discussion with both of the boys about them wanting to call her Mom. "Oh, Ray, Tommy and Jesse are so special and I love them so much. I already feel like their emotional Mom, but

I also want to be their mother legally. Do you suppose that after we're married I could adopt them?"

"I think that's a wonderful idea, Ann. You know how much they love you, and as far as they or I am concerned, you're their only real mom. I'll call Larry Ackerman, my attorney, and see if he can set it up for us."

The next day Ray met with his attorney. "Larry, I don't know if you've heard, but I'm getting married in May."

"Boy, you don't get discouraged do you?" Larry kidded.

"Not me, particularly with this woman."

"All joking aside, Ray, I've heard that Ann's one special lady, and was Tropical Citrus's honored guest at George Baker's Christmas party."

"Yes, she was."

"What can I help you with, Ray?"

"Ann wants to adopt Tommy and Jesse after we're married."

"Ray, I think that's a very good idea, particularly because it protects the boys in the event of your death."

"What do you mean?"

"As things stand now, if you died, even though you've asked that Steve and Sandy Hogan raise your boys, and you can designate who becomes their guardians as you have sole custody, if Connie could prove to a judge that she's changed and has become a suitable parent, then she could still make an effective claim for custody, since she's still legally their mother. And her motivation to do that would be to get your estate, which would go to the boys. Even though you are protecting its value through estate planning and have designated Steve Hogan as its trustee, Connie could still be motivated to get the boys for the child support payments that she would receive from the estate."

"Those are good points. How should we proceed?"

"The main thing we'll need is Connie's written consent, because even though you have custody, she's still legally their mother."

"We haven't seen or heard from Connie since she up and left after the divorce last August."

"Didn't the judge agree that, since this was Connie's first offense, if she gave them the information they requested about the drug dealers, they would release her from jail and not prosecute her?"

"That's correct. But given her lifestyle, she may not even still be alive. All I know is that she was headed to California after she married Chip Tanner, who is a truck driver. But that information is seven months old."

"I'll do what I can to find her, but it could be a long and expensive search. And when we do find her, she may not consent to the adoption."

"I don't see why she wouldn't consent. She hasn't made any effort to contact the boys since our divorce, and a few months before we ended our marriage she told me she had never wanted to have children. If necessary, I'd be willing to pay her if she'd consent to Ann adopting the boys. She's tried to use them to get money out of me before. Maybe that's the best way to handle the situation."

"I'll see what I can do, and keep you posted," Larry promised. "By the way, I'll need some background information about Ann for Connie to review." When Larry received the requested information, he called Ray and said, "Wow, she's really an impressive lady! I'm looking forward to meeting her."

Chapter Fourteen

Ann planned to move to Ruskin two weeks before the wedding so she could more easily handle the final arrangements and would already be moved in after she and Ray returned from their honeymoon. She had listed her condo for sale right after they got engaged, and it was only a month before she accepted an offer on it. The buyer also wanted her furniture, which she sold him as well. The sale closed in late March, and she rented the condo from the new owner for the month prior to her move to Ruskin. She and Ray agreed that the best place to invest the proceeds from the sale was in GSDC stock, which she did.

In April, Larry Ackerman told Ray he'd made contact with Connie, and that she was living in Fort Lauderdale and managing a massage parlor. She was willing to agree to Ann adopting Tommy and Jesse, but Ray would need to pay her ten thousand dollars[10] for her signature on the agreement. Ray called Ann and shared with her his conversation with Larry. "I can't believe she's selling the boys to us," Ann said incredulously.

"Oh, I can. I'm just glad she agreed. That ten thousand dollars is well spent."

"Cathy?" Ann asked when a woman answered her call.

---

[10] The same as $81,873 in 2014.

"Yes? This sounds like Ann."

"It is. How are you doing?" she asked her old friend.

"Great! It's good to hear your voice. How about you? Are you still at GSDC?"

"Yes, but I'm resigning."

"Why?"

"Because I'm marrying Ray Collins!"

"The Ray Collins I had dinner with all those years ago at Clemson?"

"Yeah, that Ray Collins!"

"You're kidding! Really?"

"Yeah, really."

"I want to hear all about how you met and everything."

"Okay, but first the wedding is on May ninth, in Ruskin, Florida, where Ray lives. It's just outside of Tampa. I would like you to be one of my bridesmaids.

"I'd love to."

"Cathy, I just finished reading a book about the California wine industry and would like for Ray and I to go on a wine country tour for our honeymoon."

"I think that would make a great honeymoon. You can sample wines throughout the Napa Valley, enjoy some of the best gourmet dining in the country, and stay in neat chalets and bed-and-breakfasts. It will be very romantic. How long do you plan to be out here?"

"A week. Can you make any suggestions about how to set it up?"

"I'll do more than that. If it's okay with you, after the wedding, I'll fly with you and Ray to San Francisco and you can start with our winery here in Napa. The two of you can stay in one of our guest rooms. Then I'll set you up a tour of nine wineries, as well as make reservations for you at five gourmet restaurants."

"Oh, Cathy, that would be great. Thank you so much. I can't wait to see you again."

"I can't wait to see you, either. Now tell me all about meeting Ray, the two of you dating, and everything else."

"Why don't you come to Tampa on May seventh and I'll tell you over lunch."

"Great."

"I'll meet you at the Pier restaurant in Tampa on May seventh at noon."

Next, Ann called her uncle Dave. "It's good to hear from you, Ann," he said when he answered her call. How are the wedding plans progressing?"

"Just fine. Uncle Dave, my last day at GSDC is Thursday, April 23. Ray is flying to Memphis to help me move and ride with me back to Ruskin. We'll be coming through Macon on Saturday. Could..."

"We would absolutely love for the two of you to stay with us. What time do you think you'll get here?"

"Probably around six o'clock."

"We'll be expecting you. I'm looking forward to meeting Ray."

Ann's coworkers and boss, George Martin, threw her a large farewell party on her last day at work, and Ray went with her to the party. The movers loaded her stuff on Friday and would be meeting the two of them at Ray's house in Ruskin on Monday.

Ann and Ray arrived at Oak Brook, still her Uncle Dave and Loretta's home in Macon, just before six on Saturday afternoon. "This is a really nice house," Ray observed, looking at the giant white stone columns and the bronze statues of German Shepherds as they were climbing the steps to the front door.

"Uncle Dave is a very successful attorney," Ann said as she rang the doorbell.

"Hey Ann!" Loretta said when she opened the door. "Come on in."

Loretta, this is my fiancé, Ray Collins."

"It's a pleasure to meet you, Ray. Ann has told me a lot about you."

"She's also told me a lot about you, Loretta."

Where's your daughter, Dianne?" Ann asked.

"She's spending the night at a friend's house," Loretta replied.

"Hey everyone," Dave said as he came into the foyer wearing a red apron.

"Uncle Dave, Ray Collins, my fiancé," Ann said.

"It's good to finally meet you, Ray! Come, let's go out on the terrace. We can fix some drinks, have some snacks, and talk. I'm slow-cooking and smoking a beef brisket on the grill."

"I've never been able to cook a brisket or a roast on my grill. The outside burns before the inside is cooked. What's your secret?" Ray asked Dave as he walked up to the grill.

"You have to use indirect heat," Dave replied.

"How does indirect heat work?"

"The charcoal is contained behind two steel rails on each side of the grill," Dave explained as he lifted the large dome lid on the Webber grill and pointed to the rails, each holding a mound of glowing charcoal. "A pan is then placed between the rails holding the charcoal to catch the drippings. The meat sits on a grate above the pan rather than above the coals, like it does when grilling a steak. The heat reflecting downward from the dome as well as the interior temperature of the grill cooks the meat. You have to baste the meat frequently to keep it moist. I have my own recipe for basting sauce."

"And you also smoke the meat?" asked Ray.

"Yeah, that really gives it a better flavor. It's time to put on another container of wood chips, so I'll show you."

"These hickory chips have been soaking in water for about thirty minutes," Dave explained as he drained the water from the chips. "I had these steel boxes with holes in their lids made to hold the chips," he continued as he filled the metal box with chips and put the lid on it. Then he picked up the metal box of wood chips with a pair of tongs. "Ray, would you lift the lid off the grill?"

"Okay," Ray replied as he removed the large domed lid.

Dave placed the box of wood chips on top of one of the mounds of charcoal. "In about 15 minutes, that will start to smoke," Dave explained. "Now put the lid back on the grill."

"Dave's become quite the outdoor cook," Loretta added. "His ribs, pork roast, chicken, brisket, and smoked salmon are the best I've ever had. He's the most popular outdoor cook in our neighborhood. I think he ought to open a barbecue restaurant after he retires."

"Nope. This is just a hobby for me," Dave said.

"What will you have?" Loretta asked as she went behind the fully stocked bar.

"I'll have some white wine," Ann replied.

"Great. I have a Chardonnay I think you'll love. I'll have a glass with you. Does anyone else want wine?"

"I'd like Jack Daniels over ice," Ray said.

"And I'd like a Glenlivet on the rocks," Dave replied.

Loretta returned to the table with the drinks on a serving tray, while Dave prepared a platter of cheese, crackers, smoked salmon, and navel orange slices.

"Ray, I hear you work in the citrus business," Dave began as he put some smoked salmon on a cracker.

"Yeah, I work for Tropical Citrus," Ray replied, taking a sip of his drink and munching on a cracker with cheddar cheese on top. "We produce and market orange and grapefruit juice under the Tropical Orange and Tropical Grapefruit brands, as well as blends of citrus juice with apple, grape and pineapple juices under the Tropical Blend brand.

"I frequently buy your juices. They're very good," Dave added, taking a sip of his drink.

"Thanks, I'm glad you like them," Ray replied as he took a bite of the smoked salmon. "Hey, this salmon is great! It's the best I've ever tasted."

"Thanks," Dave replied. "I smoked it last night."

"How long have you practiced law?" Ray asked as he took another bite of the smoked salmon and sipped his drink.

"If ya'll don't mind, while you and Ray discuss your work, Ann and I need to catch up on our girl talk," Loretta said as she put some of the snacks on a plate, picked up the bottle of wine, and motioned Ann to come in the house with her.

"Of course," Dave replied.

"The grill is just starting to smoke, Ray," Dave said as he pointed.

"I can't wait to try your smoked brisket."

"God, Ann! Ray's incredibly handsome! You told me he was attractive, but I never thought he'd be this good looking. You must have to beat the women off with a stick." Loretta said as she and Ann sat down on one of the sofas in the family room.

"Not really. Ray has never been unfaithful to a relationship, not even when his ex-wife, Connie, was openly cheating on him. When women come on to him or flirt, he makes it clear that he has no romantic interest in them because he's committed to a relationship. After that, they usually leave him alone.

"Ray sounds like great husband material to me. Now tell me all about how he proposed to you," Loretta requested as she refilled their wineglasses.

"That's right. I never called and told you like you asked me to. I'm sorry," Ann said as she took a bite of orange.

"That's okay," Loretta reassured her, taking a bite of smoked salmon on a cracker.

"It was the most exciting, incredible, and romantic experience of my life." And he made it a surprise, Ann began.

When Ann finished telling Loretta all about Ray's surprise proposal, the Tropical Palace Resort, and the surprise trip to the El Conquistador Resort, Loretta said, "You and Ray, and Dave and I are proof that you should always wait for the right person to marry, and if you have patience, that right person will come along."

"Well, there was some luck involved for me, and I also had a lot of help from friends that knew Ray well."

"Whatever happened to Harriett, and Blanche?" Ann asked.

"You won't believe this," Loretta began. "A couple of years after you moved away to college, Steve retired and gave the law firm to Dave. About a year later, Steve died of a heart attack. His estate was worth just over two million dollars.[11] He'd done an excellent job of estate planning, so it settled in only a few months. Harriett and Blanche were the sole beneficiaries, and each was to receive fifty percent.

"That's right, Steve's wife, Carol, died of cancer when I was in my freshman year at Wellesley," Ann remembered. "The funeral was during final exam week and I couldn't come."

Loretta continued, "At the time of Steve's death, Harriett was living with a beatnik in Greenwich Village in New York, smoking marijuana cigarettes and staying drunk most of the time. But she'd told her father that she was going back to college, studying to be a school teacher.

"Blanche married the boy, Edgar, who got her pregnant in college, and they were living in Los Angeles when she had the baby, which was a boy. They moved back to Alabama and in with his parents. You might remember that Edgar's father, Glen, was a Baptist minister. He was also very conservative and strict. The first time he caught Blanche and Edgar getting drunk on vodka, he warned them. The second time, when he caught them drunk and ignoring their baby, who was crying from soiled diapers, he threw them out of his house. Glen and his wife, Ellen, are raising their grandchild themselves.

"Edgar caught Blanche in bed with two men, and left. Blanche then hitchhiked back to Los Angeles, and got a job as a stripper in a night club. She also became a prostitute. Blanche told her grandfather, Steve, that she was married, had a fine

---

[11] The same as $16.4 million in 2014.

son, and that she and her husband were peach growers in California.

"Steve appointed Dave as the Executor of his estate. However, there was a stipulation in the will that Dave evaluate the morals and lifestyles of Harriett and Blanche, and present his findings under oath to Judge Burns, also specified in the will. If Harriett or Blanche had been lying to him about what they were doing, or were leading immoral lives, the will stated that they were not to receive anything from his estate. Half was to go to the Center for Battered Wives and Abused Children in Macon, and the other half to Steve's Baptist Church.

"Steve's will was read in Judge Burns' chambers in the Bibb County Courthouse. When the judge read Dave's description of Harriett's and Blanche's lifestyles, Harriett began screaming and threatening to get even with Dave, and to have him killed - right in front of the judge. Dave then had Harriett arrested. Blanche just got up and walked out, shouting obscenities as she left.

"After a policeman had handcuffed Harriett and led her away, and Judge Burns finished reading the will, Dave produced the tape recording of Harriett requesting that Dave have me murdered. Dave had expected Harriett to behave the way she did when she heard what he was reading about her, and so brought the tape for the judge to listen to. After Judge Burns heard it, he told Dave that in his opinion, Harriett was a dangerous woman, and if Dave would press charges, he would send her to prison. Harriett got ten years, which she's still serving. Dave was also able to get the court to approve his stopping the payment of any further alimony to her."

"Honey, the brisket is wrapped and resting and should be ready in about thirty minutes," Dave said as he walked into the room.

"Okay, dear. Ann and I will go to the kitchen and finish preparing the rest of our dinner."

"That's an incredible story, Loretta," Ann said as she prepared the coleslaw.

"Yes it is," Loretta agreed as she took the baked beans out of the oven and checked to see if they were ready. "Both Harriett and Blanche had a beautiful home, and a caring husband and father, who was an excellent provider. But they repeatedly trashed that, and ultimately lost a fortune that was handed to them. Some people are just impossible to understand."

"But I can't say that I feel sorry for them," Ann added. "They did it to themselves, and deserved what they got. They were both mean and stupid, and awful to me when I was growing up."

After a superb dinner of smoked beef brisket, baked beans, coleslaw, biscuits, and banana pudding for dessert, Ann and Ray didn't want much breakfast the next morning. After having toast with pear preserves that Loretta had made, and coffee, they said good-bye and were on their way just before nine.

They were glad to be on the final leg of their drive to Ruskin, which Ray said would take about six hours. Both of them were in a state of euphoria at finally being able to be together continuously without having those awful good-byes at the airports. They were also ecstatic about becoming husband and wife.

Reverend Bruce Godwin, the Methodist minister who was going to perform the ceremony, had long made it a practice to meet with couples before their weddings, both to get to know them better, and if necessary, to counsel them. He was familiar with Ray's background, but not with Ann's. So Ray had sent him Ann's résumé a week earlier. It was seven p.m. on the Tuesday night before their Saturday wedding, and Ray and Ann had just rung Reverend Godwin's doorbell.

"Hi, Ray," the reverend said as he answered the door. "He then turned to Ann. "And this must be Ann."

"It's good to meet you, Reverend Godwin," She said as she greeted him.

"That's Bruce. Please, come in and have a seat," he said as he led Ray and Ann into his living room. "Ann, Ray sent me your résumé and I've read it. It is very impressive!"

"Thank you."

"How did you and Ray meet?"

Over the next twenty minutes, Ann told Bruce the story of how she'd been attracted to Ray from the first time she saw him, and how she'd changed the course of her life to be with him as his wife and partner.

"That's the most unique, special story I've ever heard," Bruce said. "Ray, you, Tommy, and Jesse deserve someone like Ann as a part of your lives." Then he held the hands of both of them, and in a brief prayer, said, "We thank you, O Lord, for guiding Ray and Ann to each other and for the special love they have for one another and for you, O Lord. Guide them as they begin their lives together, O Lord, and help them to face life's challenges. We pray to you in the name of Jesus Christ, our Savior. Amen."

Steve Hogan had agreed to be Ray's best man and Sandy was going to be Ann's matron of honor. Tommy and Jesse would be ushers, while Loretta and Cathy Rossi would be bridesmaids. Ann's Uncle Dave would give her away. Since most of their guests were from out of town, Ray and Ann had arranged for all of them to stay the weekend of the wedding at the Long Boat Key Club, where they were having the reception.

"Hi, Ann," Cathy said when she greeted her friend at the Pier restaurant.

"Hi, Cathy. It's good to see you again."

"You, too."

After they'd ordered their meal, Cathy said, "Okay, tell me how you met Ray."

"We actually met at a citrus conference in California where both of us were speakers."

"Citrus?"

"Yeah, I used to buy citrus essence oils for GSDC and Ray is in charge of procurement for Tropical Citrus. Although we first met at the citrus conference, I had been in love with him for years before we met."

"You fell in love with Ray when you saw him make that presentation at Clemson, didn't you?"

"Yes, I did," Ann admitted

"I thought your interest in Ray was more than casual by the way you acted when I told you about my dinner with him."

Then Ann told her the entire story of how she'd changed the course of her life to be with Ray, about all the lonely years of waiting until they could be together, and how special their first meeting had been. "When he took me to dinner, our attraction to each other was very powerful. We spent our first weekend together a couple of weeks later."

"Details. I want all the details."

Ann then described her first weekend with Ray. "Forget the family fishing trip, limo date, picnics, and all that other stuff," Cathy urged. "How was he in bed?"

"That's really private and I'd prefer not to..."

"Oh, come on, Ann. I've shared some of my experiences with you"

"Okay," Ann agreed reluctantly. Then, somewhat bashfully, Ann described her lovemaking with Ray, and the more she revealed, the larger Cathy's eyes seemed to grow.

"It seems to me he's as good in the sex department as he is in the looks department, Cathy said."

"Better. But more than that, he's so kind and giving. He really loves me and treats me as his equal, his partner. He pays attention to the little details that are important to our relationship, and he never takes me for granted. He has this way of making me feel I'm the most special person in the world whenever I'm around him. I never knew I could be this much in love, Cathy."

"When did he propose?"

"On New Year's Eve, at the most beautiful, romantic resort. Our suite even had a hot tub on a private terrace in a garden." Ann then described the lovely way Ray had proposed, and the surprise trip to the El Conquistador Resort in Puerto Rico.

With a dreamy look in her eyes, Cathy asked, "You really have found your Prince Charming, haven't you?"

"Yes."

"Ann, I'm very happy for you."

"Thanks."

"Doesn't Ray have two children from his first marriage?"

"Yes, two sons: Tommy and Jesse. And he has full custody of them. They are little darlings. The first time I met them, they gave me a bouquet of flowers they'd picked for me. Ray's raised them to really respect women." Then Ann told Cathy about the night Tommy and Jesse asked her if they could call her Mom after she married Ray, and their prayer afterward that Ray had shared with her.

"They sound very special, just like their father."

"I'm adopting them."

"Good for you. How did you get Ray's ex-wife's consent?'

"By paying her ten thousand dollars."

"Really? What a bitch."

"Well, at least she agreed to the adoption."

"Do you want to have children with him?"

"Yeah, and so does he. In fact, we're going to start trying to get pregnant during our honeymoon."

"It sounds to me like you've found heaven."

"I have. But enough about me. What's going on in your life?"

"I'm the chief financial officer of my parents' winery, and I've met someone, too. We've been dating for a little over a year. His name is Daryl Thompson, he's thirty-two, and a surgeon in San Francisco. He's never been married, and I'm in love with him."

"Does he feel the same way about you?"

"Yes."

"Not engaged?"

"Not yet."

"Well, I'm sure you soon will be. Congratulations!"

Ann and Ray had their wedding rehearsal that Friday night at six, and a dinner for the wedding party at the Gulf Sands restaurant on Longboat Key. "Cathy Rossi, I think you know my fiancé, Ray Collins."

"Cathy, how have you been?"

"Great," she replied, thinking, *I believe he's better looking now than when I first met him.*

Ann stayed Friday night in a suite at the Longboat Key Club, and Sandy and Loretta planned to help her get ready for the wedding, which was to be at three p.m. the next day. Ray rented the same limo that he and Ann had taken on their first limo date to drive the two of them from the church in Ruskin to the reception at the Longboat Key Club. After the reception, the limo would take them to the Don CeSar Hotel, a beautiful resort on St. Petersburg Beach where they were spending their wedding night in a luxurious suite overlooking the ocean. Known as Florida's "Pink Palace," the Don CeSar, facing the powder-white sands of the Gulf of Mexico, was built in 1928 to resemble a Mediterranean-style castle. Born in the Great Gatsby era as a playground for the rich and famous, the iconic resort hotel's guests had included US Presidents, European royalty, and famous movie stars. Ray's car would be parked there.

It was Saturday afternoon, and Ann was standing at the back of the church with her uncle Dave, waiting on the start of the wedding march. And then the music began, and they walked through the doors and into the church sanctuary. *This is it!* She thought excitedly. *The moment I've dreamed of most for years. In a few minutes I'll be Ray Collins's wife!* As she started down the aisle and saw Ray waiting for her, an aura of joy like she'd never experienced came over her.

Ray was standing at the altar with Steve, Tommy, and Jesse when the pianist began to play the wedding march. Ray tried not to fidget; he couldn't remember ever being this nervous. It wasn't because he thought he'd made the wrong decision to marry Ann, but rather part of him still couldn't believe that this incredible woman had agreed to be his wife.

The first bars of the wedding march began to play. All eyes turned to the back of the church. Then Ray saw her. Ann walked in on her uncle's arm like an angel floating next to a mortal. Ray sucked in his breath, unprepared to see her exquisite beauty. Her gown fit snugly across her chest and stomach, flaring to a full skirt. The bodice was crusted with tiny pearls that caught the light from the windows. Her black hair was pulled up in a swirl with ringlets cascading around her face.

As Ann slowly paraded down the aisle, she had eyes only for him. Their gazes met and held until someone spoke words Ray didn't hear and Ann was standing before him. His angel. The rest of the ceremony was a blur. He only remembered Ann's black eyes watching him with love and trust, until at last the minister said, "I now pronounce you husband and wife. Ray, you may kiss the bride."

Ray lifted her veil. His hands no longer shook. He tilted her chin and kissed her, pouring all his love and tenderness into that one timeless gesture. There was complete silence in the church until the Reverend Godwin said, "Ladies and gentlemen, I present to you Mr. and Mrs. Ray Collins." The crowd cheered, bathing the new couple in faith and joy.

Ann and Ray opened their reception at the Longboat Key Club with a waltz that they had practiced just for this occasion. When they finished dancing, the guests applauded.

Everyone seemed to have a great time at the reception, which was still going strong when, after changing their clothes, they left about two hours later. Their bags were already packed and loaded into the limo, so they headed straight to the Don CeSar Hotel.

During the forty-five minute drive to the hotel, it was all the two of them could do to keep their hands off of each other, but given the presence of the driver, modesty prevailed. They soon arrived at the luxurious resort, checked in, and a bellman helped take their luggage to their suite. After the bellman had brought their bags into their suite, Ray tipped him, and he left. Then Ray lifted Ann into his arms and carried her over the threshold.

"Hi Cathy," Ann said when she and her new husband met her friend in the lobby to go to breakfast the next morning.

"Good morning, Cathy," Ray replied warmly.

"This place is really elegant," Cathy observed. The dining room had picture windows that overlooked the gulf and models of old ships adorned the walls.

"Was your room comfortable?" Ann asked.

"Yes, and I slept very well."

"Ann, do you remember what time our plane leaves?" Cathy asked. "I need to get to the airport in time to turn in my rental car."

"At 10:43 a.m. and we are only about thirty minutes from the airport, so we have time for a leisurely breakfast before we check out," Ray replied.

"Do you want to eat inside or outside on the beachside terrace?" the maître d' asked.

"It's such a beautiful morning, let's eat out on the terrace," Ray suggested.

"My thoughts as well," Ann added. "That ocean view is spectacular!"

"Coffee and orange juice?" Nicole, their waitress, asked them as she poured water from a glass pitcher into their crystal water glasses.

"Please," Ray replied.

"Are you ready to order?" Nicole asked when she'd finished pouring coffee and orange juice for the three of them.

"I believe we are," Ann replied.

"What will you have Miss?" Nicole asked Cathy.

"The eggs benedict, an English muffin, and steamed Gulf shrimp.

"And you Miss," she asked Ann.

"A western-style omelet with cheddar cheese, bell pepper, ham, onion, and mushrooms, a biscuit, and cantaloupe."

"And you, Sir?"

"Two scrambled eggs, grits, crisp bacon, and two biscuits."

"I thought your wedding was absolutely lovely," Cathy said as she buttered her muffin.

"Thanks. A lot of planning went into it," Ann replied just before taking a bite of her fluffy omelet.

"The reception was also great. I loved the band you selected," Cathy added as she put picked up a jumbo steamed shrimp.

"Ray's friend, Lee Hansen, suggested them. Apparently they played at his cousin's wedding in Sarasota about a year ago," Ann replied.

"Look, those are white pelicans," Ray said, pointing at eight large white birds that were landing in the water about a hundred feet from shore.

Their plane departed from Tampa International on time. They changed planes in Dallas, and arrived in San Francisco at 4:50 p.m. California time.

"I'll go get my car if you and Ray will get our luggage," Cathy suggested.

"Sure," Ann replied.

"My parents are expecting us for dinner," Cathy said once they were on their way from the airport. "Our house is just outside of Napa, and about an hour-and-a-half drive from here. So we should get there around seven."

"Great! I can't wait to see your mom and dad again," Ann replied. I haven't seen them since we were in high school."

"Once you have toured our winery and vineyards, I'll take you into Napa so you can rent a car for the rest of your trip."

"We really appreciate all this," Ray remarked.

As Cathy predicted, they arrived at her parents' house just after seven. As they drove onto the property they saw a large archway above the entrance which held a sign that said Columbia Creek Winery. "Where's Columbia Creek?" Ray asked.

"It runs through our property, just behind one of our vineyards," Cathy said. The house was next to the winery, and was a large stone and clapboard two story farmhouse with a big front porch that had rocking chairs.

Once the car was parked, everyone went inside the house, where Cathy introduced her parents to Ray. "Mom, Dad, this is Ray Collins, and I believe you remember Ann. Ray, my parents, Earnest and Jane Rossi."

"It's good to meet you," Ray told them as they all shook hands.

"Welcome to our home," Ernest told them.

"Ann, how've have you been?" Jane asked.

"Great, I just married my soul mate, and I'm looking forward to the Napa Valley wine tour that Cathy has organized."

"Ray, Ann, this is our cook, Gladys," Jane said as Gladys walked in.

"Good to meet you," the cook said. "Dinner should be ready in about thirty minutes."

"Great. I'll pour us a glass of one of our Chardonnays and we can sit down and talk before dinner," Ernest suggested.

Once they were settled, Jane opened the conversation. "So Ray, you work for Tropical Citrus?"

"Yes, I'm responsible for fruit and bulk juice procurement and operations planning."

"And Ann, you used to be the chief economist for the Global Soft Drink Company, didn't you?" Jane asked.

"That's correct. This wine is excellent, by the way," Ann commented.

"I agree," Ray replied.

"Ann, do you plan to work now that you're married?" Jane asked.

"Yes, I've decided to start a business consulting company. But once I have a baby, I'll probably only do it part-time, and no overnight trips."

Gladys then walked in. "Dinner is served," she announced.

She had prepared a prime rib roast, roasted garlic potatoes, sourdough bread, and a bean casserole.

Ernest brought out two open bottles of a nine-year-old Cabernet to enjoy with dinner. "This wine won an award two years ago for being the best Cabernet in Napa Valley. It has been open and breathing since you arrived, so it should be ready to drink," he explained as he slowly decanted the bottles, making sure the sediment stayed in the wine bottles.

"Oh, this is fabulous," Ann remarked as she sipped the wine.

"It sure is," Ray replied, as he cut a slice of the juicy prime rib.

"Okay, here is the winery and vineyard tour schedule I've worked out," Cathy explained after they'd finished their dessert of tiramisu and were having coffee.

"Tomorrow, our vineyard manager, Glen, will give you a tour of our vineyards and explain grape growing and vineyard management. Then Dad will give you a tour of the winery and explain the winemaking process. After that, we have a special surprise for dinner. We'll also give you a case of your favorite red wine and of your favorite white, as well."

"Oh, that's too much, thank you," Ray replied.

"Can I get a hint about the surprise?" Ann asked curiously.

"It involves eating," Cathy replied. Then she continued to explain the itinerary she had planned.

THE WINE QUEEN

"On Tuesday, I'll take you to rent a car. Your first tour that day will be of the Chateau Montelena winery in Calistoga, about a forty-five minute drive from here. They are an estate-bottled winery like us and most of the other wineries in the Napa Valley, so I have also arranged for you to tour their vineyards."

"What's an estate-bottled winery?" Ray asked.

"A winery that owns the vineyards that supply one hundred percent of the wines they make. These wines are labeled as estate bottled."

"I'm already getting excited, Cathy!" Ann replied.

"Next will be the Charles Krug winery in St. Helena. You'll spend the night at the Maison Fleurie hotel in Yountville. The hotel offers on-site spa treatments, gourmet dining, spacious rooms, and an outdoor pool. All the rooms have private balconies overlooking beautiful vineyards and landscaped gardens. Tea and cookies are served every afternoon, and there is a pre-dinner wine tasting with an assortment of cheeses and breads. Since it's so centrally located to all the wineries you'll tour, that is where you'll stay for the entire week.

"On Wednesday there will be tours of the Christian Brothers Winery and Pope Valley wineries. Thursday you will be free. You'll have no trouble finding lots of interesting things to do. Friday is Beringer and Stags Leap wineries. Saturday morning will be Beaulieu Vineyards in Rutherford. From there you will be an hour-and-a-half from the airport."

"Oh, Cathy, you've outdone yourself with this agenda," Ann observed.

"Yeah, thanks a lot for doing all this," Ray added. "Come to Florida and I'll give you a tour of our citrus processing plants and citrus groves."

"I'll probably take you up on that."

"We should probably get on to bed," Ernest suggested just before eleven. "Breakfast will be at seven and your tour starts at eight.

"I'm looking forward to it," Ann replied.

After breakfast the next morning, there was a knock on the front door. "That's probably Glen," Ernest said as he went to the door. It turned out he was correct. "Come on in, Glen, and let me introduce you to our guests. Ann, Ray, this is Glen Hamler, our vineyard manager. Glen, Ray and Ann Collins."

"Good to meet you, Glen," Ray said as they shook hands.

"Ready to see a wine grape vineyard?"

"Yeah. I manage fruit and bulk juice procurement for Tropical Citrus, Inc. It will be interesting to see how grape growing and winemaking differ from growing oranges and making orange juice."

Glen drove them down a winding, rutted road with breath taking scenery: rolling hills in the distance and wisps of steam rising from the dew-laden sparkling grass. They soon came to the lush, emerald-green vineyard, so Ernest parked and they got out.

"It all starts here with grape growing, called viticulture," Glen started. "The quality of any wine is dictated by the quality of the grapes it is made from. There are three grape growing regions in California, each producing different quality grapes. These regions are the Central Valley, which is the San Joaquin and Sacramento valleys, the North Coast, and the Napa Valley. The Central Valley is where the lowest quality grapes for wine come from. Most wines made from these grapes are used in blends for generic wines. A lot of Thompson seedless grapes used for raisins are also produced there. The North Coast counties are the next step up in quality, and where a number of varietal wines are produced. The Napa Valley, of course, has the highest quality wine grapes. Grape prices and yields per acre in each of these regions vary greatly, and reflect the quality of the grapes."

"That was great, Glen," Ray observed after he and Ann had spent the morning touring the vineyards and discussing grape growing. "I guess growing wine grapes and juice oranges are both major challenges. But I think growing wine grapes is more complicated, because they have to be grown to the winemaker's requirements. Juice oranges are just juice oranges - a commodity. I now know that's not true for wine grapes."

"You've both been good students," Glen replied as they entered the winery. Ernest met them at the door.

"Well, did you learn about growing grapes?"

"Yeah, and it's complicated," Ann replied.

After lunch, Ernest took Ray and Ann into the barrel room, where the wine was stored in barrels made of French oak. It was about fifty-five degrees and there were rows of barrels on their sides, stacked on top of each one another. The smell of oak was prevalent.

"Enology is the term that is used to describe the science and art of winemaking," Ernest said as he began to describe the winemaking process.

"What is the difference in generic and varietal wines?" Ray asked.

"Generic wines carry the name of a wine producing region, usually somewhere in France. California generic wines are a blend of several varieties of usually low-cost grapes from the San Joaquin Valley. One white generic is Chablis; another is Rhine wine. A couple of generic reds are Bordeaux and Burgundy and then there are the Rose wines. Currently generic wines account for about eighty-five percent of all wines consumed in the United States. Varietals carry the name of the grape they are made from. Key reds are Cabernet Sauvignon, Merlot, and Pinot Noir, while key whites are Chardonnay, Sauvignon Blanc and Johannesburg Riesling.

"Does your winery also make Champagne?" Ann asked.

"Yes, we do."

"Great. I've always wanted to know how Champagne is made and what gives it the carbonation," Ray replied.

"Champagne is also a generic wine, named for the Champagne region in France. The traditional method of making sparkling wines or Champagne is known as the *méthode Champenoise,*" Ernest began.

"How are dessert wines made?" Ray asked after Ernest had finished discussing Champagnes.

"Those are sweet wines typically served with dessert, although they can be enjoyed alone, as well as with fruit or bakery sweets." After Ernest described how port, Sherry, and late harvest wines were made, he then explained wine labels.

"When a wine waiter brings you a bottle of wine, check the label to be sure the wine is the variety, vintage year, and winery that made the wine that you chose. Also check the appellation to see that it is from the viticultural region you chose. The waiter will then open the bottle.

"Sometimes I see people smelling the cork. Why do they do that?" asked Ann.

"The cork should be examined to be sure it is not split or cracked, and squeezed to make sure it is pliable. It is supposed to keep air from getting into the wine bottle. But smelling the cork tells you nothing about that."

"What happens if air gets into the bottle?" Ray asked.

"It oxidizes the wine, which ruins it."

"How can that be prevented?" Ann asked.

"By using good quality corks and storing the bottle of wine on its side to keep the cork inside the bottle wet. Once the wine has been opened, and you have examined the cork - and allowed the wine to breathe, if appropriate - the waiter should pour a small amount into a wineglass. Swirl the wine in the glass and smell it. If it smells bad, it probably is bad, most likely due to oxygen leaking into the bottle. After smelling the wine, taste it. If it smells and tastes good, it's obviously ready to drink."

"Ernest, I believe Jacques will soon have dinner ready," Jane said as she walked into the barrel room.

"Great, I'm hungry." Ann replied.

"Who is Jacques?" Ray asked.

"The surprise for you and Ann. Jacques Pepin is a French chef we sometimes bring in for wine events, or for special guests."

"Oh, you shouldn't have," Ann replied.

"Nothing is too good for our daughter's friends."

They all went into the living room where Gladys had prepared a platter of fruit and cheese. "What types of cheeses are these?" Ann asked.

"This one is an aged mimolette from the Italian alps," Ernest explained, pointing at the cheese. "The next one to the right is provolone, also from Italy; the next is tarentaise from Oak Hill farm in New Jersey; then manchego from LaMancha, Spain; and finally Cabot, a sharp aged cheddar from Vermont."

Also on the plate, there were sliced apples and pears and an assortment of crackers.

"I believe you'll like this Cabernet Sauvignon. It is one of our best, made in 1946, just after we opened the winery. It has been aged in oak for five years and bottle-aged now for eight. It's been breathing for about an hour, so it should be ready," Ernest explained as he decanted one of the bottles of the Cabernet, carefully separating the sediment using a candle. "Cathy, will you do us the honor?" he asked his daughter.

"Of course, Dad."

Cathy swirled the wine in the wineglass, then smelled it, and took a sip. "Magnificent, Dad!"

"It should be. It won three awards last year in the Napa Valley," Jane told everyone.

"Hey, guys, after all this, you must promise me you'll come to Florida and let us treat you."

"You've got a deal, Ray," Ernest promised.

"My God! This wine is incredible!" Ann exclaimed after she took her first sip. "It's like nectar, so smooth and mellow, with hints of cherries, blackberries, all surrounded by oak."

"I agree, it is an incredible wine," Ray observed. He then took a bite of cheese on a cracker. "And these cheeses you're serving with it are excellent, too."

"I just love it when Mom and Dad go all out to entertain our guests," Cathy remarked as she put a slice of the aged mimolette on a cracker.

Ann didn't say anything. She was too busy munching on the Cabot cheddar and eating a juicy slice of apple, while still sipping the wine.

"Everyone, this is Jacques Pepin, the artist who is preparing tonight's dinner," Ernest told them. "Jacques, Ray and Ann Collins."

"It's good to meet you," Jacques said as he bowed slightly. Jacques was a round-faced chubby man in his early forties who wore the traditional white chef's frock and tall white hat, called a toque. After everyone was seated at the dining table, Jacques was ready to begin. "Your first course is amuse-bouche with caviar, which is potato gaufrettes, crème fraîche and red onion, and quail egg in brioche with peeky-toe crab," he explained as Gladys served.

"Oh, this is so wonderful. Thank you again Mr. and Mrs. Rossi," Ann said once they had finished with the first course and the platters were cleared.

"You're very welcome," Ernest replied.

Gladys brought out opened bottles of Chardonnay and Cabernet. This time, Ann did the tasting of the Chardonnay.

"Apples and figs," she replied. "How long was it oak-aged?"

"A year in oak and three in the bottle," Ernest explained.

"It's certainly excellent," Ray observed.

Then Jacques described their next course. "Now we have fennel dusted diver scallops with hearts of palm, grape tomatoes, and cucumber noodles."

"I don't think I've ever had food this good," Ann told them as she stabbed a scallop with her fork.

"I know I haven't," Ray replied, taking a fork full of the hearts of palm and a cucumber noodle.

"We're glad you like it," Ernest replied.

"Your third course is horseradish-crusted wild salmon with truffle watercress salad, ricotta gnocchi, and yuzu yogurt," Jacques told them as it was being served. The portions were small, so they could eat all seven courses of the meal. The fourth course was guava -glazed pheasant breast with foie gras ravioli and pineapple confit; fifth was a Kobe beef rib eye and short rib with jasmine rice, port wine reduction, and broccolini; and sixth was ahi tuna ceviche with warm blini, American ostera caviar, baby celery, and aged red wine crème fraîche. The seventh and final course was Chef Jacques's signature dish: grand marnier soufflé and a florentine cookie tower with citrus mascarpone and a marzipan twig.

"Before we begin our dessert, I have a port I want us to enjoy with it," Ernest told everyone as he brought out the opened bottle. "It was made in 1946, from the same Cabernet grapes as our red wine. Ray, I believe it's your turn."

"Excellent again," Ray exclaimed after he had swirled, smelled, then tasted the sweet, yet complex port. When Chef Jacques entered the room to join them for a glass of port, everyone stood and clapped. Ernest clasped his hands together and said, "Bravo, Bravo."

At breakfast the next morning Cathy told her friends, "I'll put a case each of that award-winning Cabernet Sauvignon and the Chardonnay aside for you and take it to the Maison Fleurie hotel before you leave. That way you won't have to haul them around."

"Oh, Cathy, you're too good to us," Ann said.

"Cathy why don't you and your parents join us for dinner Friday night at a restaurant of your choosing?" Ray asked. "Our treat."

"I'd love to, and I'm sure my parents would, too. So you've got a date."

"This is a very interesting place," Ray observed as he and Ann were headed to their room at the Maison Fleurie Hotel late Tuesday afternoon. "It's not like any hotel I've ever stayed in."

"Me either," Ann agreed.

Constructed of stone from local quarries in 1873, the Maison Fleurie Hotel, where they would be staying for the rest of their time in California, was an inn reminiscent of southern France. It consisted of three buildings containing a total of thirteen guestrooms situated on half an acre of beautifully landscaped gardens. Each guestroom contained finely crafted furniture, rich fabrics, a stone fireplace, and private terrace. Ray and Ann's overlooked a vineyard with mountains in the background.

The couple's winery tours were interesting and informative. And while they didn't learn anymore about the basics of grape growing or winemaking, they did see good examples of the elements that made the various winemakers' styles so different. They also enjoyed some wonderful wines and gourmet food.

"What do you want to do today?" Ray asked as he and Ann were enjoying a leisurely breakfast at their hotel on Thursday, their free day.

"I think I'd like to browse through that art museum in Yountville, then try that sidewalk bistro for lunch," Ann replied as she took a forkful of artichoke quiche.

"That sounds good to me," Ray said, pouring maple syrup over the stack of blueberry pancakes on his plate. "We're running low on cash, so we need to go by the bank and cash a check before we go to the art museum."

"Okay."

They left for the bank at nine thirty. There were nine people in line for the two tellers at the Citizens Bank. "Ann, would you get in line for a teller while I go to the restroom?"

"Sure."

THE WINE QUEEN

While Ray was in the restroom he heard a commotion outside: a woman screamed, and there was a gun shot. Ray quietly opened the restroom door and saw the bank's guard lying motionless on the floor just outside. There was a large counter where people could make out checks or complete paperwork that would keep him from being seen if he was careful. Ray crawled over to the guard, felt the man's jugular vein, and realized he was dead. The guard had fallen on his gun, which was partially exposed under his waist. Ray grabbed the revolver and checked that it was loaded. He inched as quietly as he could to the edge of the counter so he could see. There were two robbers; one was holding his gun at Ann's head, while the other was pointing his at a teller, who was putting bills into a sack.

"Next I want to get in the safe," demanded the robber holding the gun on the teller.

"It's on a timer and won't open until five p.m.," replied a man dressed in a suit, who looked like a bank executive.

"Well, you'd better figure out how to open it now or Miss America here dies," the robber threatening Ann said. Ray crawled to where Ann could see him if she looked his direction. *I hope Ann sees me before her captor does*, he prayed silently, as that robber was looking in the direction of the money being put into the sack. Ann did spot Ray, and he motioned for her to drop to the floor as he cocked and raised the revolver. When she did as he instructed, it exposed her captor's upper torso and Ray fired, shooting the robber in the center of his chest. Ray cocked the revolver again so he could shoot the other robber. But the second man was too fast, and he fired at the same time as Ray, hitting Ray in the chest as Ray's bullet killed the other robber. Ann screamed as Ray fell to the floor.

Ann went to him immediately and cried, "Oh, Ray! Ray!" Ray was still conscious but he didn't look good.

255

"Come closer, Ann," he said weakly. She sat by him on the floor and cradled his head in her hands. "Ann, you're the love of my life, my soul mate."

"Ray, you're my soul mate, too, and I love you so much," she gasped in between sobs. "The bank officer said that an ambulance will be here soon, and I'm sure you will be okay."

"I don't think I'm going to make it. Ann, promise me you won't let this destroy you. Be brave and make a success of your life. Raise Tommy and Jesse to be honorable men with the values we hold important. Find a good man and remarry; don't stay alone. Just know that I'll always love...always lo...al..." Ray's head turned to the side, and he was dead.

"No! No!" Ann screamed. Then she began to cry loudly.

A man came over to her and said, as he felt Ray's jugular vein, "I was a medic in the Korean War." But he only shook his head.

"I'm sorry, miss. Was he your husband?"

"Yes, and we were on our honeymoon," she sobbed.

"I'm so, so, sorry ma'am. The police have been called. Both robbers are dead. Your husband is a hero."

"YES, BUT IT COST HIM HIS LIFE!" she shrieked. The police soon arrived. The officers got the information they needed from others who had been in the bank and didn't bother the hysterical, grief-stricken Ann, who wouldn't have been a reliable source of facts in her state of mind, anyway. When the ambulance arrived, the emergency technician gave Ann a sedative and took her to the hospital, while another ambulance came and picked up Ray's body. The hospital admitted Ann, where she was given another sedative and left to sleep.

The nurse found Cathy Rossi's phone number on the itinerary Cathy had written on Columbia Creek Winery stationary and dialed it. "Is this Cathy Rossi?"

"This is she. Who am I speaking to?"

"Vicky Weldon. I'm a nurse at Providence Hospital in Yountville. Do you know an Ann Collins?"

"Yes, she's a good friend. Is she okay?"

"She's here in the hospital, sleeping. We have her sedated. Her husband, Ray, was killed during a bank robbery today."

"Oh my God! I'll be there as soon as I can!"

"Okay, ask for me when you get here."

"Dad, Ray Collins was killed during a bank robbery today in Yountville."

"What? That's awful! Is Ann okay?"

"A nurse just called. Ann's at Providence hospital, sedated and sleeping."

"Let me get your mother and we'll go right now."

"Dad, I think it would be better if I went alone. She's not going to want to see many people now. I'll call you and let you know what's going on."

"Okay, if you think that's best."

Forty minutes later, Cathy walked into the hospital and went up to the receptionist. "I'm Cathy Rossi and would like to see Nurse Weldon, please." The receptionist called the nurses' station, and in about five minutes, Vicky Weldon arrived.

"Cathy Rossi?" she asked.

"Yes. You must be Nurse Weldon."

"Yes. I'll take you to Ann's room, but I suggest you let her sleep off the sedative."

"Okay."

A short while later, Cathy entered Ann's room and sat down in a chair beside the bed. After about fifteen minutes, she got up and went to the nurses station, where she got a newspaper to read, and then returned to Ann's room.

Around four o'clock that afternoon, Ann woke up. "Where am I?" she asked, groggily.

"You're in Providence hospital," Cathy replied.

"Oh, oh no! Cathy, Ray was killed this morning!" She shrieked, as she now was remembering things.

"I know. I came as soon as the nurse called and told me."

"What time is it?"

"Just after four."

"I'm ready to get out of here."

"Good. I'll take you to the hotel to get your things, then we'll go back to my parents' house. You get dressed while I go get Nurse Weldon."

Once she found the nurse, Cathy told her, "I think she'll be okay now. She's going to stay at our house until she can travel back to Florida."

"Good. The doctor will have to release her, though."

A few minutes later, Nurse Weldon escorted one of the hospital's doctors into Ann's room. "I'm Dr. Watson. How are you feeling?" he asked Ann as he listened to her heart. Nurse Weldon checked the thermometer she had put in Ann's mouth.

"I'm okay," Ann replied. "I just want to go stay at Cathy's now."

"Okay. And I'm sorry for your loss, Mrs. Collins. Here is a sedative to help you sleep, if you need it," the doctor explained handing her a brown bottle. "There is a five- day supply here. More than that and you run the risk of becoming addicted."

"Thanks, doctor," she mumbled.

"Ann, Detective Mulligan wants to speak with you before you leave," Nurse Weldon said. "He asked us to call him when you woke up, which we have. He should be here any minute."

About five minutes later, a tall man dressed in a suit came into the room. "Hi, I'm Detective Mulligan."

"How can I help you?" Ann asked.

"I just have a couple of questions for our records. What was Ray's occupation?"

"He was vice-president of procurement and operations planning for Tropical Citrus, based in Florida."

"Had he been married before, and did he have any children?"

"Yes, he was previously married and has two sons, Tommy and Jesse."

"Okay, that's all I need."

"Where did Ray get the gun?" Ann asked.

"According to one of the witnesses at the bank, he took it off the guard who was shot. He obviously knew how to use it."

"Yes, shooting and hunting were Ray's favorite hobbies."

"Ma'am, Mr. Collins was a hero. He saved the lives of everyone in the bank. Those two robbers have hit half a dozen banks in California, and they've always killed everyone in the bank before they left, so there wouldn't be any witnesses. That's why they weren't wearing masks. I've kept the press away from you, and we've provided them with the information they've requested. If they bother you, just give me a call," he said, handing Ann his card.

"Okay, and thanks, Detective Mulligan," Ann said, still in the denial phase of grief.

After she and Cathy arrived back at the Rossi home, and she had talked to Ernest and Jane, Ann took one of the sedatives and soon fell asleep.

The next morning at breakfast, Cathy said as she handed Ann the newspaper, "The robbery made the front page of the *Napa Valley Register*."

The headline read, "RAY COLLINS THWARTS ROBBERY OF CITIZENS BANK, KILLS ROBBERS." She then scanned the accompanying story. "Yesterday Ray Collins, the vice-president of procurement and operations planning for Tropical Citrus in Florida and father of two, was on a Napa Valley wine tour for his honeymoon with his second wife, Ann, when their trip was tragically interrupted by Elgin Sims and Rory Thompson, who attempted to rob the Citizens Bank where the couple had stopped to cash a check. Ray Collins had been in the restroom when Sims and Thompson arrived and was able to get the fallen guard's gun and kill the two robbers, but not before one of them fatally shot Collins. According to Detective Mulligan of the Napa Police Department, these thieves are the same ones who had been robbing banks throughout California and killing everyone in the banks they robbed. Mr. Collins not only saved the lives of the fifteen people in the Citizens Bank, but also the lives of those in whatever banks Sims and Thompson would have subsequently robbed. He was a hero."

The phone then rang, and Ernest answered it. "This is Detective Mulligan," the caller said. "Can I speak to Ann Collins?"

"Yes, I'll get her," Ernest replied.

"Ann, Detective Mulligan is on the phone."

"Hello, this is Ann," she said when she picked up the phone.

"Ann, there was a reward of ten thousand dollars[12] for the capture of those two thieves. If you'll come down to the station before you leave for Florida, we'll give you a check."

"Okay, and thanks, detective."

"What did he want?" Ernest asked after Ann hung up.

"There was a ten thousand dollar reward for those thieves that I can collect before I leave."

"Small price for a good man's life," Jane observed.

"When are you going to tell Tommy and Jesse?" Cathy asked.

"When I get home. I prefer to tell them in person. It's just five a.m. there, so they're still asleep."

"You'd better call their nanny and tell her not to say anything because it's all over the news. Students at their school will also know," Cathy explained.

"They'll just have to miss school today," Ann decided. "I plan to leave on that Saturday flight, if I can make arrangements today to get Ray's body sent to Tampa. Excuse me," she said as she hurriedly went to her room, sobbing as she was reminded of Ray's death. About an hour later, Cathy tapped lightly on her door.

"Come in." Cathy entered to find Ann sitting on the bed, her face stained with tears, twisting a tissue nervously in her hands.

---

[12] The same as $81,873 in 2014.

THE WINE QUEEN

Cathy went over and hugged her. "Ann, my dad has offered to handle everything with regard to Ray, so just don't think about it anymore."

"Okay, tell him I said thanks." Then the tears began again. Cathy quietly left the room. Her mother was in the living room reading a book. "How's Ann?" Jane asked.

"She's taking this very hard."

"I know it must be almost unbearable. I don't know how I would handle it if I lost your father."

"It has to be unbearable for her, especially considering how much she loved him." Then Cathy told her mother the story of how Ann had changed the course of her life to be with Ray, and described how intense and romantic their relationship had been and the kind of man Ray had been.

"That poor girl," Jane remarked. "Is there anything else we can do for her?"

"Handling the shipment of Ray's body back to Florida helps her a lot. But I'm going to watch her closely, and if she needs anything, I'll tell you."

Ernest then came in and said, "Adam, the mortician embalming Ray's body, suggested it would be best if the body goes back on the same plane Ann's taking back to Florida."

"There's no way she can handle that, Dad."

"I agree, so I have made arrangements for it to be sent on another flight that leaves on Sunday morning."

"Okay. I'll fly back with Ann and meet that second flight in Tampa with the funeral director that Ann chooses to handle the services and the burial. Then I'll take care of the arrangements, because I don't think Ann is in any condition to do that," Cathy explained.

"Good. I figured you'd want to," her father said.

Chapter Fifteen

It was almost midnight when Ann and Cathy arrived at Ann's house in Ruskin. The boys and Norma had made a banner that said, **"Welcome Home Mom and Dad!"** and it had been hung across the columned entrance to the house. "Everyone's asleep, so I'll talk to Tommy and Jesse at breakfast in the morning," Ann whispered. She then led Cathy to the guest room and helped her settle in before she went to the master bedroom, put on her pajamas, and laid down. Then the tears came again. Being in Ray's bedroom reminded her how special their relationship had been and how much she loved him. She cried herself to sleep.

"Ann," Cathy said softly as she tapped on Ann's door the next morning at seven.

"Yes," Ann replied, sleepily, yawning as she got up and walked to the bedroom door.

"Tommy and Jesse are up and asking where their dad is. They remember me from the wedding. I told them you would tell them at breakfast."

"Okay, I'll be in the kitchen in a few minutes. Tell Norma to go ahead and fix breakfast."

"Mom!" Tommy said when Ann walked into the breakfast nook. He and Jesse went to her and each gave her a hug and card they had made. Ann read Tommy's first:

Mom,

It makes me real happy to have you as my mom now. We have a lot of fun when you are here, and I used to miss you a lot when you had to go back to Memphis. It sure is good that you will be here with us all the time. Now we can all be a happy family together.
I love you, Mom!
Tommy

Jesse's card read:

Dear Mom,

My teacher asked me why I was smiling all the time, because I used to be sad a lot. I told her that I was getting a mom who loved me a lot and that she was a lot of fun to do things with. My teacher said she was glad that I was getting a mom, because she likes to see me so happy. When I say my prayers every night, I've been thanking God for letting you marry my dad and be our mom. I think God is happy that you are our mom. And I'm happy too.
Love,
Jesse

When Ann finished reading the cards she said, "Oh, Tommy, Jesse, come here." She gave both of them hugs and said, "I love both of you, and I'm so proud to be your mother." Then she passed the cards to Cathy, whose eyes became glassy with emotion as she read them.

"Mom, where's Dad?" Tommy asked.

"Yeah, where's Dad?" Jesse asked also.

"Boys, last Thursday morning your dad and I went to a bank in California to cash a check and get some spending money." Then she told them what had happened. "According to the police, your dad saved the lives of the fifteen people in the bank and any others who would have been killed until the robbers were caught," she said in conclusion.

"But why didn't Dad come home with you, Mom?" Tommy asked.

"Tommy, Jesse... your dad was killed when he killed those bank robbers."

"*HE WAS KILLED*?" Tommy cried. Jesse began to cry also.

"Yes," Ann replied as she started to weep also.

Next was the most astounding thing that Cathy and Ann had ever seen. Tommy looked up at Ann, blinked back his tears, and asked, "Mom, what can we do to help you?"

"Yeah, we don't want you to cry," Jesse said, rubbing the tears from his eyes. Ray had talked to both boys right after him and their mother got divorced and told them that if for some reason he died, they should be brave, because they would be the men of the family. And he also told them that if there was a woman in their lives, they should comfort and help her deal with what had happened. They could cry later in their room, and that he would be in heaven, watching over them. It is one of the things he taught them to ingrain his philosophy of always putting the welfare of your family and others first.

Ann momentarily pulled out of her depression and said, "Come here, boys." As she again hugged them tightly, she continued. "You are the most special boys in the world to me, and I love you very much."

"We love you, too, Mom," the boys said in unison.

Cathy began to cry softly, in awe of what she had just witnessed.

Ann went back to her bedroom after breakfast and stayed there for the rest of the day and into that night.

Later that morning Cathy drove back to the airport with the mortician, Ron Jones, retrieved Ray's body, and took it to Jones' Funeral Home. "Ask Mrs. Collins to come here at nine tomorrow morning and we will make the funeral and burial arrangements," Ron suggested.

"If Mrs. Collins isn't up to it, can I come instead?"

"Yes, as long as you accurately reflect her wishes."

After she got back to the house, Norma explained to Cathy that she had told Ray and Ann that after they returned from their honeymoon, she was going to resign and move to Orlando to help her daughter, who was expecting her first baby in early June.

"Yes, I know," Cathy said. "Ann told me on the flight back from California."

"If it's okay with you, then, I'll plan to move out tomorrow. But I will be back to attend the funeral."

"Sure, that's fine, Cathy replied."

"Thank you," Norma said. "You're a special friend to help this family out."

Cathy took the boys to get a hamburger and see a Western that afternoon, even though both Tommy and Jesse were very sad. She just wanted to get them out of the house.

That night after dinner, as she passed the boys' room on the way to hers, she could hear them crying quietly, so as not to disturb the rest of the household. She heard Tommy say, "Please, God, give Jesse and me the strength to deal with our dad's death and help comfort our new mom. And help Dad to watch out over Mom and us, and protect us. And, God, thanks for having Miss Cathy come and take care of us."

This was too much for Cathy, and she got to her room as her own tears began. She closed the door and fell onto her bed, sobbing. *Tommy and Jesse are saints,* she thought. *Ray must have been a wonderful father.* She then cried herself to sleep.

Cathy woke up just before five a.m. She had nothing to do and had not brought anything to read. Ann had told her about the scrapbook and films she'd assembled about Ray, and had told her during the flight that they were in Ray's study and she could look through them if she wanted. Cathy quietly went into the study, closed the door, and found the scrapbook and the films. She set up the projector on the desk so the movies would play on the wall about six feet away. Then she watched all of the films. She was surprised that Ray was a national football star, because he had never said anything about it, but she was not surprised that he had been voted the Most Handsome Man on the University of Florida campus. But what affected her the most, as it had Ann, was the film of his farewell to the GSDC board, as well as the film of him going fishing and on a picnic at the beach with Tommy, Jesse, and Steve and Sandy Hogan. The film effectively showed how close Ray and his boys were, and to be reminded of how much it must hurt for Ray's sons to have lost him and the way they were dealing with it, brought out Cathy's tears again.

The boys woke up at seven, and when they walked into the kitchen Cathy was already there. She asked, "Boys, what do you want for breakfast?"

"I'm not very hungry. Just a glass of milk," Tommy said.

"I'll have the same," a sad Jesse replied.

"Boys, you can stay home from school all this week."

"No, if Mom is going to stay in her room most of the day we should go to school," Tommy explained.

"Yeah, other than taking care of Mom, school is our responsibility," Jesse agreed.

Again, Cathy was astounded. They were not going to let their dad's death allow them to avoid their responsibilities, no matter how devastated they were.

Norma said good-bye to Tommy and Jesse before they left for school. When she was packed and ready to leave, she tapped lightly on Ann's door. But Ann was still asleep, and so didn't answer. "I'll say good-bye to Ann at the funeral, Norma told Cathy as she was leaving.

The viewing of Ray's body was to be at Jones' Funeral Home in Ruskin on Wednesday from six until nine p.m. The funeral would then be at the First Methodist Church in Ruskin - where Ray, Tommy, and Jesse had been members - on Thursday morning at ten. Ann called George Baker, Ray's boss, and explained that she was not up to going to the viewing, and asked him to attend, along with Cathy, Tommy and Jesse, which he sympathetically agreed to do.

She then called her uncle Dave and told him about Ray's tragic death, and gave him the dates of the viewing and the funeral.

"I'm so sorry," Ann," Dave said. "Is there anything that Loretta and I can do?"

"No, my friend, Cathy Rossi is here helping out."

"Well, just let me know if there's anything we can do," he said sympathetically.

The next morning, with Tommy and Jesse's help, Cathy got Ann out of her bedroom and dressed for the funeral.

The pall bearers at Ray's funeral were George Martin, Jack Lovelace, Steve Hogan, George Baker, Joe Simms, who was Ray's director of juice procurement, and Fred Jackson, one of his and Ann's former agricultural economists. Cathy got them together and, with the help of Fred Jackson, introduced those from Tropical Citrus to those from GSDC and to Steve Hogan. After the morticians had taken the casket out of the hearse and carried it to the front of the church sanctuary, the pall bearers gathered just outside the sanctuary in the foyer of the church. There were about one hundred fifty people at the funeral. Many were citrus growers from whom Ray had bought fruit. Most gathered in the foyer of the church before going into the sanctuary.

"What a tragic waste of a good man in the prime of his life," George Martin observed.

"Yeah, Ray was a very talented businessman, and as honest and ethical as they come," George Baker said.

"He certainly had a rotten personal life up to when he met Ann," Fred said.

"And now, just as he found his soul mate and happiness, he's killed," Steve Hogan said.

"Same for Ann. Look at all the years she waited for Ray and how she changed her life to be with him, and now this," Sandy observed. "They had only been together about six months."

"The limo has arrived," Cathy told them all. Ann, Tommy, and Jesse, followed by the pall bearers and their wives, went with Ann into the church sanctuary, which was filled with Ray's many friends and associates. Ann, crying and carrying a tissue to wipe away her tears, was wearing a black silk dress with a matching veil that covered her face. Tommy and Jesse were wearing dark blue suits.

"Death is not an easy thing to accept," Reverend Godwin said as he began the service. "Even under the best of circumstances, death is a terrible thing. Nature has its seasons but death can come to anyone, at any time, in any place. Truly we know not what a day may bring forth. We come here today with sorrow in our hearts and questions on our minds as to why these things happened. Why did Ray Collins have to die? A man in the prime of life, newly married, with two young sons and a prosperous career. Can we really know why? There are many unexplainable sorrows in life and we must simply leave these in the hands of God who knows all things.

"All of us here today are sorrowful, but the Bible teaches us of sorrow. First Thessalonians, fourth chapter, thirteenth verse says, 'But I would not have you to be ignorant, brethren, concerning them which are asleep that ye sorrow not even as others which have no hope.' Some here may have a sorrow with no hope beyond the grave while others have the sorrow of a friend that has gone on a long journey and will be joining that friend shortly. The Christian who dies and the believer who remains will one day meet again. That will be a glad reunion day. To comfort your hearts and ease your pain of loss, I want to make two statements.

"First, Ray Collins did not die. God's children do not die. Jesus said it himself in John chapter eleven, verse twenty-six. 'Whosoever liveth and believeth in me shall never die.' Second Corinthians, fifth chapter, eighth verse says, 'Absent from the body and present with the Lord'. Ray Collins did not die. He simply went to a better place.

"Second, if my Bible is right and if I understand anything of the glories of Heaven, then I believe that it is safe to say that, with only two exceptions, Ray Collins would not want to come back into this world of sin, pain, trial, and sorrow. The two exceptions are one, maybe to ease your sorrow, and two, maybe to urge some loved one to turn to the Lord.

"I was thinking Ray has already seen the angels for the first time. He has heard the angelic choirs, seen sights man has never seen, walked the streets of gold, talked to the people of the Bible. But best of all, he has seen Jesus.

"Ray Collins was a hero. His act of bravery in that bank saved many lives, but the price of that was his own life. He leaves behind his newly-wedded wife, Ann, and two sons, Tommy and Jesse. Let us pray."

After the burial service, there was a get-together at Ray's house. Cathy had arranged to have the food catered, and there was an open bar. About forty couples came, mostly citrus growers and their wives. Ann made a brief appearance, but everyone understood when she excused herself to go to her bedroom.

During the get together, Cathy approached Sandy Hogan and said, "Sandy, I need to return to California tomorrow."

"Okay. Steve has to go back, too. But I'll stay here for a couple of weeks. I brought some extra clothes in case I needed to stay and help out. Ann's in no condition to take care of Tommy and Jesse."

"I agree. She needs more time to grieve."

Ann mostly stayed in her bedroom and seldom came out. She wasn't eating, and lost weight as a result. Sandy focused on Tommy and Jesse, helping them with their homework and consoling them. They were all worried about Ann. But nothing Sandy, Tommy, or Jesse said to Ann helped. Finally, on Saturday morning just after eight thirty, nine days after the funeral, in desperation Sandy stormed into Ann's room out of desperation and flung open the window curtains, letting the bright sunlight stream into the dark bedroom.

Ann sat up in bed and winced at the sudden light, while shielding her eyes.

"Okay, Ann. You have a decision to make!" Sandy announced. "You can either stay in this room and die of self-pity, while Tommy and Jesse go without the love and support they need from you, or you can choose to live and be a mother to those wonderful boys. Do you think Ray would want you to be this way, or Tommy and Jesse to have to grieve alone?"

"Go away and leave me alone," Ann pleaded.

"No!" Then Sandy pulled Ann out of bed, pushed her into the bathroom, turned on the shower, and pushed Ann into it.

"This water is COLD!" Ann shouted.

"Good! You need to be shocked back to reality."

After Ann had finished taking a shower, in what eventually became warm water, she toweled off and dressed. Then she came into the kitchen where Sandy, Tommy, and Jesse were preparing a breakfast of bacon, eggs, oatmeal, and toast. A pot of coffee was also brewing.

"Well, look who's decided to rejoin the living," Sandy said.

"Mom, are you okay?" Tommy asked.

"Yeah, we were worried about you," Jesse added.

"Boys, come here," Ann said as she opened her arms to them. They both came over to hug her. "I'm sorry that I haven't been here for you. I know how much you must be hurting."

"That's okay. We know you were hurting, too. And Miss Sandy has been helping us," Tommy replied.

"Well, that's my responsibility now and I will be here for both of you from now on."

"I love you, Mom, Jesse said.

"I love you, too," Tommy added.

"And I really love both of you," Ann replied, struggling to hold back tears. At the sight of Ray's special little family beginning to come together and console each other over his death, Sandy choked up and had to leave the room.

When she came back, everyone was just sitting down to have their breakfast. Sandy poured herself a cup of coffee and joined them. "I'm glad to see you're okay, Ann," Sandy said as she buttered a piece of toast.

"Sandy, I can never repay you for all you've done. I don't know how I would have dealt with all of this if you hadn't been here for us," Ann replied, putting scrambled eggs from the platter on her plate.

"That's what friends are for."

Ann was indeed okay. Remembering Ray's dying words to her gave her strength and purpose. He'd said, *"Ann, promise me you won't let this destroy you. Be brave and make a success of your life. Raise Tommy and Jesse to be honorable men with the values we hold important."*

On Monday, June1, feeling that Ann was okay now and that she needed to be alone with Tommy and Jesse, Sandy made plans to fly back to California. Her flight left Tampa the next day at ten a.m. Since school was out for the summer, Ann, Tommy, and Jesse took her to the airport.

As they were saying good-bye, Ann told Sandy, "You're the best friend I've ever had. You saved my life."

"I was glad that I could be there for you and Tommy and Jesse. And like I said, that's what friends are for."

"Thanks for taking care of us, Miss Sandy," Tommy said.

"I'll miss you," Jesse added.

"Oh, boys, I'll miss both of you. And Ann also."

"Call when you get home to let us know you got there okay," Ann said as Sandy was leaving to board the plane.

"I will," Sandy shouted back.

As Ann knew, Ray had appointed Steve Hogan as executor of his estate in the event of his death, and Steve then handed over that responsibility to Ann. Ray's estate was relatively easy to settle, since he had all of his assets, except the house and checking account, in a trust for Tommy and Jesse. His assets included $228,155 in GSDC stock, roughly $1,000 in a checking account, $4,210 in a savings account, and an estimated $19,500 in equity, after estimated selling expenses, in his house, all of which totaled $252,865.[13] Ray had driven a company car, which Tropical Citrus took back. Ann left the trust in Tommy and Jesse's names, signed a number of papers, and the estate was settled.

Ann also finalized her adoption of Tommy and Jesse during these legal proceedings. Fortunately, Ray had already signed all the necessary forms.

Ann called Cathy Rossi on Monday, July 6. "Cathy, its Ann Collins," she said when her friend answered the phone.

"Ann! How are you doing?"

"I didn't think I would make it at first, but Sandy helped me deal with everything. I'm fine now. And I also want to thank you sincerely for helping me. Both you and Sandy were life savers."

"No thanks necessary. I know you would have done the same for me. How are Tommy and Jesse?"

"They're fine. Our grieving together has brought us closer as a family."

"What are you planning to do? Are you going back to GSDC?"

---

[13] The same as $2.1 million in 2014.

"That's one of the reasons I called. I want to move to Napa and get a job in the wine business. I think that being in the area where Ray and I went on our honeymoon and spent our last days together will give me comfort."

"What a coincidence! You may remember that I have been dating Daryl Thompson, a surgeon in San Francisco. Well, Daryl and I are engaged now, and we are getting married in October. I was going to call to ask you to be one of my bridesmaids. After we're married, I will be moving to San Francisco. My parents haven't found anyone to replace me as their chief financial officer. You're more than qualified, if you want the job."

"That sounds perfect! The house is already up for sale and we have an offer on it. If that sale goes through, we should be able to move out in August."

"That timing will be good for Tommy and Jesse, too, because school out here starts the day after Labor Day, which is Tuesday, September 8. I'll have Dad call you so you and he can make plans."

"Mr. Rossi, it's Ann Collins," she said when he answered the phone on Monday, July 13.

"Hi, Ann. Please, call me Ernest. Cathy said you were going to call."

"Did you get my résumé?"

"Yes, and it's very impressive. I would love to hire you for our CFO, but I'm not sure I can afford to pay you what you're worth."

"I would really like this job to be a part of the Napa wine industry, so I'm sure we can agree on satisfactory compensation for me."

"Great! We'd certainly like to have you as part of our senior management team."

Ernest and Ann were indeed able to agree on a compensation package that included a base salary and an annual bonus tied to company profits. She sold Ray's possessions and put the money into a savings account for Tommy and Jesse.

The sale of the house closed on Thursday, July 31, and she put the proceeds into a savings account for her, since she would need to use the funds as a down payment on a house for them in California. After selling her car, she bought three one-way plane tickets to San Francisco.

She and the boys were scheduled to arrive in San Francisco at 4:10 p.m. on Saturday, August 8. A moving van loaded their furniture on Friday, and Ann and the boys checked into a hotel in Tampa that night. The van would then take their furniture to a storage facility in Napa, where it would be stored until Ann could find them all a house.

Tommy and Jesse had never flown in an airplane before and were glued to the window during most of the flight and asked endless questions. When the plane was circling to land in San Francisco, Tommy pointed and said, "Is that the Golden Gate Bridge?"

"Yes, it is," Ann replied.

"We studied about it in school," Tommy said.

After their flight landed, Cathy met them in the terminal. "How was your flight?" she asked.

"It was good," Tommy replied.

"Airplanes are neat," Jesse remarked.

They then got their luggage, loaded it into Cathy's car, and headed for her family's winery in Napa.

"So this is Tommy and Jesse," Jane Rossi said as she greeted them at the front door about an hour-and-a-half later. "Cathy has told me what wonderful boys you are. Welcome to California!"

"Thanks Mrs. Rossi," Tommy replied.

"We have something for you," Jesse said as he handed Jane a box of Whitman's Samplers chocolates.

"That's so thoughtful. Thank you, Jesse and Tommy! Cathy was right; you are wonderful boys."

After dinner, while Jane, Tommy, and Jesse played Monopoly, Cathy, Ernest, and Ann discussed Ann's plans.

"Ann, we've planned for you and the boys to stay in our guest house next door until you find a place of your own," Ernest said.

"It's nice. I think you'll be comfortable there, Ann," Cathy added.

"First thing on my list is to find a house," Ann said.

"I've found two for you to look at," Cathy told her.

"I also have a real estate agent who can show you more houses if you don't like either of those," Ernest added.

"I also need to enroll Tommy and Jesse in school." Ann said.

"How old are they?" Cathy asked.

"Tommy's ten and Jesse's eight."

"Then they will go to Browns Valley Elementary. It's for grades one through six. Napa Junior High is grades seven and eight, and Napa High School is for grades nine through twelve," Cathy explained.

"Cathy, when are you leaving your job here?" asked Ann.

"My last day will be Friday, October 9, which is a week before my wedding."

"Great, that will give us plenty of time for you to teach me your job."

"Ann, as smart and well-educated as you are, you could probably learn it on your own."

"Maybe, but I'm glad you will be here to help me in the transition."

"Staying in your job for another nine weeks also gives Ann time to buy a house, get moved in, get the boys started in school and get settled," Ernest noted.

"I can't tell you how much I appreciate all your help," Ann told them both.

THE WINE QUEEN

"We're happy to do it, Ernest said. "I'm just glad you're going to be my CFO. Cathy is hard to replace."

On Monday morning, Cathy called the real estate agent who was selling the houses she had picked out for Ann and the boys and told her that she and Ann were ready to look at them.

"That's fine. Since you told me Ann would arrive this weekend and would be looking at houses, I already made arrangements with the owners to show them. How about ten o'clock for the house in Browns Valley and eleven for the one on Elm Street?"

"We'll see you at ten," Cathy replied.

Ann liked the first house they showed her. It was Cathy's favorite, too. It was a four bedroom with two bathrooms. The master bedroom with its bathroom and one of the other bedrooms was on one end of the house, while the last two bedrooms and their bathroom were at the other end of the house. It had a two-car garage and sat on a half-acre lot. The large fenced backyard had a giant oak tree with a rope swing and two navel orange trees. The house was only five blocks from Browns Valley Elementary, where Tommy and Jesse would be going to school. This meant they could ride their bicycles to and from school. It was also only a thirty-minute drive from Columbia Creek Winery. Ann didn't need to look any further, and she made an offer on the house that afternoon. The offer was accepted, and the closing was set for Wednesday, September 9, a month later. The owners were moving out the week before the closing, so Ann and the boys would be able to begin moving in the day after the closing.

On Tuesday, Ann bought a new Chevrolet Impala.

"Ann, this is Mr. Porterfield," Cathy said as she introduced Ann to the principal of Browns Valley Elementary School when they visited on Tuesday, September 1.

"It's a pleasure to meet you, Mr. Porterfield."

"Please, call me Jim."

"Jim, these are my two sons, Tommy and Jesse."

"Hi, boys."

"Hey, Mr. Porterfield," Tommy said.

"Will you be my teacher?" asked Jesse.

"No, but both of you will be able to meet your teachers in a few minutes," Jim replied. "First, I have some forms for your mother to complete. How old are you and what grades were you in last year?"

"I'm ten and will be eleven on September 20," Tommy replied. "I was in the fifth grade last year."

"I'm eight and will be nine on October 5. And I was in the third grade last year," Jesse replied.

"Good. Ann, you can take these forms with you to finish and bring them back later if you'd like," Jim told her as he gave her a short stack of papers.

"Okay. I brought the boys' report cards for each year they have been in school and the results of their achievement tests from last year."

"Great. Let's go meet their teachers and you can show them the report cards and test scores."

"Ann, I'm going back to the winery now, if that's okay," Cathy said.

"Sure. Thanks for introducing us to Jim."

Jim took Ann and the boys to one of the classrooms. "Ann, boys, this is Mrs. Lena Woods and Mrs. Cynthia Milton," he said as he introduced the teachers. "Mrs. Woods will be Jesse's fourth grade teacher, and Mrs. Milton will be Tommy's sixth grade teacher."

"Here are their report cards and the results of last year's achievement tests," Ann explained as she handed the materials to Mrs. Woods and Mrs. Milton

"You sure are smart boys!" Mrs. Milton said as she and Mrs. Woods looked at the report cards and test scores. "Straight As for both Tommy and Jesse, and scores in the top two percent on their achievement tests!"

"Dad always told us it was our responsibility to do well in school and finish our homework," Tommy explained.

"Yeah, and he helped us with our homework every night, as well as with our school projects," Jesse said.

"Now that your dad's no longer with us, I will do that," Ann said.

"What happened to their father?" asked Mrs. Woods.

"He was killed last May in that bank robbery in Yountville," Ann explained.

"That was your husband?" asked Mrs. Milton.

"Yes."

"Boys, your father was a hero," Mrs. Woods told Jesse and Tommy. "His bravery in that bank saved a lot of lives."

"We know," Tommy replied.

"And we're very proud of him," Jesse said as a tear trickled down his cheek.

"I'm sorry. I wasn't thinking. I didn't mean to bring back painful memories," Mrs. Woods said.

"That's okay. We will always love him and he'll always hold a special place in our hearts. But our job now is to start the new school year, work hard, and make good grades," Tommy explained.

"Yeah, that's what Dad would want us to do," Jesse added.

"And our new Mom, too," Tommy reminded his brother.

"Well, school starts on September 8, the day after Labor Day. That's only a week away," said Mrs. Milton.

After Tommy and Jesse had left to go see Tommy's classroom with Mrs. Milton, Mrs. Woods said, "Ann, they are both fine boys. And smart, too. From the newspaper article I read about your late husband's act of bravery, I take it they are his children from a previous marriage?"

"That's correct, but I've adopted them."

"I look forward to having Jesse as one of my students, and I'm sure Cynthia will be glad to have Tommy in her class this year as well.

Over the next week, Ann and the boys moved into their new house and they started school. Ann hired Alice Gray, a widow and retired nurse in her late fifties, to stay with Tommy and Jesse in the afternoons after school. She would also fix the boys' meals and stay with them overnight or on a weekend if Ann had to be away on business, as well as do the housework.

Now that Ann was settled in, she, Cathy, and Ernest agreed that it was time for Ann to begin learning the wine business. That would start with learning viticulture (grape growing) and enology (winemaking).

At eight on Wednesday morning, as Ann rode with Ernest out to the vineyard, where she would meet Glen Hamler for her lesson in viticulture, she said, "I've noticed that you've been harvesting grapes for about a week now. When will the harvest be completed?"

"Harvest dates vary by a few weeks from year to year, but this year our harvest will be from August 31 to the end of October."

"So I'll be able to see all of the winery's operations – grape growing, harvesting, crushing, and winemaking."

"That's right. Your timing to start this job couldn't have been better." As they pulled up to the entrance to the vineyard and got out of Ernest's truck, he said, "I believe you know our vineyard manager, Glen Hamler."

"Yes. He gave Ray and me an interesting tour of the vineyard last May."

"I'll leave you in his capable hands," Ernest said before he got back in his truck and left.

"Welcome back to wine country, Mrs. Collins."

"Thanks, and that's Ann."

(Ann's detailed lesson about viticulture is shown in Appendix A at the end of the book).

...and that's the end of your lesson in viticulture."

"That was great, Glen," Ann replied. "I guess growing wine grapes can be a major challenge."

"Yes, it can. You've been a good student," Glen told her as they entered the winery. Ernest met them at the door.

"Well, did you learn about viticulture?" Ernest asked.

"More that I'll ever remember," Ann replied. "But while both of you are here, I have a few more questions."

"Shoot," Ernest replied.

"Where are most of the wines in the United States and the world produced?"

"In the US, wine grapes are grown and wine is produced primarily here in California and in New York State, although Washington State and Oregon are continuing to increase their production of quality wines," Glen replied.

"What percent of US wine production is from California?"

"About eighty, and most of the rest is from New York State," said Glen.

"I've heard that France is the largest producer of wine in the world. Is that true?"

"Yes. France produces over forty percent of the world's wines. The other major wine producing countries, in order of the amount produced, are Italy, Spain, the US and Germany. Together these five countries account for almost eighty percent of world wine production," Ernest explained.

Ernest took Ann into the barrel room, which Ann remembered from its cool temperature and smell of oak.

"I covered some of this on your wine tour during your honeymoon, so I will try not to be repetitive," Ernest began.

"That's okay. I think this is fascinating. I won't mind hearing it a second time."

(Ann's detailed lesson about enology is shown in Appendix B at the end of the book).

"That concludes the lesson on enology, Ernest said. Cathy will familiarize you with our financial and cost accounting systems, accounts receivable and payable, our budgeting and financial planning process, and purchasing. Then Darrel Hayes, our sales manager, will explain our wine pricing process."

Chapter Sixteen

It was just before six p.m. on Thursday October 15 when the Rossis' doorbell rang.

"Well, hello there, Daryl," Jane said as she greeted Daryl Thompson, Cathy's fiancé.

"Hi, Jane. How have you been?"

"Fine, come in and have a seat while I get Cathy."

A few minutes later Cathy came in, followed by Ann. "Hi, love," Daryl said as he gave Cathy a hug.

"Hey. I'd like you to meet Ann Collins, my matron of honor."

"Hi, Ann. Cathy's told me lot about you," Daryl said. He was tall, with broad shoulders, blond hair, blue eyes, and a mustache.

"I hope it wasn't all bad," Ann kidded.

"It was very complimentary," Daryl replied.

"How's my future son-in-law?" Ernest asked as he came into the room.

"Great. How's my future father-in-law?"

"Very busy these days."

"That's right. You are harvesting and processing grapes now. When does it look like you will be finished?"

"The harvest will probably be finished by October 27."

"Cathy tells me you're going to Hawaii on your honeymoon," Ann said.

"Yeah, we're taking a fifteen-day cruise from Los Angeles," Daryl replied. "We leave on Sunday, and arrive in Hilo, one of the islands, on Friday. Then we'll go to Honolulu, Nawiliwili, and Lahaina. Then four more days at sea before we get back to Los Angeles."

"I know you'll have a wonderful time," Jane observed.

"I'm certainly looking forward to going," Cathy added. "I'm also looking forward to the cruise. I've never been on one before."

"I've always wanted to go to Hawaii. Maybe we will one day after Jane and I retire," Ernest said. "Is everything all set for the rehearsal dinner at the Royal Oak?"

"Yep," Daryl replied. "There will be eighteen of us, and it will begin at seven."

"I checked the weather forecast and it still looks like the weather will be good on Saturday, so we'll be able to have the wedding under the oaks out by the vineyard," Jane said.

"It seldom rains here in the fall," Ernest observed.

"That's why I was okay with an outside wedding," Cathy said.

Gladys then came into the room. "Dinner is ready," she announced.

On Monday morning, November 16, Ernest came into Ann's office and handed her a glass of wine. "This is the Merlot we made from this year's crop," he said.

"Oh, that's bitter," she said after tasting the wine.

"Of course, that's the tannin from the grape skins and seeds. But after five years of aging in our French oak barrels, that bitterness will be replaced by a mellow fruitiness that you'll love."

"Is there a school that I could attend where I can learn to taste wines?"

"Yes, there's one in the Languedoc-Roussillon region in southern France taught by the French Wine Academy. It's five days long. I get their newsletter, and that will tell me when the next class is. I'll get the last one and find out right now."

"Great! Thanks."

A few minutes later, Ernest returned holding the newsletter. "It says the next class starts on Monday, April 11."

"Okay. If it's all right with you, I will plan to go," Ann said.

"Sure, I think you should. Tommy and Jesse can stay with Jane and me while you are gone."

"Thanks."

"Jesse, you look kind of melancholy this morning. Is everything okay?" Ann asked on Saturday morning, December 19, as Jesse was eating a bowl of cereal.

"Yeah. Just missing Dad. This will be our first Christmas without him."

"I know. I miss him a lot, too. All the time."

"What's this? The sad bunch?" Tommy asked as he walked into the kitchen.

"We're just talking about how much we miss your dad."

"Yeah, I miss him, too, but I try to not let myself dwell on it, or it makes me feel bad. Are we going to get a Christmas tree today?"

"That's the plan. After breakfast I thought we'd ride out to Mr. Ryder's tree farm and pick one out," Ann suggested.

Later, Ann and the boys were busy decorating their Christmas tree. There was a warm, crackling fire in the fireplace and Christmas music playing on the stereo. "Jesse, that bell is too heavy for the branch it's on. The branch is bending. Move the ornament to the stronger branch just below," Tommy suggested.

"Okay."

"Mom, what are our plans for Christmas Day?" Tommy asked while he took a sip of hot chocolate.

"I thought we'd open our gifts and have breakfast here. Then the Rossis' have invited us to have Christmas dinner with them. Cathy and Daryl will also be there."

"Mom, this is really neat!" Tommy said as he admired his new red Schwinn ten-speed bike. It was sitting near the family's Christmas tree when they all came into the family room on Christmas morning.

"Yeah!" Jesse agreed as he looked at his matching green one, his voice loud with excitement. "Thanks, Mom!"

"Those ten-speeds will make it a lot easier for both of you to handle that hill between here and your school."

"I agree," Tommy said.

"Mom, I believe Santa left you a gift under the tree," Jesse pointed out.

"Yes, I believe you're right," Ann replied as she picked up the gift.

The card said, "Merry Christmas, Mom. Tommy and Jesse." The gift was a gold necklace with a gold, heart-shaped locket on it. She opened the locket and inside was a photo of Ray when he was a boy. He looked to be about eight or nine years old.

"Boys, this is so very special. I've never seen a picture of Ray as a boy. How old is he in this picture?"

"He's eight," Tommy replied.

"Thank you, Tommy and Jesse. I'll wear this every day."

It was eight a.m. on Monday, April 11. Ann was in the barrel room of the Domaine De L' Angeliere winery in Bezounce, France. "Good morning, class." The instructor began in a heavy French accent. "My name is Alexis Fontaine and I will be your teacher for this five-day wine school. There are eighteen students attending, eight from France, four from Italy, one from Great Britain, and five from the United States. The classes will be taught in this barrel room. Class will be from eight a.m. until six p.m., with a one-hour lunch break. Lunches will be provided for you by the Domaine De L'Angeliere winery, our host for this course. Are there any questions?"

"I have a question," Ann said.

"Please identify yourself, Madame," Alexis requested.

"Ann Collins from the Columbia Creek Winery in Napa, California. When we complete this wine school, will we get a certificate?"

"Yes. Yours, for instance, would read, 'Ann Collins completed the French Wine Academy Professional Wine Tasting Course and is hereby granted the distinction of **French Wine Scholar,** April 15, 1960.'" Then the instructor began the class.

(Ann's detailed lesson about wine tasting is shown in Appendix C at the end of the book).

"Hi, Ann. I'm Bridgette Spencer," a young woman dressed in tan slacks and a blue, long-sleeved blouse with a British accent said when she introduced herself during lunch.

"I'm pleased to meet you, Bridgett. Where are you from?"

"London. I am a buyer for Harrods."

"I've read about Harrods, and they're huge."

"Yeah. The store sits on a five-acre site and has over a million square feet of shopping space."

"Why are you going to wine school?"

"I want to become a wine buyer for Harrods. We carry hundreds of wines, and our current wine buyer is retiring."

"Does Harrods carry any of our wines?"

"Columbia Creek, correct?"

"Yeah."

"No, we only carry wines from Europe, primarily France."

"When I get back to California, I would like to send you some of our wines to try."

"You're on. If I like them, I'll plan to come to Napa and see your vineyards and winery."

"Tomorrow, we will meet here in the barrel room again and discuss the taste characteristics of white and red generics, white and red varietals, Champaigns and dessert wines," Alex said as he concluded the first day's class. "We'll spend Wednesday in the vineyards. A key to evaluating wines is understanding how the grapes they are made from were grown. On Thursday and Friday we will be tasting flights of various wines to give you examples of the things we have discussed today and will discuss tomorrow. By the time you finish this course, each of you will have tasted more than a thousand wines."

"I want to send a bottle of our Cabernet Sauvignon and Chardonnay to Bridgette Spencer in London," Ann told Ernest when he came into her office on Monday morning, April 18, after she had returned from wine school. She was hanging her French Wine Scholar certificate on the wall behind her desk.

"Who is Bridgette Spencer?"

"I met her in wine school. She was training to be the wine buyer for Harrods in London."

"Okay. But they're not going to carry our wines."

"Why?"

"Because California wines aren't recognized as high quality wines in Europe."

"Well, it can't hurt to try. By the way, I have an idea for a new line of wines."

"New wines?"

"Yeah. Generic wines are currently almost ninety percent of the US wine market, but only account for about half of our wine sales."

"That's because our focus is on the higher quality varietals."

"I believe there could be a market for wines in between the generics and the varietals," Ann said.

"What type of wine would it be?"

"A higher quality generic. Between a premium generic and an ordinary wine. We could call the line Columbia Creek Cellars. There would be a Burgundy and a Chablis. The grapes it would be made from will be twenty percent North Coast Counties, five percent Napa Valley, and seventy-five percent Central Valley. The grapes from the North Coast Counties and the Napa Valley will give it a taste that's superior to other generic wines."

"How will consumers know that?" Ernest wondered.

"We'll advertise on TV and in magazines. The advertisements will feature wine experts that compare its taste to that of other leading generic wines, and ours will win because of the superior grapes in its blend. I'm sure Columbia Creek Cellars will also win awards in real wine contests. Between its advertising and winning awards, Columbia Creek Cellars could become the nation's best-selling wine."

"I don't like the idea. First, the grapes from the North Coast Counties and the Napa Valley will increase the wine's cost, and thus the price we will have to charge for it compared to other generic wines in the marketplace. And second, most consumers will not be able to tell the difference in these wines and other less expensive wines, and they will choose the less expensive wines."

"But our advertising will explain the difference in the quality of Columbia Creek Cellars and other generic wines."

"Advertising wines is a Pandora's box. If we start advertising on TV, our competitors will do the same thing, and the result will be intense price competition. Soon the California wine business will become unprofitable and a number of wineries will be forced out of business. I don't want us to be one of those forced out of business. I don't want to discourage you from trying to find ways to grow our business, I just don't think this new line of generic wines is one of them."

"Okay," Ann replied reluctantly

"Ernest, you were right about Harrods," Ann said to him a month later. "Here's a letter I just got from Bridgette. She says our wines were among the best they sampled. But California wines are not recognized among Harrods's customers as high quality wines, so they will not carry them."

"I wish it were different," Ernest said with a sigh." Our wine industry has been trying to gain recognition in Europe as a producer of high quality wines since the end of World War II, but we haven't been successful."

"I have another idea to grow our business," Ann said. "This would be a line of wines targeted to people in their twenties and thirties. It would be made from Central Valley grapes. These wines would be light, fruity, slightly sweet, and carbonated. They could be designed to compete with beer, which would make them popular with young females who don't like the taste of beer. It could be called Columbia Creek Farms."

"I don't like this idea either. It will cheapen our image as a producer of high quality Napa Valley varietal wines, and attract competition from the beer companies. They are much larger than we are, have more marketing funds, and are well known by consumers. They will win in competition against us, and Columbia Creek Farms will be a financial failure."

"I understand, Ernest," Ann replied glumly.

"Are you and the boys going to join us for dinner Friday night?"

"Yeah."

"Good I want to take them fishing with me on Saturday, if that's okay."

"Absolutely. I'm sure they'd love to go."

"Tommy, Jesse, would you boys like to go fishing with me in the morning?" Ernest asked when they were all having dinner at his house that Friday night.

"Yeah!" the boys both said enthusiastically at the same time.

"Where are you going?" Ann asked

"To Lake Berryessa. It's about an hour-and-a half drive from Napa."

"What will you be fishing for?" asked Ann.

"Rainbow trout and bass. Do Tommy and Jesse have any fishing tackle?"

"We have rods and reels. Dad used to take us fishing at the Anna Maria Island pier in Florida," Tommy explained.

"He also took us fishing on a boat out in the ocean," Jesse added.

"Their fishing has all been in salt water. There are no lakes near Ruskin," Ann explained.

"I'll be by to get you at six tomorrow morning," Ernest told the boys.

"You finally have boys to go fishing with you," Jane said later as she and Ernest were getting ready for bed that night.

"Yeah. Cathy never liked fishing, and I got bored going alone. I was getting ready to sell my boat, but then Tommy and Jesse came along. I was hoping they would like to go fishing with me."

"I think they'll make good fishing buddies."

It was just before six a.m. when Ernest's pickup truck pulled into Ann's driveway. He was pulling an eighteen-foot Skeeter bass boat with a seventy horsepower Mercury motor. Tommy and Jesse heard him drive up and came out to meet him. They were each carrying a Garcia rod with a Mitchel 300 reel attached. "You boys ready to go?" Ernest asked.

"Yeah," Tommy replied.

"Give me your fishing rods and I'll put them in the rod holders on the boat."

"That's a neat boat," Jesse said as he and Tommy handed their rods and reels to Ernest.

"They've had breakfast," Ann said as she walked up.

"Okay. We should be back around five thirty or six," Ernest told her.

"I'll have the grease ready to fry fish," Ann kidded.

It was just before seven thirty when Ernest and the boys arrived at the boat ramp. He unhooked the strap holding the boat to the trailer and put it in the back of his truck, then backed the truck down the ramp until the boat and trailer were in the water. While he was unwinding the crank and pushing the boat off the trailer farther out into the water, he said, "Tommy, now that the boat's in the water, crank the cable back into the winch while I get in the boat and start the motor."

"Okay," Tommy replied and then began cranking the winch.

After he'd gotten the motor started, Ernest pulled the boat up to the dock and tied it there, then climbed out of the boat. Jesse had unloaded their gear from the truck, as well as the lunches that Jane had packed for the three of them. While Ernest parked his truck with the empty trailer in a spot near the boat ramp, Tommy and Jesse loaded all their gear and the lunches into the boat.

A short while later, they were pulling away from the dock. "Tommy, do you want to drive the boat?" Ernest asked.

"Yeah!" was Tommy's excited reply

"I'd like to drive it too," Jesse requested.

"Our fishing spot is about twenty minutes away, so that will give each of you ten minutes to drive the boat."

"This is fun!" Tommy exclaimed as he followed Ernest's instructions and powered the boat to get it onto a plane.

"It's my turn," Jesse said about ten minutes later.

"Pull into that cove where the stump is sticking out of the water," Ernest told Jesse a little later. "That's our fishing spot."

They pulled up about seventy feet from the stump and Ernest quietly lowered the anchor while Tommy turned the motor off. "We'll start out fishing for bass," Ernest explained.

"We've never been bass fishing," Tommy said.

"But we've watched bass fishing shows on TV," added Jesse.

"We'll use plastic worms," Ernest said as Tommy and Jesse took their rods and reels out of the rod rack.

"Boys, put the hook into the large end of the worm, then push it through the length of it and out about an inch from the back. Like this." Ernest then demonstrated by putting the plastic worm on Jesse's hook. After both of the boys were finished baiting their hooks, Ernest continued, "Cast over near that stump. Let the worm sink to the bottom, then slowly reel it in."

Tommy cast his worm to the left side of the stump while Jesse cast his to the right side.

Tommy had reeled his worm up to the boat and was getting ready cast it back out when something hit Jesse's bait. "Wait a minute while the fish swallows the worm, Ernest instructed. Then jerk the line to set the hook."

Jesse followed Ernest's instructions, and after he had set the hook, a large bass erupted out of the water. "Don't let the line go slack," Ernest said. "Let him take it out on the reel's drag, then reel him in when the line starts to go slack."

Jesse fought the fish for several minutes, then as he reeled it up to the boat, Ernest dipped it up into a net. "He's a nice one!" Ernest said as he held the large bass up by its gills. "Tommy, hand me that scale and let's weigh him." Tommy did as he was asked.

"Five pounds, three ounces," Ernest said as he read the scale. Ernest then unhooked the bass and put it in the boat's live well while Jesse put another plastic worm on his hook.

"Aren't you going to fish?" Tommy asked Ernest as he cast his worm back out near the stump.

"Maybe later. For now, I'd rather watch you and Jesse fish."

After a few minutes, Tommy had hooked a bass, too. It weighed four pounds, six ounces. Over the next two hours they caught five more, ranging from three to six and a half pounds. "Boys, we've got plenty of bass, let's go catch some rainbow trout," Ernest suggested.

"Okay," Tommy replied, so Ernest pulled in the anchor.

As Ernest maneuvered the boat out into the mouth of Putah Creek that the lake fed into, he said, "Tommy use the net to get up some minnows out of the other live well and put them in that bucket. We'll use smaller hooks with cork bobbers for the rainbows.

After the boys had tied the smaller hooks onto their lines, Ernest continued his instructions. "Put the bobber about three feet above the hook. Then put the hook through the minnow's tail like this," Ernest said as he baited Jesse's hook. "That way, the minnow will stay alive longer."

"Where should we cast?" Tommy asked.

"Anywhere. According to the fishing report, trout have been feeding all over the mouth of this creek lately," Ernest replied.

Tommy cast his minnow and bobber about forty feet from the boat. The bobber moved back and forth as the minnow swam about. Then the bobber suddenly sank, and Tommy set the hook. The rainbow trout jumped about a foot out of the water. Tommy reeled him in, and then Jesse dipped the trout into the net. "He's a nice one!" Ernest observed.

They stopped for lunch at twelve thirty. "How many have we caught?" Tommy asked.

"I've counted seven bass and six rainbow trout," Jesse replied.

"That's what I got too," Ernest said. "How about we eat these sandwiches that Jane fixed for us, then head back to Napa. We have more than enough for a fish-fry. When we get back to the dock, I'll call Jane and tell her to plan on having fish for dinner."

"We'll clean the fish in that sink over there," Ernest said when they got back to the dock and were pulling the boat out of the water. He then pointed at a stainless steel sink at the end of the dock.

A short while later, Ernest was showing the boys how to fillet their fish. "Slide the blade along his backbone like this," Ernest explained as he showed Tommy the proper technique. They filleted the seven bass, but not the rainbow trout. Since they were smaller than the bass, Ernest preferred to cook the trout whole, after scaling them and removing the head and insides.

After they had washed their hands and put the fish on ice, Ernest went into the bait and tackle shop near the boat ramp and called Jane. "How many did you catch?" she asked.

"Seven bass and six rainbow trout"

"You've had a pretty successful trip. How about if I call Ann and we have a fish-fry tonight?"

"That was my thought as well. We should get back to Napa around four. I'll just come straight to our house with the boys."

"Okay. I'll plan dinner for six thirty. You want me to fix hush puppies, baked beans, and Coleslaw to go with it?"

"That sounds good to me."

"Tommy, would you and Jesse like to go camping after school is out?" Ann asked at dinner on the night of May 27, 1960.

"Yeah! We love camping. Dad used to take us camping on a ranch owned by one of Tropical Citrus's growers."

"Where are we going?" Jesse asked.

"To Yosemite National Park."

"Where is it located?" Tommy asked.

"In California, about a four-hour drive southeast of here."

"Did you bring our camping gear when we moved?" asked Jesse.

"Of course. Your tent, sleeping bags, two-burner kerosene cooking stove, and Coleman lantern are all in the attic. I don't have a sleeping bag or fishing gear, so I'll need to get those. Then we'll have most of what we'll need."

"When are we going?" Tommy asked excitedly. "How long are we staying?" Jesse asked, also excited.

"Calm down, boys. I thought we'd leave here on Saturday, June 11, and stay a week. Tommy, get some paper and a pencil, and let's make a list of what we'll take on the trip."

"Is that the last duffel bag, Jesse?" Ann asked as her son carried the bag to the car.

"Yeah. It's got Tommy's and my clothes."

"Hand it to me and I'll strap it to the luggage rack with the other stuff," Tommy said.

"Okay," his brother replied.

"I think that's everything. Are you ready to go?" Ann asked.

"Yep," Tommy replied.

"Wait! I forgot my pocket knife," Jesse said as he remembered.

"Here's the house key," Ann said and handed it to him.

"Okay, are we ready to leave now?" asked Ann when Jesse returned.

"Ready," he replied.

They arrived at an entrance to the park at two p.m., and Ann pulled up to a log building just inside the park, which had a sign that said, ***All Campers Must Register Here Before Entering the Park***. Ann parked their car, and she and the boys went inside the building.

"May I help you ma'am?" a middle-aged man in a ranger uniform asked.

"Yes, we want to camp in the park for the week." "Okay. You'll need to fill out these forms," he said as he handed her two-page forms for her, Tommy, and Jesse, and a pencil. "Once you've finished, I'll get you and your sons registered."

He looked over the forms when Ann handed them back. "That will be ten dollars," he said. "Oh, you forgot to put down the make, model, and tag number of your vehicle."

"I'll go out and get the tag number," Tommy offered.

"Thanks, Tommy," Ann said.

"Here's a map of the park" the ranger said as he unfolded one of the maps for Ann. "Since you will be camping in a tent instead of a camp trailer, I recommend the Valley View campground." He said as he pointed to it on the map. "It's about seven miles from here. It's on a large glacier lake with excellent fishing. And the view is breathtaking. The lake water's very pure and safe to drink. Each campsite has a large picnic table. There are only twenty-six campsites at this campground, and they are spaced about a hundred yards apart, so you'll have privacy."

"That sounds great," Ann said. "That's where we'll go. Can we pick any site we want?"

"Yeah. There are only two campers out there, but there will probably be more later this summer. If you decide you don't like it, come back here and I'll send you to another campground."

Ann took the map, and she and the boys got back in the car and headed down the gravel road toward the campground. About thirty minutes later, they saw a sign nailed to a post that read, **Valley View Campground to the left.** An arrow pointed down a narrow winding rutted road that led through a dense forest.

"This is great!" Tommy observed.

"Yeah, I think we're in the middle of nowhere," Jesse said.

"That's why it's called wilderness camping," Ann replied.

About fifteen minutes later, the rutted road came out of the dense forest and opened up into a meadow filled with wild flowers. A nearby sign said **Campsites Ahead**. They drove another half mile and came to the lake. As the ranger had said, it was a pristine glacier lake with crystal-blue water and sweeping vistas of snowcapped mountains in the distance and was bordered by dense forest canopies and granite cliffs that rose a thousand feet into the air. Water was cascading off one of the granite cliffs from a stream and into the lake.

"This is fabulous!" Tommy observed.

"I've never seen anything like this before," Jesse said.

"It's definitely breath-taking," added Ann. They were at campsite number one, which they chose as theirs. The grassy meadow it was on went right down to a sandbar that bordered the lake, and there was a picnic table about fifty yards from the shore shaded by large oak trees. There was a five foot by seven foot stone-lined fire pit off to one side of the picnic table.

"Boys, let's unpack," Ann suggested. "We'll put up our tent near the picnic table, under the oak trees."

"When can we go fishing?" Jesse asked.

"After we're unpacked and the tent is up," Ann replied.

"Tommy, this cold glacier lake will be our refrigerator. I brought a stainless steel box with iron weights in the bottom that we can put food and drinks in and sink. There's a seven-foot chain attached to it that we can fasten to a tent stake and drive into the ground on the bank of the lake. Let's put two six packs of Coca-Colas, the bacon, the butter, and the eggs in it."

"Mom, can we go fishing now?" Tommy asked after they had put up their four-man tent, put their sleeping bags in it, and had finished unpacking the rest of their gear.

"Okay. In case you don't catch any fish, I have canned beef stew for dinner."

"Boy, Jesse, that makes me want to catch fish even more," Tommy said.

"Me, too," Jesse replied.

"While y'all are fishing, I'll gather wood for a fire and make cornbread," Ann said.

"Jesse, since its summertime and warm, I think the bass will be feeding near the surface, so let's try top-water lures." Ernest had been taking them bass fishing frequently, and the boys had begun to study bass fishing techniques. They had also acquired a number of bass fishing lures.

"I agree. I think I'll start with a repala walleye runner," Jesse said.

"I'll try a repala flicker shad."

Tommy cast about seventy feet from the bank and began to work his lure with short jerks. Immediately it was hit by a bass. He set the hook, and began to fight the large fish, which jumped out of the water. Jesse got the dip net, and a few minutes later, Tommy had landed a nice bass. "I bet he's at least six pounds," Jesse observed.

"Let's weigh him and see," Tommy suggested.

"Seven pounds three ounces," Jesse said as he weighed the fish.

"Wow! Now it's your turn, Jesse."

Jesse cast his walleye runner near the base of the waterfall and began to reel it in, popping it in the water as he did. As with Tommy's cast, a bass hit the lure after it had gone only about ten feet. Jesse set the hook and the large fish erupted out of the water. "He's bigger than mine was!" Tommy exclaimed as he got the dip net ready. "Eight pounds, eleven ounces," Tommy said after he'd weighed the fish on their scale.

"Wow, Tommy. This in the best fishing I've ever seen! It's even better than on the TV fishing shows."

"It sure is. Let's get Mom to go fishing with us in the morning. This great fishing will be perfect for teaching her how to fish." They had enough for dinner with their first two catches, and so they released the other seven bass they caught over the course of the afternoon, which ranged from four to seven-and-a-half pounds.

When they returned to their campsite, the boys showed Ann the two bass they'd decided to keep. "Wow, they're huge!" Ann observed.

"We caught seven more, but threw them back because we had enough for dinner," Tommy explained.

"That's good sportsmanship," Ann said.

"Mom, why don't you come fishing with us in the morning?"

"Okay. With fishing this good, it will be ideal for me to learn how to fish for bass." While Tommy and Jesse filleted the fish, Ann started two fires in the large pit. Once the flames died down to red-hot coals, they would add more wood to one to keep the fire going, and put hot coals from it into the other one, which they would cook over. The boys returned with the fillets, and all of them sat on folding camp stools around the large crackling fires, the calls of lake loons in the distance mixed with the gurgling of the waterfall as the day faded into night.

"This is wonderful, Mom," Tommy observed.

"It sure is," Jesse agreed.

When the fires had died to glowing embers, Ann said, "Tommy, scoop half of the coals from the fire on the left and put them into the other one, then put more wood on the fire on the left. Jesse, get the metal fire grate and put it over the coals on the right. I'll get the frying pans, the cans of pork and beans, the shortening, and the cornbread." Ann dipped the bass fillets into a mixture of cornmeal and flour, then put them in the pan of hot grease over the coals to fry. Then she put the cornbread in an iron skillet, and leaned the skillet against a stone, facing the fire, for the bread to bake. Jesse opened the three cans of pork and beans and set them near the fire to heat. Tommy set the picnic table with their metal camp plates, metal cups, forks, knives, and spoons. Once he had set the table, Tommy retrieved three Cokes from the steel box in the lake, opened one and took the other two to Ann and Jesse.

"Thanks, Tommy," Ann said when he handed her an ice-cold Coke.

The afternoon's activities had made everyone hungry and they feasted on the fried bass, hot buttered cornbread, and pork and beans. When they'd finished, they put some more wood on the fire and sat around it sipping hot chocolate as the whip-poor-wills called in the distance. "Thanks, Mom," Tommy said.

"Yeah, thanks for taking us on this camping trip, Mom," Jesse added.

"You're welcome. I want us to spend time doing things together, and I hoped this camping trip would be the start of that."

"It is. We're having lots of fun. The fishing's great and food always seems to taste better cooked outside over an open fire," Tommy said.

"Did Ray take y'all camping a lot?"

"Not a lot. Jesse how many times did Dad take us camping?"

"Let's see, there was the time in June when we had to leave early and go home because of a major lightning storm," Jesse remembered.

"Yeah, after that we only went camping in the winter, when there weren't lightning storms."

"Then there was the time you were stung by a storm of honey bees and Dad took you to the doctor. But after that there were no more mishaps, and if I remember correctly, we went camping maybe four more times."

"Yeah, that's what I remember, too."

"I know how much you miss your dad, and I know I'll never be able to replace him. But I hope spending time together on trips like this makes up for some of your loss," Ann said.

"Mom, we love you. You're the only mom we've had who loved us."

"Yeah, and even though we like this camping trip, we'd love you no matter what we were doing," Jesse added.

"Come here. I'm just glad that I have two sons as wonderful as you," she said as she gave both of them hugs. "Would you like us to go camping for a week every summer? We can come back here, or go to other national parks like Yellowstone or Glacier."

"The fishing's so good and the scenery is so great, I'd like to come back here," Tommy said.

"Me, too," said Jesse.

"This is also the closest national park to where we live, so this is also my choice," Ann added.

They enjoyed the rest of their week, with the boys teaching Ann how to fish for bass, hiking to the top of a mountain, and exploring a cave. And they enjoyed fresh fish for dinner around the campfire every night.

Chapter Seventeen

"Ernest, I have another idea for how to grow the business," Ann began as she walked into his office on Monday morning, June 20.

"Okay, let's hear it."

"We need to increase our focus on two additional high quality varietals: Merlot and Sauvignon Blanc," explained Ann.

"We already make an excellent award-winning Cabernet Sauvignon and Chardonnay. Why do we need two more varietals? Besides, Merlot is a blending grape, it's not made as a varietal. And Sauvignon Blanc has a grassy flavor, and aromas that are too aggressive."

"The Merlot and Sauvignon Blanc I tasted in wine school were excellent. I think Merlot would be ideal as a first red varietal for new wine drinkers because it's softer and fruitier than Cabernet Sauvignon or Pinot Noir."

"You may have a point there. Our soils produce better Merlot grapes than Cabernet Sauvignon. We blend it with Cabernet Sauvignon and and Petit Verdot for our Bordeaux. We could substitute more Cabernet and Petit Verdot and use the extra Merlot to try a varietal with it. But I'm not sure about the Sauvignon Blanc."

"When we tasted Sauvignon Blanc in wine school, it was very good, so I asked what had been done to improve the flavor.

Alex, our teacher, said the wine had been made in a fruitier style, aged in oak for a year, and bottled aged for another three."

"So the aging improved the flavor?"

"That's what our teacher told us."

"But why should we take a chance with a new white varietal?"

"Most white wine competition is over Chardonnay. The only competition with Sauvignon Blanc is in Europe. If we can produce a high quality Sauvignon Blanc, maybe we can get it into competition in Europe," Ann explained. "That would give us international exposure. "

"Okay, you've convinced me that it's worth a try. I heard that the twenty-three acres adjoining our vineyard is for sale. Let's buy it and plant more Merlot and some Sauvignon Blanc vines there."

"Great!"

September 11, 1964. Four Years Later

"Tommy, do you have enough money saved to buy Mr. Rossi's old Chevy pickup?" Jesse asked on Friday when they were riding their bicycles home from school. Tommy would be sixteen on September 20, and he'd been driving with a restricted license for two years. Both boys were hoping Tommy could buy Ernest's 1952 Chevrolet pickup truck. Ernest had recently bought a new truck, but had kept his old one for Tommy to buy. Both boys had been working at Columbia Creek Winery on Saturdays and over the summer for the last two years to earn money.

"I've got two hundred five dollars saved, but that still leaves a hundred ninety-five to go."

"I've saved a hundred fifty-two. You can have that."

"Thanks, Jesse, but we'll need to use that money to help us buy a used bass boat."

"But the truck is more important than a boat. Maybe Mr. Rossi will let you pay for part of it now and the rest later, or reduce the price so you can buy it now."

"No, the four hundred dollars he's asking is about a hundred less than he could normally sell it for, so he's doing me a favor. And I don't want to owe money to anyone. So we'll just have to make do with borrowing Mom's car."

"But we can't go fishing in her car."

"We can't go fishing anyway without a boat."

"I was hoping we could borrow Mr. Rossi's boat, but I don't think Mom would want us to pull it behind her car."

The following Monday morning, Ernest came into Ann's office. "Ann, have you found a pickup for Tommy's birthday present yet?"

"As a matter of fact I have. It's a 1964 green Chevrolet C-10, half-ton Fleetside. Since the 1965 models are coming out in October, the price of this one was reduced by two hundred dollars to forty-one hundred. I paid for it on Saturday. Have you located a bass boat?"

"Yeah, it's an eighteen-foot Skeeter with a ninety horsepower Evinrude motor. It has two live wells, a dry well, two swivel seats for casting, a trolling motor, and a Lowrance electronic fish finder. It's at Napa Valley Marine. I paid for it on Saturday, too."

"I really appreciate this. The boys are going to love the boat, and it's very kind and thoughtful of you to give it to them on Tommy's birthday."

"Tommy and Jesse are both wonderful boys, and I feel like their grandpa. They've been great fishing partners. I'm going to enjoy their excitement when they get this new bass boat as much as you will."

"I'll call Vasser Chevrolet today and get them to install a trailer hitch and light connection on the truck. Tommy's birthday is next Sunday, but I thought we'd celebrate it on Saturday. Since I would like to make the pickup and bass boat a surprise, I was thinking that I would drive the new truck to Napa Valley Marine, hook up the new boat, and park them both in the Anderson's driveway three houses down. They're leaving Saturday morning to visit Mrs. Anderson's mother in San Francisco, so I'm sure they'll give me permission to park the truck and boat there.

"Okay. I'll pick the boys up at seven thirty Saturday morning, but they'll only work until noon. I'll tell them I'm giving them the afternoon off with pay as Tommy's birthday present. Then Jane, Tommy, Jesse, and I will come to your house for his birthday. We should get to your house around twelve thirty."

"Okay. After I get the truck and boat, I'm going to bake a birthday cake. I was planning to bake a ham and have that with mashed potatoes and green beans for lunch."

"That sounds good. But as excited as they're going to be, I doubt if the boys will have much of an appetite."

"Oh, before I forget, would you sign this birthday card? I'm going to tape it to the boat."

"Sure." Ernest's inscription in the card read, *Happy Birthday, Tommy. Jane and I hope you and Jesse enjoy your new boat.*

"Boys, let's go. It's time to go to your house and celebrate your birthday, Tommy," Ernest said at noon on Saturday. They were in the winery where grapes were being crushed.

"Okay. I'll go get Mrs. Rossi," Jesse offered.

"Good. Tommy and I will start the car," Ernest replied.

They got to Ann's house a little while later. "Hi, Mom," Jesse said as he walked in.

"Something sure smells good," Tommy observed.

"Baked ham and birthday cake," Ann replied as she handed Ernest the keys to Tommy's new truck when the boys weren't looking. "Tommy, do you want your birthday presents before or after we eat?"

"Before."

"Ernest, would you go and get them?"

"Certainly."

About ten minutes later, Ernest came back inside. "Where are Tommy's presents?" Jesse asked.

"They're outside," Ernest said.

"Well, Tommy, let's go outside so you can get them," Ann suggested.

They all walked out to the driveway, led by Tommy. There in the drive were the new truck and bass boat, each with a red bow and card attached.

"Mom, are these my birthday presents?" asked an excited Tommy.

"Yep."

"Tommy, it's a new bass boat and a new truck!" exclaimed Jesse.

"YEAH!" Tommy replied excitedly as he walked up to the shiny new truck and ran his fingers over the hood. He read the cards that were attached to the truck and boat. "Thanks, Mom. Thanks Mr. and Mrs. Rossi."

"You're very welcome," Ann replied.

"Tommy, it's even got a fish finder!" exclaimed Jesse as he examined their new red and gray fiberglass bass boat.

"If a feller gets a new truck, he needs a new bass boat for it to pull," Ernest said jokingly.

"Mom, since I won't have my driver's license until I take, and hopefully pass, my driving test on Monday, would you come with me so I can take the truck for a short drive?" Tommy asked.

"Of course, but I don't want us to be gone long because your birthday lunch is ready," Ann replied as she handed him the key.

"Come on Jesse, let's go for a spin," Tommy suggested as he climbed into his new truck.

"You're on pal!"

"Ann, it's been five years since Ray's death," Jane began after they had finished Tommy's birthday meal and she and Ann were washing the dishes. "You're a very attractive, well-educated woman, and I know a number of eligible, handsome men have asked you out, but you keep refusing. It's none of my business, but why are you unwilling to get into a romantic relationship?"

"Ray was the love of my life, my soul mate. There's just no one else for me but Ray.

"Cathy told me your special story right after Ray was killed. I greatly admire your strong convictions."

"Columbia Creek is the winner in both the white and red varietals," the head judge announced at the 1964 Grand Harvest Awards wine competition in San Francisco on October 24. Their Cabernet Sauvignon and Chardonnay also won in competition against a number of French hybrids from New York State, making Columbia Creek's the best table wines in America."

Ernest walked to the stage to accept the award as cameras flashed. The first certificate he was presented read, *First Place Red Table Wine in the 1964 Grand Harvest Awards Wine Competition*. The other certificate was the same, but for white table wine.

"I'm so proud of you, Ernest," Jane said after he had come off the stage.

"You did it, Ernest," Ann said as she congratulated him.

"Congratulations, Dad," Cathy said as she joined the group.

"Thanks, Cathy. What time do you want us to be at your house?" he asked.

"I've planned dinner for seven. If we leave now, we'll get there about six."

"Okay."

"Ann, you're going to join us, aren't you?" Cathy asked.

"Yeah."

THE WINE QUEEN

Later that day when they entered Daryl and Cathy's large, beautiful home, Daryl met them all in the foyer. "Congratulations, Ernest. Cathy called and told me Columbia Creek had been awarded top wines in America."

"Thanks, Daryl," Ernest said as they followed him into the living room.

"Congratulations Ernest!" seven couples shouted as he entered the room.

"We figured you'd win, so I invited some of your friends to come to your celebratory dinner," Cathy explained.

"What if I hadn't won?"

"Then we'd have had almost as good of a time getting together for dinner," Daryl replied. "Antonio has prepared a wonderful feast. But first, let's all enjoy Columbia Creek Cabernet Sauvignon and Chardonnay with some imported cheeses, and freshly baked sourdough bread."

"Jane, I don't feel very good, I think I'll lie down for a while," Ernest said just after eight a.m. on Friday, November 27, the day after Thanksgiving.

"Are you okay?" asked Jane.

"I think so. It's probably just indigestion from the Thanksgiving feast we had last night."

An hour later Ernest was still feeling bad. "Jane, I'm feeling worse, and I'm having chest pains," he told her.

Jane went to the phone and called the doctor. "Dr. Kilgo, it's Jane Rossi," she said after his receptionist had transferred Jane to him.

"You sound upset."

"Ernest is nauseous and having chest pains."

"Can you bring him to my office?"

"Okay, we'll see you as soon as I can get us there."

"Ernest has had a mild heart attack," Dr. Kilgo told Jane after he had examined Ernest.

"Is he going to be all right?"

"I think so. I gave him a mild sedative. He's asleep now and will sleep for a couple of hours. You need to fill this prescription for heart medication. Dosage instructions will be on the label."

"What can we do to prevent him from having a worse attack in the future?"

"I need to think about that and consult one of my colleagues. How about if you and Ernest come see me on Monday morning, and I'll give you my advice then."

"Okay."

After Jane and Ernest got home that afternoon, Ernest laid down.

As instructed, they met with Dr. Kilgo at ten a.m. on Monday.

"Ernest, the medication I gave you will control your high blood pressure, but you also need to start walking about twenty minutes daily, and lose at least twenty pounds. But the best thing you can do is to retire and move away."

"Retire? Why?" Ernest asked.

"To reduce your level of stress."

"Okay, but why should we leave the Napa Valley?"

"Because as long as you live here, you won't really retire. You'll stay involved in some way with the wine business, and the stress from that will continue to create health problems for you. That's not only my opinion, it's also the opinion of Dr. Smuckler."

"The famous heart surgeon at Johns Hopkins?" Jane asked. Jane knew of him because her son-in-law, Daryl, had trained with him at Stanford.

"That's him. We did our residencies together and have remained in contact over the years." He then turned back to Ernest.

"You can try to ignore our advice if you want, Ernest, but if you do, you will have another heart attack, and this one will probably kill you.

THE WINE QUEEN

Ann was at a meeting at the Wine Institute in San Francisco and didn't return home until Monday night. The next morning, Ernest told her about his heart attack and the doctor's advice to retire.

"Oh no. Just as our wines are gaining national prominence."

"Well, that's my reality, and I've accepted it. Jane and I have talked it over and discussed it with Cathy and Daryl. We'd like to sell Columbia Creek Winery, the vineyards, and this house to you, if you'd like to buy them."

"Yes, I would very much," Ann replied, as she thought, *Now I can try my ideas to grow this business.* "Do you have a price in mind?"

"What were our last three years' average profits?"

"About a million dollars a year."

"So a ten multiple would give a value of ten million dollars. I think ten million[14] for the winery and vineyards plus another seventy-five thousand[15] for the house and guest house would work for us."

"I think that's fair. Can you give me a couple of weeks to work out the financing?"

"Of course."

"Global Soft Drink company, executive offices," a female voice said when Ann called.

"This is Ann Collins. I would like to speak to George Martin."

"Mr. Martin's office," another female voice said when Ann had been transferred.

"This is Ann Collins, I used to work for Geor.."

"Hi, Ann. This is Donna Casper," Ann's secretary when she worked at GSDC said when she greeted her.

"Donna! How have you been?"

"Great. And you?"

"Never better. I would like to talk to George, if I can."

---

[14] The same as $76.9 million in 2014.
[15] The same as $576,411 in 2014.

"He's in a meeting, but I will have him call you. I don't know if you've heard, but George was promoted to executive vice-president and chief financial officer. He replaced Harry Davis after Harry was killed in that accident.

"Yes, George called when he was promoted and told me."

An hour later Ann got a phone call. "Ann, this is George returning your call," he said.

"Hey, George. How have you been?" After they had exchanged pleasantries, Ann said, "George, my boss, Ernest Rossi, is retiring and wants to sell Columbia Creek Winery. And I want to buy it."

"How long has it been since you started working there?" "I started in September of 1959 as their Chief Financial Officer, so I have been here five years."

"As smart as you are, I'm sure you thoroughly understand the business."

"Yes, I do. I'm looking for an investor. Would GSDC be interested in owning a minority share, say a third?"

"Possibly. Could you send me a proposal? Include the last five years of financials, and a projection of revenues, costs, and profits for each of the next three years."

"Okay. I'll get it in the mail to you tomorrow afternoon, so you should have it to review on Monday. I'll also include some of my ideas to grow the business."

"Ann, George Martin," he said when he called Ann a little after four p.m. the following Monday.

"Did you get the proposal?"

"Yeah, great job. I just discussed it with our mergers and acquisitions group, and we are interested in becoming a minority partner. We really like your ideas about growing this business and would like a thirty-five percent interest. Can you come to Memphis on Thursday to discuss it?"

"My next call will be to the airline."

"Ann, this is Chris Cohen, the head of our M&A group; Tom Snyder, our treasurer; and Gloria West, our vice-president of strategic planning," George told her as he introduced her to the group just after two p.m. on Thursday afternoon.

"Excellent proposal, Ann," Chris said.

"I concur," said Gloria. "I also like your plans to grow this business. Did you share them with Ernest Rossi?"

"Yeah, a few years ago, but he ..."

"He didn't like them because he is resistant to change and risks," George interrupted.

"I think you are correct," Ann replied. "But I think the risk of implementing these ideas is minimal and the potential is enormous. If you think about it, the population in the United States is mostly Europeans. Most of our ancestors came here from Europe. That suggests that our tastes in wine will follow that in Europe, once we become more experienced as wine drinkers. Currently, US per capita consumption of wine is 3.7 liters, just under a gallon, and only a fourth that of Europe's. Even if we can grow US wine consumption to half that of Europe, it would double the size of the market."

"I agree," George replied. "That's enormous growth potential."

"Also, the seventy-six million post World War II baby boomers who are now consuming soft drinks will soon be getting old enough to consume alcoholic beverages. They are now forty-six percent of our population," Ann explained.

"Considering the potential for per capita US wine consumption to grow as large, or almost as large, as it is in Europe, and adding a potential seventy-six million new wine drinkers to that, makes the possibilities mind-boggling," Gloria added.

"The wine business is also a perfect strategic fit, because it enables GSDC to broaden its beverage base by moving into a business that can capitalize on changing demographics, tastes, and preferences that will likely be brought about by the baby boom generation, who are a large and growing share of its consumers," George pointed out.

"At a purchase price of ten million, thirty-five percent equity would be three-and-a-half million. Do you know where you're going to borrow the remaining six-and-a-half?" Tom asked.

"Not really. I was thinking maybe an insurance company that makes loans to agriculture, such as Prudential."

"We have a good relationship with Morgan Stanley and can probably help you get a very competitive interest rate," Tom explained.

"Great. What are our next steps?" Ann asked.

GSDC's board approved the $3.5 million investment in Columbia Creek Winery. With their assistance, Ann was able to secure a $6.5 million ten-year loan from Morgan Stanley at an interest rate of 4.5 percent. The closing on the purchase of Columbia Creek Winery was at Morgan Stanley's offices in New York City on February 12, 1965.

Ernest and Jane bought a house in Sarasota, Florida and moved there in March. Ann sold her house in Napa and used the proceeds of the sale, plus another $10 thousand of her own funds, as a down payment on Ernest's house. She financed the remaining $49 thousand through the Napa Savings and Loan, and in April, she, Tommy, and Jesse moved into the five-bedroom stone house at the winery.

"Boys, would you like to go to New York City and see a Broadway play?" Ann asked her sons as they were all having breakfast on a Sunday in May of 1965.

"That could be fun," Tommy replied. "We've never been to a city as big as New York, so it would be an opportunity for us to experience that for the first time."

"Could we also go see the Statue of Liberty?" Jesse asked.

"Yes, and I thought we'd also go see a comedian, and enjoy some gourmet dining," Ann explained.

"How long would we be there?" Tommy asked.

"Probably three days and two nights, but let me put a schedule together.

"Okay, here's the schedule I've put together," Ann began after they'd finished dinner on Monday night. "We'll see *The Glass Menagerie* at the Brooks Atkinson Theater on Broadway Friday night, June 18. On Saturday morning, we'll tour the Statue of Liberty and have lunch at the Four Seasons. I don't have anything scheduled yet for Saturday afternoon. On Saturday night, we'll see comedian Lenny Allen perform at the Copacabana nightclub. On Sunday, I've planned for us to attend the Park Avenue Methodist Church, and after church, we'll go to a baseball game at Yankee Stadium. We'll have dinner at Lacoste Basque, a gourmet French restaurant. We'll return home on Monday. What do you think?"

"Who are the Yankees playing?" Jesse asked.

"The Minnesota Twins. The game starts at three o'clock," Ann replied.

"Great! I've always wanted to go to a baseball game at Yankee Stadium," Jesse said.

"I have an idea for Saturday afternoon," Tommy said. "Let's go shopping at Abercrombie & Fitch."

"What's Abercrombie & Fitch?" Jesse asked.

"A store that specializes in high quality fishing tackle and casual wear," Tommy replied.

"I'm glad you thought of that, Tommy. I've always wanted to see their line of outdoor clothing for women."

"It sounds like we're going to be busy having fun and doing interesting things," Tommy added.

Their plane arrived at LaGuardia Airport in New York at 1:35 p.m. on Friday, June 18. After retrieving their luggage, Ann and the boys were waiting in line for a taxi. "The next one's ours,

Mom," Tommy said as the next yellow cab pulled up in front of them.

"Waldorf Astoria," Ann said as the cab pulled away from the curb.

A short while later, they arrived at the hotel. "Welcome to the Waldorf," the bellman said as he loaded their luggage onto a cart. "How long will you be staying with us?"

"Until Monday," Jesse replied.

As they entered the expansive lobby, they all were awestruck by the elegance. A large gold and crystal chandelier hung from the ceiling in the center of the lobby, and a spiral staircase descended from the second floor. On the marble floor, under the chandelier, was a large circular art deco mosaic. Dominating the lobby was an ornately carved bronze clock set on an octagonal base made from marble and mahogany and topped with a Statute of Liberty. A small plaque below the clock read, "The Waldorf Astoria Clock was made by the Goldsmith Company of London for exhibition at the Chicago World's Fair in 1893. It weighs approximately two tons and stands nine feet tall. Around the eight sides of its base are likenesses of seven American Presidents - Cleveland, Harrison, Washington, Grant, Lincoln, Franklin, Jackson - and Queen Victoria. Under these are bronze plaques depicting various sports scenes. Westminster chimes ring on the quarter hour." Along the sides of the lobby were upholstered chairs that looked like giant seashells, massive square black marble columns, and big vases of potpourri on square, gilt-edged coffee tables. Allegorical murals lined the walls, and a massive Art Deco-inspired light fixture hugged the ceiling.

"Do you have a reservation?" the check-in clerk asked when Ann went to the front desk. Tommy and Jesse continued to explore the lobby.

"Yes, Ann Collins. We have two rooms for tonight, Saturday, and Sunday nights."

"Yes, I have it right here. How many are in your party?"

"Myself and my two sons. Could we get adjoining rooms?"

"Yes, we can accommodate that. Here's a map of the hotel. Will you be seeing a play during your stay with us?"

"Yes, we're seeing *The Glass Menagerie* tonight at seven."

"That's at the Brooks Atkinson Theater, which is only a five-minute cab ride from here. If you haven't made dinner plans, I would suggest our Bull and Bear Steakhouse. They have a theater menu served from five until six o'clock."

"That sounds good. Can you make a reservation for us for five o'clock?"

"Sure. Your rooms are on the ninth floor, and the elevators are over there," he said, pointing. "I'll have a bellman bring up your luggage."

"Mom, this is the nicest place I've ever seen!" Jesse said as they got into the elevator.

"Yeah, thanks for bringing us," Tommy added.

"You're more than welcome. I just wanted us to experience the glamor and excitement of New York City."

"Dad said once that you used to work in New York while you were in college," Tommy said.

"That's right. I was a fashion model during the summers."

"Did you ever stay in this hotel?" Jesse asked.

"No, I had an apartment."

The bellman with their luggage arrived at their rooms at the same time they did and he opened Ann's room with her key. The deluxe room had floor-length curtains and densely patterned carpeting. It also had a wood desk, an upholstered chair, matching bedside tables and a cherry wood dresser. There was a TV on a wooden table. The cream-hued, marble-tiled bathroom had a tub-shower combo and a pedestal sink. The boys' room was the same, but with two double beds instead of a queen. Both rooms had a view of Park Avenue.

"Would you like me to bring you some ice?" the bellman asked as Ann was tipping him.

"No, we're fine," Ann replied. She then turned to Tommy and Jesse. "Boys, it's just after three o'clock. The play starts at seven, but we need to be there thirty minutes early because there will probably be a line to get in. We are only about a five-minute cab ride away. We have dinner reservations at the Bull and Bear Steakhouse for five. So let's unpack and relax. I'll knock on your door at four forty-five. Remember, we need to dress up tonight."

When Ann knocked on their door at four forty-five, Jesse opened it. "Ready?" asked Ann.

"Yep," Tommy replied.

While they were waiting on the elevator, Ann looked at Tommy and Jesse. She hadn't seen them in suits since she and Ray had gotten married. When they dressed up for church, and other occasions they had worn blazers and ties. She'd bought them suits for this trip, a gray one for Tommy and a blue one for Jesse, and both looked handsome in them. Tommy was growing into manhood, and looked a lot like Ray. He was just over six feet tall now, with black wavy hair, inquisitive brown eyes, broad shoulders, and a lean, muscular build, evidence that he lifted weights and played football for Napa High. He had an infectious grin that had caused female hearts to spontaneously flutter since he was thirteen. Jesse was not as tall, about five ten, slender, and somewhat favored his birth mother. He had blond hair, crystal-blue eyes, and was not as outgoing as his brother. He played baseball for Napa High. Both boys were very smart and hard working. In spite of working Saturdays at Columbia Creek Winery, as well as participating in athletics, both made straight As. Tommy, who would enter his senior year at Napa High in September, had decided to pursue a degree in chemical engineering at the University of California at Davis, fifty-five miles from where they lived.

"Mom, the elevator's here," Jesse said as a soft *bong* preceded the twin doors sliding open.

"What were you thinking so hard about?" Tommy asked Ann.

"How proud I am of both of you."

"Thanks, Mom. We're glad you're our mother," Jesse said.

"We sure are," Tommy added.

As they entered the Bull and Bear Steakhouse, the uniformed maître d' met them. "Ann Collins, reservations for three at five."

"Yes, ma'am, please follow me."

The dimly lit room had rectangular tables with white table cloths, water and wine glasses made of crystal, and china dinnerware with silver utensils. Autographed photos of famous movie stars and past American presidents adorned the walls.

After the family was seated, a uniformed waiter walked up. "I'm Tony, and I will be serving you this evening. May I bring you something to drink?"

"Yes. I'll have water with lemon, and I'd also like to see your wine list," Ann replied.

"I'd like a Coke," Tommy said.

"So would I," added Jesse.

"Mom, this is a very nice restaurant," Tommy observed after the waiter had left.

"It looks like a lot of famous people ate here," Jesse added

"I agree," Ann replied.

"I take it you asked for their wine list to see if they offer any of our wines," Tommy said.

"Yeah."

"Our wine list," Tony said as he handed it to Ann. It was divided into wines by the bottle and those by the glass. There was a Chardonnay and a Cabernet Sauvignon from Columbia Creek Winery, both by the glass and by the bottle.

"I will have a glass of the Columbia Creek Chardonnay," Ann told him.

"That's an excellent choice. The Columbia Creek Chardonnay and Cabernet Sauvignon are our most popular wines."

"I'm glad to hear that, because we own the winery," Ann replied.

"Really? Well, you produce some excellent wines."

After their drinks had been served, Tony then asked, "Are you ready to order?"

"I am," Ann replied.

"We are, too," Tommy said.

"What will you have, ma'am?"

"The Waldorf salad, roasted half chicken, mashed potatoes, and steamed broccoli."

"What's a Waldorf salad?" Jesse asked.

"It's a salad consisting of candied walnuts, slices of apple, celery, and mayonnaise served on a bed of lettuce. It was first served here at the Waldorf in 1896," Tony explained. "And what will you have sir?" he then asked Tommy.

"I also want the Waldorf salad, with the beef tournedos crusted with blue cheese, a baked potato with butter and sour cream, and mixed vegetables," Tommy replied.

"How would you like your steak prepared, sir?"

"Medium."

Tony then looked at Jesse. "And for you sir?"

"I'll have the same thing my brother is, but I want my beef cooked medium rare, and I want béarnaise sauce on it."

After they had finished their superb meal and the bus boy was clearing the table, Ann said, "It's only five forty-five. Would you boys like to order dessert?"

"Sure," Tommy replied.

Ann signaled to Tony, and he brought over three dessert menus. "We'd like to order dessert and coffee," Ann said. "But only if we can be ready to leave at six thirty."

"We are going to see *The Glass Menagerie*," Tommy said.

"If you order something we don't have to prepare, like the New York cheesecake, I can have you out of here by then," Tony explained.

"You okay with that, boys?" Ann asked.

"Yeah," both said at once.

"Then it's three orders of New York cheesecake, with fresh raspberries," Ann instructed Tony.

"Mom, I think that was the best meal I've ever had," Tommy observed as they rode in a cab toward the Brooks Atkinson Theater.

"I agree," Jesse added.

"I'm glad you enjoyed it. Now it's on to our next adventure!" Ann said as the cab pulled up to the curb in front of the theater.

A neon sign above the entrance to the theater said: *The Glass Menagerie, a play by Tennessee Williams, starring Eddie Dowling, Laurette Taylor, Julie Haydon, and Anthony Ross. Directed by John Tiffany, now through October 21.*

The three of them walked into the huge carpeted lobby and got in line to find their seats. The lobby had a concessions area where soft drinks, alcoholic beverages, candy, and sandwiches were available. They soon entered the theater, where hundreds of people were finding their seats among row upon row of red folding seats.

"How many people can this place hold?" Tommy asked as they were waiting for an usher to take them to their seats.

"Over a thousand," Ann replied.

"Wow!" exclaimed Jesse.

"Ma'am, I can seat your party now," the uniformed usher said as he walked up. Ann handed him their tickets. "Seats one twelve, one thirteen, and one fourteen; the first three seats in the fifth row," the usher said.

The room soon grew dark and as the curtain rose, the audience was faced with the dark, grim rear wall of the Wingfield tenement during the 1930s depression. This building, which ran parallel to the footlights, was flanked on both sides by dark, narrow alleys that ran into murky canyons of tangled clothes lines, garbage cans, and the sinister lattice-work of neighboring fire escapes. It was up and down these alleys that exterior entrances and exits would be made during the play. At the end of Tom Wingfield's opening commentary, the dark tenement wall slowly revealed - by means of a transparency - the interior of the ground floor of the Wingfield apartment. Soon Ann and the boys were absorbed by the story.

"Do you want to get something from the concession stand?" Ann asked during the first intermission.

"I'd like a Coke," Tommy said.

"Me, too," Jesse added.

"And I'll have white wine," Ann said as she got up to go.

"I can go, Mom," Tommy offered.

"Thanks, Tommy. But I doubt if they'll let you buy the wine."

After the play ended, the three of them left the theater amid the crowd of people. "Well, what did you think of the play?" Ann asked as they were in a cab heading back to their hotel.

"I thought it was depressing," Tommy said. "The poverty during the depression, their dingy apartment, Tom's nagging mother, him being forced to stay in a job he hated."

"I agree," Jesse added. "And Tom's sister, Laura. Too shy to get a boyfriend, and too insecure to go to college or get a job."

"But I didn't like it that Tom abandoned his mother and sister. They were his responsibility," Tommy said.

"I agree with what both of you think about the play," Ann replied. "But unfortunately, it's reality. Most families were very poor during the depression and many men abandoned their families. Amanda in this play reminded me of my Aunt Harriett, who was a nagging witch to my Uncle Dave."

THE WINE QUEEN

At nine thirty the next morning, they all took a boat from Battery Park to the Statue of Liberty on Ellis Island. Ann had secured Crown tickets, which enabled them to visit the crown of the statue, the pedestal, the museum, and the Fort Wood level. Access to the crown was by stairs only, no elevators. But since both boys were high school athletes, and Ann jogged regularly, they had no trouble climbing the 377 steps to the crown.

"Did you enjoy the Statue of Liberty tour?" Ann asked later while they were having lunch at the Four Seasons restaurant.

"Yeah," Jesse replied as he took a bite of his crab cake sandwich. "But I didn't think we'd ever make it to the top. Those stairs were endless."

"I liked the view of New York City," Tommy added before taking a large bite of his grilled red snapper. "But why did France give the Statue of Liberty to America?"

"In recognition of the friendship established during the American Revolution," Ann replied, buttering a yeast roll. "France fought alongside the US against Britain in the Revolutionary War. French money, munitions, soldiers, and naval forces were essential to America's victory over Great Britain and to America winning her independence," Ann explained.

"It seems to me we should have given France a Statue of Liberty instead of France giving it to us," Jesse said as he dipped a French fry in ketchup.

"But we have been an important ally to France. In fact, we liberated them during World War II," Tommy added, taking a forkful of rice from his plate.

That afternoon they went shopping at Abercrombie & Fitch. When the store announced that their weekly fly-fishing lesson would start in fifteen minutes, Ann, Tommy, and Jesse decided to take the one-hour lesson. After it was over, they all decided to take up fly-fishing, and bought fly rods, reels, and flies with which to fish. Ann also bought a pair of khaki shorts and a blue Polo shirt.

"I'll have an egg roll, and the moo goo gai pan," Ann told the waitress that night at the Copa Cabana nightclub. Ann and the boys were seated at a round table with a candle in the center in the dimly lit club. It was almost seven thirty p.m. and they were ordering dinner before Lenny Allen's comedy routine was scheduled to start at eight o'clock.

"What's in the Happy Family?" Jesse asked their waitress

"Jumbo shrimp, crab meat, sliced pork, beef, chicken, lobster meat and vegetables in a brown sauce."

"Okay. I'll have that."

"Me, too," Tommy added. "I never thought that a New York night club would have Chinese food for dinner."

"Our guests really like our Chinese food," the waitress replied.

"Ladies and Gentlemen, Mr. LENNY ALLEN!" the announcer bellowed a while later after Ann and the boys had finished eating. The band played a drum-roll and the comedian strode onto the stage. There was loud applause and a few whistles from the audience.

"In the world of romance, one single rule applies: make the woman happy. Do something she likes and you get points. Do something she dislikes and you lose points. You don't get any points for doing anything she expects. That's the way the game is played. Here is a guide to this point system:

SIMPLE DUTIES

You make the bed – gain one point.

You throw the bedspread over rumpled sheets – lose one point.

You go out and buy her what she wants - gain five points; in the rain – gain eight points; but return with beer – lose five points.

You check out a suspicious noise at night – gain one point; it is nothing – no points; it is something – gain five points; You pummel it with an iron rod – gain ten points; it's her pet – lose 20 points.

SOCIAL ENGAGEMENTS

You take her to a party and stay by her side the entire time – no points; you stay by her side for a while. Then leave to chat with an old school friend – lose two points; named Tina – lose 10 points; Tina is a dancer – lose 20 points.

A NIGHT OUT

You take her to a movie – gain one point; it's a movie that she likes – gain three points; you take her to a movie you hate – gain six points; you take her to a movie you like – lose two points; it's called "Death Cop" lose three points; you lied and said it was a foreign film about orphans – lose 15 points.

YOUR PHYSIQUE

You develop a noticeable pot-belly – lose 15 points; you exercise to get rid of it – gain ten points; you develop a noticeable pot-belly and resort to baggy jeans and baggy Hawaiian shirts – lose thirty points; you say, "It doesn't matter, you have one too" – lose 8,000 points.

COMMUNICATION

When she wants to talk about a problem, you listen displaying what looks like a concerned expression – no points; you listen for over thirty minutes – gain fifty points; without looking at the TV – gain 500 points; she realizes this is because you have fallen asleep – lose 4,000 points.

And you ladies thought the guys didn't understand you."

The audience is roaring with laughter, as are Ann, Tommy and Jesse.

"Curtis and Leroy saw an ad in the local newspaper advertising a mule for sale. They subsequently bought the mule for a hundred dollars, and the farmer agreed to deliver the mule the next day.

"The next morning the farmer drove up and said, 'Sorry fellers, I have some bad news, the mule died last night.'"

"Curtis and Leroy said, 'Well, then just give us our money back.'

"The farmer said, 'Can't do that. I spent it already.'

"Okay, then just bring us the dead mule."

"What in the world ya'll gonna do with a dead mule?" the farmer asked.

"Curtis said, 'We're gonna raffle him off.'

"The farmer said, 'You can't raffle off a dead mule!'

"Leroy said, 'We shore can! Heck, we don't hafta tell nobody he's dead.'

"A couple of weeks later, the farmer ran into Curtis and Leroy at the grocery store and asked, 'What'd you fellers ever do with that dead mule?'

"Curtis said, 'We raffled him off like we said we wuz gonna do.'

"Leroy said, 'Shucks, we sold five hundred tickets fer two dollars apiece and made a profit of $998.'

"The farmer said, 'My lord. Didn't anyone complain?'

"Curtis said, 'Well, the feller who won the dead mule got upset. So we gave him his two dollars back.'

"Curtis and Leroy now work for the government."

"There comes a time when a woman just has to trust her husband. For example, a wife comes home late at night and quietly opens the door to her bedroom. From under the blanket she sees four legs instead of two. She reaches for a baseball bat and starts hitting the blanket as hard as she can. Once she's done, she goes to the kitchen to have a drink. As she enters, she sees her husband there, reading a magazine. 'Hi darling,' he says. 'Your parents have come to visit us, so I let them stay in our bedroom. Did you say hello?'

"Little Larry attended a horse auction with his father. He watched as his father moved from horse to horse, running his hands up and down the horse's legs, rump, and chest. After a few minutes, Larry asked, 'Dad, why are you doing that?'

'Because when I'm buying horses, I have to make sure that they are healthy and in good shape before I buy.'

"Larry, looking worried, said, 'Dad, I think the mailman wants to buy Mom.'"

The audience roars with laughter again.

Tommy was laughing so hard he was coughing, and Ann was laughing so hard tears were running from her eyes. Jesse's laughter had given him the hiccups.

"Let's sleep in tomorrow morning," Ann suggested once they were back at their hotel. "We need to be at church at eleven, so I'll knock on your door at nine forty-five for breakfast."

"Yankee Stadium," Ann told the taxi driver on Sunday afternoon just after two p.m.

When they entered the massive stadium along with thousands of fans, Ann turned to her sons, "Boys, let's stay close together so we won't get separated in this crowd."

"Mom, can we get a hot dog and Coke?"

"Yeah. Since we haven't had lunch, I'm hungry," Jesse added.

"Okay, but let's find our seats first," Ann suggested. "According to this, they are on the field level in Section one twenty-five, row sixteen."

"Here they are, Mom," Jesse said after they navigated their way through the stadium.

"It's almost fifteen minutes until the game starts, so how about if Jesse and I go get drinks and hot dogs for us?" Tommy suggested.

"Great. I just want a hot dog and a Coke," Ann replied.

A little while later, the boys came back and Jesse handed Ann her food and drink. "Here, Mom. I wasn't sure what you wanted on your hot dog, so I put mustard and relish on it."

"That's fine."

"Strike three, you're OUT," the umpire yelled later, after the game had started. The New York Yankees went to the field as the Minnesota Twins came in to bat.

The first player came up to bat. *CRACK!* The ball sailed into the air and, before the batter made it to first base, it was caught by the Yankees shortstop. The next batter for the Twins came to the plate. After two strikes, he slightly changed his position. Then came the pitch. *CRACK!* This time the ball sailed over the center fielder and into the stands as Tony Oliva trotted around the bases for a home run.

The final score was the Twins – 7 and the Yankees – 4, with the game ending at 5:13 p.m.

"That was fun, Mom," Jesse said as they rode back to their hotel.

"Yeah, that pitcher for the Twins threw four no-hit innings," Tommy said.

"That was Dave Boswell," Jesse added. "He signed with the Twins last year for fifteen thousand dollars, even though the Yankees offered him the same amount to sign with them."

After they got back to their rooms, Ann told the boys, "Our dinner reservations are at seven. Since the restaurant is only about half a mile from here, I thought we'd walk."

"Suits again?" Tommy asked.

"Yep. Let's leave here at six thirty."

The restaurant had a brown awning out front, with a red carpet under it that led to a formidable oak door with the words *LaCôte Basque* on a brass plate in the center. Inside, large chandeliers hung from the high oak ceilings and a brown-and-red-patterned carpet covered the floor. White table cloths, cut-crystal water and wine glasses, china, and silverware sat on tables, that each had four leather chairs.

"May I see your wine list?" Ann asked the waiter who had brought them their menus and filled their water glasses.

"Of course, madam."

"I've never heard of most of the items on this menu, but it looks like it will be good,"

Tommy said.

A little while later, when the waiter returned, Ann told him, "I'll have a glass of the Beringer Cabernet."

"Jesse and I will have Cokes," Tommy said. "A Beringer Cabernet? Checking out the competition, huh, Mom?"

"You'd better believe it."

The waiter brought their drinks and said, "I'll go over our menu now if you'd like."

"Yes, please do," Ann replied.

"Tonight appetizers are crab and lobster-stuffed mushrooms, bacon-wrapped dates stuffed with blue cheese, Thai banana leaves with meatball stuffing, avocados stuffed with gorgonzola cheese and walnuts, Cantonese-style pork and shrimp dumplings, and our signature appetizer – Maine lobster cocktail. It consists of fresh Maine lobster tossed in citrus mayonnaise, with micro greens, avocado, mango, and potato gaufrettes.

"What are potato gaufrettes?" Jesse asked.

"Wafers of crisp fried potato cut to resemble a small waffle," the waiter replied.

"Our entrees include paillard of sea bass with citrus avocado and tomato, caviar, and hearts of palm ceviche. Ceviche is a seafood dish spiced with chili peppers and onions. Our other dishes are roasted squab with pheasant ravioli and red beets; pepper-seared buffalo tenderloin with jasmine rice grits, broccoli, and fig chutney; potato-wrapped snapper with celery root crush, and slivered garlic tomato fondue; and pepper-seared rib-eye Wagyu beef with green pea risotto, garlic butter, and steamed broccoli."

"What is Wagyu beef?" Tommy asked.

"It comes from Japan, and is beef from exceptionally well-fed steers that have beer added to their feeding regime and are massaged daily. The beef is highly marbled and very flavorful," the waiter replied. "Next is butter-poached Maine lobster with lemongrass essence and wild rice. For dessert, there's a Grand Marnier soufflé, the Florentine cookie tower with raspberry compote, and almond lace filled with marinated strawberries and lemon cream marzipan twig."

"I'll have the crab and lobster-stuffed mushrooms for my appetizer, the poached Maine lobster, and Grand Marnier soufflé for dessert," Ann said.

"I want the Maine lobster cocktail, Wagyu beef cooked medium, and the Florentine cookie tower," Tommy said.

"I'll also have the Maine lobster cocktail, and the buffalo tenderloin medium rare, and Florentine cookie tower," Jesse said.

"Well, now that you've experienced New York City, what do you think?" Ann asked the boys when they were on their way to the airport the next morning.

"It's definitely an exciting place, with lots of things that are fun to do. And the gourmet dining is superb. But I wouldn't want to live there," Tommy said. "It's too crowded and everything is too expensive."

"I agree," Jesse added. "I enjoyed everything we did, especially the ball game, the play, and the comedian. But I'll be glad to get back home."

"My thoughts as well," Ann added.

Chapter Eighteen

"Loretta? It's Ann Collins," she said when her Uncle Dave's wife answered the phone. It was Monday, July 12, 1965.

"Hi Ann, how have you been?"

"Great. I've bought Columbia Creek Winery!"

"What? Did the Rossis' sell it to you?"

"Yes, Ernest retired and moved to Florida and now I own the winery and its vineyards. I need a chief financial officer since I no longer have time to do that job. Are you interested?"

"As a matter of fact, I am."

"Are you still with the CFO for the Rayonier Timber Company?"

"Yeah, for the past four years. But I'm ready for a change. I'm bored with my job, and Dave recently retired and turned the law firm over to your old boyfriend, Eric Carver."

"Eric is an attorney, now?"

"Yep, law school at Notre Dame. And he's now the senior partner at your uncle's law firm."

"Eric must have changed, and improved his morals."

"He became religious while he was in college. After he graduated from law school, he married a girl from a well-to-do family in Atlanta, Ruth Muller. She's also very religious, and a graduate of Agnes Scott College.

"Dave wants to move away from Macon, and I'll agree if I can find a job. I'm only fifty and not ready to retire."

"When could you and Uncle Dave come to Napa? We have a five-bedroom house and plenty of room, so you can stay with us."

"I'll check with Dave and see, but this weekend works for me."

"Great. Unless I hear otherwise, I will be expecting you and Uncle Dave this Friday night. You'll need to fly into San Francisco, which is about an hour-and-a-half from here. I'll have Tommy meet your flight. Just let me know your flight schedule when you have it."

"This is a very nice house," Loretta said as she and Dave entered the foyer just after six p.m. on that Friday. "When was it built?"

"Ernest and Jane Rossi built it in 1948, two years after they moved here," Ann replied.

"Mom, do you want me to take their luggage up to their room?" Tommy asked.

"Yes, please," Ann replied.

"I'll help you, Tommy," Dave offered.

"Do you play football?" Dave asked as he and Tommy ascended the stairs to one of the guest rooms.

"I play quarterback for the Napa High Indians. I'm going to apply to UC – Davis next year, and I hope I'll get an opportunity to play for the Aggies."

"You look athletic, so I figured you played football," Dave observed. "Does your brother also play?"

"Jesse plays baseball. He's a pitcher."

"What do you plan to major in at UC-Davis?"

"Chemical engineering."

"That's a difficult major, but as smart as your mother says you are, I'm sure you'll do well."

"We'll have some wine and cheese with sourdough bread while Jenny's finishing dinner," Ann told them once the group had reassembled.

"This wine is excellent," Loretta said as she took another sip of their Chardonnay.

"So is this wine," Dave observed, taking a sip of the Columbia Creek Cabernet Sauvignon.

"Those two wines were voted the best in America at the 1964 Grand Harvest Awards wine competition in San Francisco on October 24," Ann replied.

"Wow! They certainly merit an award like that," Dave said.

"My plan is to give both of you a tour of our vineyards and winery in the morning, then I'll go over our financial information with Loretta tomorrow afternoon. Uncle Dave, if you'd like, Tommy will take you bass fishing while Loretta and I are going over the books."

"That would be great. It's been years since I went bass fishing. Jesse, are you coming with us?"

"No, I'm going to spend the night at a friend's house tomorrow."

"Well, are you interested in the job?" Ann asked Loretta after they had toured the vineyards and winery and gone over the financial records.

"Yes, if we can agree on compensation."

"I was thinking it would be the same pay and benefits as I had in that job. A base salary of twenty-eight thousand dollars[16], plus a twenty-five percent bonus tied to the performance of the business. Three weeks paid vacation, nine paid holidays, health insurance, and life insurance equal to twice your base salary. We will also reimburse you the closing costs for selling your house, the cost of moving your furniture and personal belongings in a moving van, and the closing costs for the house you buy in Napa."

---

[16] The same as $211,778 in 2014.

"You have your new CFO!" Loretta replied.

"Great! When can you start?"

"In three weeks."

"That will be on Monday, August 9."

Later that night, just after midnight, Ann heard a noise coming from the kitchen. After putting on her robe, she went to see what it was. "Uncle Dave?"

"Hey, Ann. I couldn't stop thinking about Jenny's superb blueberry pie, so I came down to get another slice," he explained as he poured himself a glass of milk.

"I'm glad you like it," Ann replied as she joined him at the kitchen table.

"Ann, I am very proud of you," he said. "You've been a terrific success at everything you've done. You survived the Harriett and Blanche years without ever openly losing your temper; introduced me to Loretta, the love of my life; excelled in college and graduate school; didn't marry until you found Ray, your true soul mate; dealt with his death bravely and responsibly; have been a loving and responsible mother to Tommy and Jesse; and now own your own successful business. I wish your mother and father could have seen what a wonderful woman their daughter has become. They would have been extremely proud as well."

"Thanks, Uncle Dave. I couldn't have survived the Harriett and Blanche years as well as I did without your help and support. And you were a great role model for me when I was growing up. You instilled in me the drive to be successful."

The next morning at breakfast, Ann asked her uncle, "What time is your flight out?"

"Eleven forty-five," Dave replied.

"Okay. Let's plan to leave for the airport in half an hour, at nine fifteen," Ann suggested.

"Wine Institute," a female voice answered when Ann called the next Monday morning. "How may I help you?"

"This is Ann Collins. I'd like to speak to your executive director, Ken Gunter." There was a pause while the receptionist connected Ann with Ken.

"Ken, this is Ann Collins at the Columbia Creek Winery."

"Hi Ann. How can I help you?"

"Now that Ernest has retired and moved to Florida, I'm looking for a head winemaker to replace him. I would prefer someone with a degree in enology and at least ten years of experience."

"I think I know someone who would be perfect for that job. His name is Ed Peterson. He completed his college education at the University of California at Davis. He has been the number two winemaker at Beringer for nine years. But since Todd Beringer is the head winemaker and also owns the company, Ed can't advance to head winemaker. I'll have him contact you if you'd like."

"That would be great, thanks."

"Ann Collins," she said as she answered her phone that afternoon.

"This is Ed Peterson. Ken Gunter at the Wine Institute said you wanted to talk to me about a job."

"That's right. When could you come for an interview?"

"How about Wednesday morning at nine?"

"That works for me. I'll see you then.

"One more thing, I want this kept confidential," Ed requested.

"No problem."

"Mrs. Collins, Mr. Peterson is here for his nine o'clock meeting," Ann's secretary, Jonell, said the day of their meeting.

"Okay, send him in."

After she and Ed had exchanged pleasantries. Ann started the interview. "Tell me about yourself."

Ed stood just over six feet, had dark brown hair and hazel eyes, and a calm, pleasant expression on his face.

"I grew up in Napa and graduated from Napa High," he began. "I worked summers in the Beringer vineyards and winery while I was going to the University of California at Davis. I graduated with a bachelor's degree in viticulture in 1950 and a master's degree in Enology in 1952. My master's thesis was about changes in wine chemistry during production, and wine drinkability as a function of aging time in bottles. It also developed a practical method for planning the optimum times of bottle aging, both before and after shipment from the winery. It won the *Outstanding Thesis Award at UC – Davis* in 1952. I have been the Director of Winemaking at Beringer for the past nine years, but can't be promoted because Todd Beringer is the head winemaker. So I'm ready to move on."

"In 1960, we reduced the portion of Merlot in our Bordeaux, planted more Merlot, and also planted Sauvignon Blanc. Since then we have made a varietal Merlot out of the grapes not being used in the Bordeaux. We age each Merlot for three years in oak, and they are still being bottle aged. We are currently using our new plantings of Merlot and Sauvignon Blanc as blending grapes, but I want to make varietal wines out of them. How do you feel about that?"

"Just after prohibition, when the wine-drinking public was small and more sophisticated, Sauvignon Blanc was the most popular California varietal wine, even considering red varieties. I would love to make it into a varietal.

"What about Merlot?"

As I'm sure you know, Merlot is the primary variety used in Bordeaux, both here and in France. It is also one of the most popular varietal red wines in Europe. In fact, in the early history of California wine, Merlot was used primarily as a varietal wine, until California winemakers began to encourage taking the grape back to its blending roots with Bordeaux style blends. In my opinion, the problem with most of this industry is that everyone is too risk-averse and set in their ways. Nobody wants to try something new – even if it is a success somewhere else. I believe it's time for a good California varietal Merlot. And I would love the opportunity to make it."

I can see that Ed and I are going to get along very well, Ann thought.

"What would you want as compensation if we hired you?"

"Currently my annual salary is twenty-three thousand dollars. I would like twenty-eight."

"Done. You'll also have a twenty-five percent bonus added to that, based on our profitability. Do you need a moving and relocation reimbursement package?

"No. I live only thirty minutes from here."

"When can you start?"

"The Monday after I give my two weeks' notice, on August 9."

"Good, that's also the same day our new CFO, Loretta Robinson, will start."

"Are you and Uncle Dave settled in yet?" Ann asked Loretta on Friday morning, September 24.

"Yeah, for the most part, Loretta replied. We still have a few things in boxes. That house you helped us find is perfect. It's spacious, has a large back-yard, it's close to shopping, and only twenty minutes from here. Dave is already planning a fall vegetable garden."

"Good. Loretta, I want to discuss a business idea I have."

"Okay."

Ann shared her idea about a generic wine that was higher in quality with a better taste than other generic wines because it would have more grapes from the Napa Valley and the North Coast Counties. "This new line of wines would be called Columbia Creek Cellars," Ann told Loretta.

"In order for consumers to know that it is a higher quality wine, we'll advertise it on national TV and in popular magazines such as *Life* and The *New Yorker*. The advertisements will feature winetasting experts who compare its taste to that of other leading generic wines, and ours will win because of the superior grapes in its blend. Columbia Creek Cellars should also win awards in actual wine contests. Between its advertising and winning awards, I hope that Columbia Creek Cellars will become the nation's best-selling wine."

"That sounds like a good idea to me. Have you discussed this with GSDC?"

"That idea is one of the reasons they bought a thirty five percent interest in our business."

The next day Ann met with Ed and Glen. "Well, what do you think?" she asked after she'd finished discussing her idea about Columbia Creek Cellars.

"We have no extra grape crushing capacity, so we'll need to add a considerable amount of equipment for grape crushing, winemaking, and tanks, and that will be very costly," Ed replied.

"Yeah," Glen agreed.

"We're not going to crush these grapes," Ann said. "I'm going to pay another winery to crush them, and store the wine there until we are ready to bottle it."

"How will you control the quality of the wine if you don't make it?" Glen asked.

"Glen, you're going to buy the grapes for these wines, which as we know is the most important part of making quality wine. Ed's going to put precise winemaking specifications in our contract with this winery. In addition, Ed will visit the other winery monthly to taste our wines. If their flavor deteriorates, we won't be obligated to purchase the wine. That should be more than enough checks, balances and incentives for this other winery to make quality wines for us.

"Any more questions or concerns?"

"No, I believe you've thought of everything," Ed replied.

The next day, Ann called Ken Gunter at The Wine Institute. "Can you tell me which wineries could process our grapes for a fee?"

"There are several. That outbreak of leaf roll a couple of years ago killed a lot of grape vines and reduced the California grape harvest by over twenty percent. Consequently, a number of wineries have excess capacity."

"Ed, here are six wineries that Ken Gunter at the Wine Institute said could be potential processing candidates for us. I would like you to visit each one and give me a recommendation on which one to choose," Ann told him the next morning.

"I'm already familiar with all of these wineries," he said. "My recommendation is Grape-Co. They've been in business for twenty-seven years. I went to college with their winemaker, Scott McBride, and their business is supplying the brands with bulk wines from San Joaquin Valley grapes."

"They sound ideal. Set up a meeting with Scott for you, Loretta, and myself for next Friday."

"Here is our proposal," Ann said as she handed copies of the document to everyone in the meeting the following Friday. Bill Moyer, Grape-Co's CFO, was also in the meeting.

"We will buy grapes from the Central Valley, and Lake, Marin, Mendocino, Solano, Napa and Sonoma counties and deliver them to your winery, according to an agreed upon schedule," Ann began. "We will provide you with specifications for the wines you will make for us. Ed will make several visits while you are processing our grapes, and once the wine made from them is stored, he will conduct monthly inspections of the wines. We will pay you a processing fee thirty days after you have completed processing our grapes. We will then pay you a storage fee thirty days from when we ship the wine to our winery for bottling."

"When would you want us to begin processing for you?" Scott asked.

"Next season. Probably in September of 1966," Ed replied.

"What quantity of grapes will you be sending us?" Scott asked.

"Approximately two thousand tons," Ed replied.

"What will you charge us to process our grapes?" Ann asked.

"Seventeen dollars per ton," Bill replied.

"That's reasonable," Ann replied thinking, *our processing costs are about that.*

"And for wine storage?" Ed asked.

"Half a cent per gallon per month," Bill replied.

"That works for us," Ann said. "I'll have this proposal worded into a contract by our attorney and get a copy to you."

"I have the new Sauvignon Blanc and Merlot for you to try, as well as our oldest Merlot, which has aged in oak for three years, but only bottle aged for two," Ed said as he walked into Ann's office on a Friday morning the following March. "It still needs three to five more years of bottle aging to mellow its tannins. The new Sauvignon Blanc and Merlot are aging in French oak barrels and are too young to judge, but I thought I'd let you try them anyway. I've brought a Chardonnay and Cabernet Sauvignon that were also made from last season's harvest, and so are just as young, for comparison. I also have a Cabernet Sauvignon that has bottle aged only two years for you to compare to our five year old Merlot."

"Great!"

Ed placed six beakers of wine on the round table in Ann's office while she took wine glasses from a closet. "Let's try the Sauvignon Blanc and Chardonnay first," Ann suggested.

Ed poured the wines for each of them. Ann lifted her two glasses toward the florescent light in her office to look at the wines' color. Then she swirled each wine in its glass and smelled it. Next she took a sip of each.

"Ed, this is phenomenal! This Sauvignon Blanc is better than our Chardonnay!"

"Thanks. I agree."

"What are your plans for aging?"

"Same as the Chardonnay in oak - twelve months. Then four years in the bottle, about a year less than the Chardonnay."

"That means it should be at its optimum for the 1971 Los Angeles National Wine Competition."

"My thoughts exactly."

"Okay, now let's try the newest Merlot."

Again, Ann looked at each wine's color, smelled it and tasted it. "This Merlot is also superb! It's every bit as good as the Cabernet!"

"I plan to age it in oak for three years, than in the bottle for five."

"I can't wait to try it when it's at its peak," Ann said, thinking, *if this Merlot ages the way I think it will, I want to enter it in the 1974 Paris Wine Tasting competition.* "Now let's try the five year old Merlot."

Ann repeated the steps she'd followed in evaluating the other wines. "It's excellent. But not as good as the Cabernet Sauvugnon. Why?"

"I'm not sure. But I think it's either that Ernest's heart was not really into making the best Merlot, or the soils it grows on don't produce as good of a Merlot as the soils the new Merlot is grown on."

"Even though the older Merlot is excellent, it's not as good as I think our younger Merlot will be. I don't want to sell it, because it doesn't represent our best Merlot. At the next harvest, blend it into our Bordeaux, and from now on we'll use the Merlot grown on that soil for blending into our Bordeaux like we did before. We'll only make our varietal Merlot from grapes grown on that new twenty-three acres of vineyard."

"Do you want me to go back to the blend Ernest was using before we reduced the portion of Merlot in it?"

"That's up to you. If you like that blend, then go back to it. If not, develop another blend."

"Mom, I just received my acceptance to UC-Davis," Tommy told her as he handed her his letter of acceptance. It was Thursday, April 14, 1966.

"Congratulations, Tommy," Ann replied.

"I've also completed an application for a draft deferment covering the four years I will be in college," he said as he handed her the form.

"That's probably a good idea. Nobody knows what's going to happen in Vietnam, but with the passing of the Gulf of Tonkin Resolution in 1964, and the escalation of conflicts over there, we don't want to risk an interruption in your education."

"George, I'd like to come to Memphis and work with your marketing people on an advertising campaign for Columbia Creek Cellars," Ann said to her partner at GSDC. It was Monday, May 16, 1966.

"Okay. Our vice-president of marketing is Eric Teasley. I'll have Donna transfer you to him."

Eric agreed to help Ann design an advertising campaign. She was scheduled to meet with Eric and his creative director the following Monday.

After several written drafts, the final copy was completed the following Wednesday. Ann would shoot scenes in one of their vineyards and on their bottling line. She would then return to GSDC to put the advertisement together.

The opening scene was Ann walking in a vineyard, sipping white wine from a crystal wineglass. "This is Columbia Creek Cellars, part of our new line of wines. It is made from much higher quality and flavorful grapes than any other Chablis in America." The scene then switched to the bottling line, where Ann was sipping red wine from a crystal wineglass. "This is Columbia Creek Cellars Burgundy, and it's also made from higher quality, more flavorful grapes than any other Burgundy in America. In fact, Columbia Creek Wines were voted the best in

America at the 1964 Grand Harvest Awards. Sure these wines cost a little more than other Chablis and Burgundy wines, but you deserve the best." The closing scene is of Columbia Creek Chardonnay and Cabernet Sauvignon, each bottle with a red, white and blue striped ribbon with a gold medallion draped around its neck with a sign in the background that read, *1964 Grand Harvest Awards.*

Wine sales had always been very seasonal. Almost 80 percent of sales were in November and December because of the holidays. Consequently, the rollout of Columbia Creek Cellars Chablis and Burgundy was scheduled for November 19, the Saturday before Thanksgiving, as was the TV advertisement. Within two weeks, liquor stores, supermarkets, and grocery stores that sold wine were a mob scene. Everyone wanted to try the new higher quality Columbia Creek Cellars wines.

"Ann, I don't think we have enough Columbia Creek Cellars wine to get through the rest of the holidays," Darrel Hayes, her sales manager said. "Sales are double what we projected."

"I figured that might happen, so I have a backup plan. How much more wine do we need?"

"About a hundred and twenty-six thousand cases." "That's an additional three hundred thousand gallons. But with only a month's sales to project from, I think we'll need more. I'm going to try to get six hundred thousand gallons of additional wine.

A little later, she placed a call to Grape-Co. "Scott, this is Ann Collins. You're on my speaker phone and our sales manager, Darrel Hayes, and Ed Peterson are here with me."

"What can I do for you?" Scott asked.

"I want to exercise our option to purchase additional bulk wine from Grape-Co."

"How much do you need?"

"Six hundred thousand gallons."

"That's a lot! Columbia Creek Cellars must be off to an incredible start."

"It is. Can you supply that much made to our blend and specs, in the same proportions of Burgundy and Chablis?"

"I'm pretty sure we can, but I'll check our inventory to be sure. We may be a bit short on the on French Colombard, but it's only five percent of the blend and we can substitute Chenin Blanc."

That extra purchase option was sure worth its price, Ann thought.

"Ann, sales of Columbia Creek Cellars are three times as much as we projected," Loretta told her the following March. "It sure is good that you were able to get that additional bulk wine from Grape-Co. Sales of our varietals are up twenty-three percent as well."

"It's the effect of our advertising program for Columbia Creek Cellars with that end scene where we showed our award-winning Chardonnay and Cabernet Sauvignon," Ann explained.

"I agree with you. But we will probably need to expand our grape crushing and wine storage capacity here to meet the extra demand for our varietal wines, as well as well as secure more bulk wine processing capacity at Grape-Co.

"I agree. Ed and I are going over there to meet with Scott and Bill tomorrow to increase our toll processing volume. If Grape-Co can't process more grapes for us, we'll have to take our additional bulk wine processing needs to another bulk winery."

Grape-Co was glad to process more grapes for Columbia Creek Winery. Ed managed the project to increase Columbia Creek winery's capacity by 35 percent to cover their increased sales of varietals.

"Allen Lester," he said as he answered his phone.

"Allen, this is Ann Collins. I'm calling to see if you would be interested in a position as director of grape and wine procurement for Columbia Creek Winery."

"Possibly, could we meet and discuss it?"

"How about this Friday here at our winery?"

"That works for me."

"I grew up in Clermont, Florida," Allen began as he started his interview on Friday. "My parents were citrus growers. But a freeze destroyed our five hundred and seventy acre grove when I was a senior in high school and we sold the land to a real estate developer. I got my degree in agricultural economics from the University of Florida in 1954 and accepted a job in grower relations for Florida Citrus Mutual, a large trade association with eight thousand grower members. In 1958, I accepted my current position with Paul Masson as manager of grape and bulk wine procurement.

"Why did you leave Florida Citrus Mutual?"

"Paul Masson offered me a higher paying job."

"What training have you had in viticulture and wine tasting?"

"I have taken courses at UC-Davis. We buy from about two hundred growers and three bulk wineries."

"What compensation would you want?" asked Ann.

"Twenty-two thousand per year plus a company vehicle. Grape and bulk procurement require about seventy-five thousand miles of driving a year. I will also need a moving and relocation package since I live almost two hours' drive from here."

"Okay. When can you start?"

"In two weeks."

"Mom, I'm trying to decide whether to major in agricultural economics or viticulture at UC – Davis," Jesse said on Saturday morning, January 20, 1968, as he was working on his college application. What made you and Dad decide on agricultural economics?"

"We liked business better than the physical sciences."

"I really like working in our vineyards and winery. But I've never given much thought to business before now.

"Why don't you enter with an undeclared major, take a course in agricultural economics and one in viticulture, and see which you like best. It won't really matter if you don't decide on a major until your sophomore year."

"I like that idea, thanks, Mom."

"One other thing. With the Vietnam War escalating, I think you should complete an application for a draft deferment to cover the four years you will be in college."

"I agree, I'll contact our draft board and have them mail me the form."

"This is Mary Saunders," Ann began in the Monday morning staff meeting on Monday, January 6, 1969. Present were Loretta, Ed Peterson, Glen Hamler, Allen Lester, Darrell Hayes, and Mary. "Mary comes to us from the Global Soft Drink Company where she was a brand manager. Mary is our new director of marketing and this is her first day on the job. Glen, after this meeting I want you to give her a tour of our vineyards and after that, Ed, I want you to give her a tour of the winery.

"I want us to create another new line of wines," Ann said, in a staff meeting three weeks later.

"Our total sales have quadrupled since we launched Columbia Creek Cellars. We don't have the grape crushing capacity," Ed pointed out. "And Grape-Co has no extra capacity either."

"I want to discuss the Grape-Co capacity issue with you after this meeting, Ed. But we won't have the grapes for this new line processed at Grape-Co. We'll find another winery to process them," Ann explained. She then described her idea for the Columbia Creek Farms line of light, fruity, slightly sweet, and carbonated wines, that she called wine coolers, which would be targeted to young adults who didn't like beer.

"What will the alcohol content be?" Ed asked

"Six percent," Ann replied.

"What size bottles will these wines be packaged in?"

"Twelve ounce, just like beer."

"Have you thought about label design?" Mary asked.

"I want the label to have a picture of a vineyard with mountains in the background," Ann replied.

"What will be the launch date?" asked Mary.

"November 22, the Saturday before Thanksgiving," Ann replied.

After the meeting about Columbia Creek Farms was over, Ann met with Ed to discuss grape processing capacities. "Ed we need to increase our processing capacity again here at Columbia Creek for our varietal wines, and we need Grape-Co to increase their capacity to process our bulk wines," she began.

"I agree. I'll schedule a meeting with Scott and Bill at Grape-Co. How much do you want to increase our processing and packaging capacity here?" Ed asked.

"I want to double it. Even though we don't have enough varietal sales to fully utilize that much capacity, I believe we soon will."

"I agree," Ed said. "The growth in sales of all of our wines is astounding."

"It's the TV advertising that's made the difference," Ann concluded.

"Yeah. And even though a few of our competitors are now advertising on TV, they can't make the claims that we can."

Grape-Co agreed to increase their processing capacity to meet Columbia Creek Winery's additional needs. By August 11, 1969, between both Grape-Co and their own facilities, Columbia Creek Winery had the capacity to crush 287,000 tons of grapes into approximately 43 million gallons of wine, and package that into 18 million cases. That would give them 15 percent of the US wine market.

Ed and Allen chose the Alcoma winery in Modesto, California to process the grapes for Columbia Creek Farms' new wine coolers. Allen secured contracts for 5,000 tons of grapes, predominantly Thompson seedless and Chenin Blanc. They would be processed in September and October. If sales were greater than anticipated, they would have no problem obtaining additional wine; the majority of generic wine sold was from Thompson seedless and Chenin Blanc grapes.

Mary and Ann designed the TV advertisement. "I don't like the taste of beer," began an actress in her twenties at a party with young adults. "If you don't, either, Columbia Creek Farms wine coolers are for you. Light, fruity, slightly sweet, and carbonated, they have the same alcohol content as beer. Try one, I know you'll like it," the young woman said as she takes a sip.

Sales took off like a rocket. Available in liquor stores, supermarkets, grocery stores, and convenience stores, everyone wanted to try the new Columbia Creek Farms wine coolers. By June, sales of Columbia Creek Farms wine coolers had reached $73 million. Unlike wine, consumption of wine coolers was not seasonal, although Mary expected wine cooler sales to be slightly higher in the summer.

Meanwhile, Tommy graduated from UC-Davis with a bachelor's degree in chemical engineering in June of 1970, and entered Stanford in September to pursue an MBA.

"Ann, our total sales of all our products will be $162 million[17] this year and our pre-tax profits are going to exceed $15 million, [18] Loretta said in September of 1971. "Also, we are out of office space. We can't keep adding on house trailers for offices. We need to build a new office building."

"I know. We now have two hundred and two employees that have offices and half of those are in trailers. It's time to build additional offices, and I would like you to manage that project."

---

[17] The same as $953 million in 2014.
[18] The same as $88 million in 2014.

"I'll get started right away."

"Columbia Creek Winery has won the competition in red table wines with its Cabernet Sauvignon," the head judge for the 1971 Los Angeles National Wine Competition announced to a packed room. Columbia Creek's new Sauvignon Blanc also tied with its Chardonnay for first place in white table wines. Mrs. Collins, would you please come up to the podium?"

"Yes, but I want Ed Peterson, our chief winemaker, to accompany me," Ann replied.

Ann and Ed went up to the stage amidst flashing cameras. Ann whispered something to the judge, and he nodded his head.

"Mrs. Collins, I am presenting Columbia Creek Winery with three plaques and three gold medals," the judge began. "The first plaque and gold medal each read, *Columbia Creek Cabernet Sauvignon is Awarded the Best of Class for Red Table Wine in America at the 1971 Los Angeles National Wine Competition*." He handed her the plaque and shook her hand while his assistant hung a ribbon with a large gold medallion on it around Ed's neck. There was a standing ovation while cameras continued to flash. "The second plaque and gold medal each read, *Columbia Creek Chardonnay and Sauvignon Blanc are Awarded the Best of Class for White Table Wine in America at the 1971 Los Angeles National Wine Competition*," he said as he and his assistant repeated their presentations of the plaque and gold medal. The crowd again roared with applause. And the third plaque and gold medal each read, *Columbia Creek Winery is Awarded Best Red and White Table Wines in America at the 1971 Los Angeles National Wine Competition*." The crowd, still standing, continued their thunderous applause while the last awards were presented to Ann and Ed.

"Mrs. Collins," several reporters shouted at once as they raised their hands.

"You," Ann said, pointing to a man on the front row.

"Jack Engles, Los Angeles Times," he said as he stood. "What led you to decide to include a Sauvignon Blanc in the wines you entered in the competition?"

"I believe that Sauvignon Blanc can be made into a wine as good as Chardonnay if the grapes are grown in the right microclimate and soils, and if the winemaker has the skills and talent to do it," she replied. "But my chief winemaker, Ed Peterson, can explain how he did it much better than I can."

"Mr. Peterson...," several reports began at the same time.

"Congratulations, Ann," George Martin said as he walked up to her after she had come off the stage.

"Thanks George. But the credit goes to Ed. He styled and aged the wine."

"I agree. But it was your idea back in 1960 to talk Ernest into going against common wisdom and planting Sauvignon Blanc vines. By the way, I'm treating you and Ed to dinner tonight at the Au Petit Café on Sunset Boulevard."

"Great, that will be a good occasion to give Ed the bonus I have for him for winning those awards. It's equal to a year of his salary."

"You always have realized the benefits of rewarding hard work, talent, and success."

"I learned from the best," Ann said, remembering Harry Davis.

Jesse graduated from UC-Davis with a bachelor's degree in viticulture in June of 1972, and entered graduate school there in September to pursue a master's degree in enology.

"Ed, I want to get Columbia Creek wines entered in the 1974 Paris Wine Tasting competition," Ann said on a Monday morning in December of 1973.

"When is it?"

"Next May."

"I don't know anyone connected with the wine industry in France. How can we get our wines in the contest?"

"The wine buyer for Harrods in London is a friend of mine. I thought we'd call her and see if she can help. I sent her a telegram that we would be calling this morning at ten our time, which is one p.m. her time, so I'll dial her number."

"Okay, it's worth a try," Ed agreed.

Later that morning, Ann put in the call. "Bridgette? It's Ann Collins and my winemaker, Ed Peterson."

"Hi, Ann, I was expecting your call."

"Can you help us get our wines in next year's Paris Wine Tasting competition?"

"I read the letter you sent me about that, and I think I'll be able to. I talked to my boss about it, and he was supportive. Harrods is the biggest buyer and seller of wines in Europe, and we are the largest sponsors of that competition. We are going to insist that they allow you to enter your wines in the contest, or we will withdraw our support."

"Great! Thanks. What are the next steps?" asked Ann.

"Select two bottles of each variety you want to enter, and send them to me. I will send them to the people organizing the contest."

"Thanks, Bridgette! I owe you one."

"You'll have an opportunity to return my favor after the contest. If your wines win, and I think they will because I've tasted them, I want exclusive distribution rights in Europe for the first year."

"No problem. Ed will get the wines in the mail to you tomorrow." After they ended the call, Ann started her planning.

"Ed, let's send our Chardonnay, Sauvignon Blanc, Cabernet Sauvignon and Merlot."

"Okay. I'll get right on it."

Ann and Ed's plane arrived in Paris at 4:55 p.m. on Sunday May 19. The contest was the next day. Bridgette and her boss,

Ross Dickenson, met them at their hotel for breakfast that morning.

"Are you nervous, Ann?" Bridgette asked after the introductions had been made and they'd ordered breakfast.

"Not really. I'm confident that we have an excellent chance to win with at least one of our wines."

"I wish I had Ann's confidence," Ed said. "I've read a lot about how talented the winemakers in Europe are."

"They have to be. They don't have the consistency in grape quality from year-to-year that you have in California," Ross pointed out.

They arrived at the building where the wine tasting was being held at nine fifteen, and the staff was setting everything up for the tasting. The nine tasters in the blind taste tests were France's top wine experts. White wines would be tasted first, followed by red. The tasting would begin at ten. *Time* magazine's Paris correspondent was there, and there were several newspapers, including *The New York Times, The Washington Post*, and *The London Times*.

The French tasters were stunned when the winning wines were revealed to be California wines. All four of Columbia Creek's wines had won, which catapulted their wines onto the world stage. Ann and Ed were interviewed by all of the reporters there. That night, Bridgette and her boss treated Ann and Ed to a celebratory gourmet dinner.

"Ed, we need to increase our processing capacity again," Ann began when they were on the plane headed back to California.

"I agree," Ed replied. "Do you want us to start making the wines for Columbia Creek Cellars and the wine coolers for Columbia Creek Farms?"

"No, let's leave that processing at Grape-Co and Alcoma Let's focus on high quality varietals at our winery," Ann replied.

THE WINE QUEEN

"Congratulations on taking the Paris wine tasting by storm, Ann!" George Martin said during his phone call with her when she was back in her office on Wednesday.

"Thanks, George. I would like to change the name of our company to the Columbia Creek Wine Company."

"That's a good idea. You're certainly no longer a boutique winery, you're a major corporation, and getting ready to go international."

"Good, I'm glad you agree."

The impact of Columbia Creek California wines winning top honors at the 1974 Paris Wine Tasting was like "the shot heard round the world." In anticipation of the enormous demand that had been created for Columbia Creek's wines, Harrods placed a very large order. They not only ordered the four wines that won the contest, they also ordered Columbia Creek Cellars Burgundy and Chablis. Ann had to raise the prices of these wines to allocate their scarce supply.

Tommy graduated from Stanford with an MBA in June of 1972, and started working for the Columbia Creek Wine Company as a financial analyst in Loretta's department.

Jesse graduated from UC-Davis in June of 1974 with a Master of Science degree in enology, and began working for Ed Peterson as an assistant winemaker.

In 1975, Tommy and Jesse were married. They married sisters, Amy and Carolyn Lesser. At their wedding reception, Loretta joked that their children would be double cousins.

Loretta retired in July of 1979, and Ann hired Mike Way to replace her. Mike, who had an MBA from The University of Pennsylvania's Wharton School of Business, had been vice-president of financial planning for the Global Soft Drink Company.

By 1982, Columbia Creek Wine Company was the largest wine company in the world, commanding a forty-two percent market share in the US and a twenty-six percent market share in Europe. Sales were approaching two billion dollars. In 1983, *Forbes* published an article about the Columbia Creek Wine Company's successes, with Ann on the cover, pictured with her award-winning wines. Beneath her picture was the caption "The Wine Queen." Shortly after that, in 1984, the news show *60 Minutes* interviewed Ann, Tommy and Jesse about their success story on national television.

Inquiries about buying the Columbia Creek Wine Company began to pour in, and one of those calls was from the partners at GSDC.

"Ann, this is George Martin," he said when she answered her phone.

"George, I was planning to call you. I'm being inundated by investment bankers that want to buy our company."

"That's what I wanted to discuss with you. Would you consider selling it to GSDC?"

"Yes, I would - for a fair price."

"Of course. Can you be in Memphis next Thursday to discuss this?"

"Yes."

"Tommy, Jesse, GSDC wants to buy our company," Ann began when they were having dinner the night before she was going to Memphis.

"Do you want to sell it?" Tommy asked.

"For the right price."

"What price is that?" asked Jesse.

"About two billion. My share would come to seven hundred million. And since each of you owns fifteen percent, you would each receive three hundred million. GSDC will probably pay us with a mixture of stock and cash, and in my opinion, GSDC stock is a very good investment. "

"Do you think that Jesse and I could continue to work here if GSDC buys our company?"

THE WINE QUEEN

"I don't know, but I will find out. I'm flying to Memphis tomorrow."

"Ann, how have you been?" George asked as he greeted her.

"Great, and you?"

"Never better. Ann, this is Murray Goldman, our treasurer."

"We know each other well," Ann said.

"I'm familiar with the financials, so I'll just ask you. What do you want for the company?" George asked

"Two billion dollars," Ann replied.

"That's very fair, given your annual profits are just over two hundred million and you are growing fourteen percent a year. Would two-thirds in GSDC stock and the rest in cash work? Our stock is growing seven percent a year and paying a dividend of nine percent."

"That works for me."

"If I remember, Tommy and Jesse each own fifteen percent."

"That's correct."

"Will they be okay with receiving a mix of GSDC stock and cash?"

"Yes."

"One other thing, will your management team agree to stay after the acquisition?"

"I'm sure they will, particularly if Tommy and Jesse remain with the company, which is what they want to do."

"What are their positions again?"

"Jesse is vice-president of operations and Tommy is the chief operations officer. I would recommend promoting Tommy to president and Jesse to chief operations officer."

"Didn't Tommy get his MBA from Stanford?"

"That's right, and Jesse has a Master of Science degree from UC-Davis in enology."

"I respect your opinion Ann, and I know you are objective even though they are your sons. So consider it done."

"I called this staff meeting to announce that GSDC is buying the Columbia Creek Wine Company," Ann said to the management team the following Monday morning. "They want all of you to stay after the acquisition. I assume none of you have a problem with that."

"Will GSDC be replacing anyone?" Mike asked.

"No. With our profitability and growth, they know better than to replace anyone on our management team. After the acquisition, I will be retiring, but Tommy and Jesse will stay. They are promoting Tommy to president, and Jesse to chief operations officer."

"Ann, the closing on the acquisition is scheduled for Friday, November 9," George Martin told her when she answered her phone later that day.

"That's in two weeks. Okay, I'll schedule a flight to Memphis."

"Jim, you look like the twin of Ray Collins," George Martin said when he was being introduced to GSDC's new president, Jim West.

"Does Ray work here?"

"Not now, but he did from 1953 until 1955. He was very talented and had a great future here, but had to leave because of family issues. In fact, in 1959, Ray married Ann Robinson, now Ann Collins, who also used to work here, and now owns the Columbia Creek Wine Company?"

"Aren't we buying that company?" Jim asked.

"Yeah. The closing is in a week. You can meet Ann then."

When Jim got back to his office, he became lost in his thoughts. *I was adopted when I was six months old, and when I served on the board of the agency I was adopted through years later, the Children's Home Society, I obtained my birth records.*

From them I learned that my parents were both killed in a train wreck, and that I also had a twin brother who was adopted a month after I was adopted. Knowing I had a twin brother, George's remarks about Ray Collins looking like my twin makes me curious.

"I think I might be Ray Collins's twin brother," Jim told George later that afternoon. "Do you have any pictures of him?"

"I have some films of him making presentations to our board. If you'd like, I'll have one of them set up for viewing in the conference room tomorrow morning."

"Great. Thanks."

The film began and there was Ray, making his farewell speech. *He appears to be the same height and weight as me, and has the same hair color,* Jim thought. *And we do look just alike. Even our voices sound the same. I believe we are twins.*

"George, I'm now almost certain Ray and I are twins. Will he be coming to the closing with Ann?"

"No, Ray was killed in an accident while he and Ann were on their honeymoon in Napa. He was shot when he prevented a bank robbery, though he saved a number of lives. Ann adopted his sons, Tommy and Jesse, who now both work for Columbia Creek. After the acquisition, Ann plans to retire and Tommy will be promoted to president and Jesse to chief operations officer."

"Ann, this is Jim West, our new president," George said when Ann came into the board-room for the closing. Murray Goldman was also there, as was Steve Soran, a GSDC attorney.

Ann almost fainted. Jim looked exactly like what she thought Ray would have looked like at sixty-one if he were still alive. Jim's face was impossibly handsome, its features appearing to have been carved in stone, and he had blackish hair, that was going gray at the temples. She regained her composure and said, "It's good to meet you, Jim."

After the closing, Jim went over to Ann and said, "Would you come to my office? There's something I want to discuss with you."

"Okay." *He even sounds like Ray,* Ann thought.

"Ann, I'm Ray Collins's twin brother," he announced once they were alone. Ann grew weak in the knees and stumbled. Jim caught her before she fell.

"Would you like a glass of water?" he asked after he'd helped her sit down.

"No, I'm okay now. But Ray never told me he had a twin brother."

"That's because he didn't know he had one." Jim then told her the story about how he and Ray had been separated at birth and adopted by different families. "I never knew Ray was my twin until George Martin told me that I looked like Ray's twin and then showed me a film of Ray making a presentation to the GSDC board."

"That's an incredible story, Jim," Ann said, as she thought, *I would like to get to know Jim, but he's probably married.*

"Would you go to dinner with me tonight, Ann?"

"As a date, or professionally?"

"As a date. And don't look so concerned. I'm a widower. My wife, Cathy, died of cancer over two years ago."

"I'm sorry for your loss. Yes, I would enjoy having dinner with you."

"Great, I'll be at your hotel at seven."

"Jim West, reservations for two at seven thirty," Jim told the hostess at the restaurant.

"Mr. West, yes. Welcome back, sir," the uniformed maître d' said as he led Jim and Ann to their table. "I take it you will have a bottle of the Columbia Creek Chardonnay?" the maître d' asked once the two were seated.

"That okay with you, Ann?"

"Of course."

THE WINE QUEEN

After the maître d' brought their drinks, the waiter came by to take their order. "I'll have the Caesar salad, steamed Maine Lobster with red skin potatoes, and sweet corn," Ann told him.

"I'd like a tossed salad, the New York strip - medium rare - and a baked potato with butter and sour cream," Jim said.

"Ann, what you accomplished is incredible," Jim began once the waiter had left. "A widowed single mother of two and you built the largest, most profitable wine company in the world."

"Thanks. It was a labor of love."

"What type of background did you have that enabled you to do that?"

"I completed my bachelor's degree in economics at Wellesley in 1950," Ann began as she described her background to him.

"Very impressive."

"Now it's your turn," Ann said.

"I was raised in a Christian home in Atlanta, Georgia, by two loving parents. My father was a lawyer and my mother a high school teacher. I got my bachelor's degree from Georgia Tech, worked for GSDC for three years, then went to business school. I got my MBA from Harvard in 1950. From there I went to the consulting firm McKinsey & Company, and became a partner in 1957. GSDC hired me away from McKinsey."

On the ride back to her hotel, Ann was lost in her thoughts. *Jim is like Ray reincarnated. I'm already falling in love with him. I can't help it.*

Meanwhile, Jim was having similar thoughts. *Ann's so smart, accomplished, beautiful. I've never been so attracted to someone on a first date.*

It was after eleven when he walked her to the elevator in the deserted hotel lobby.

"Jim." Ann's voice was barely a whisper and echoed with uncertainty. This was their first date, and yet... and yet she had a lifetime of feelings for him already. "I'm glad we met. I..."

His lips hushed the words. He kissed her with aching tenderness, a long, lingering kiss that pulled at the secret places inside her. They were beyond words now. Suddenly, only this moment mattered. This moment, this man, this coming together of two spirits. Her hands circled his neck, entwining in the hair at his nape, just as she had wanted to all evening. His arms circled her, their kiss deepening, searching, exploring, defining.

She sank against his hard chest. There was no use denying her feelings now. Her body spoke her need. Her skin prickled with desire and her fingers gripped his shoulders. Her tongue reached for his. And in return, he wrapped her in a joy so intense, her knees weakened. They were cocooned in desire and she never wanted to leave.

He finally broke the kiss to catch his breath, which came raggedly. With his forehead pressed against hers, he stared deep into her eyes. The corners of his eyes crinkled with a smile when Jim said, "I've wanted to do that ever since I met you."

Appendix A. Viticulture

"There are 4,800 wine grape growers in California that last year harvested 580,000 tons of wine grapes from seventeen grape growing districts. These seventeen districts can be grouped into three regions according to grape quality," Glen told her as he began his lesson on viticulture. "The three regions are the Central Valley, which encompases all or parts of nineteen counties and includes the San Joaquin and Sacremento Valleys where Madera, Modesto, Fresno, Sacramento, and Visalia are located; the North Coast which is four counties north of San Francisco - Lake, Marin, Mendocino, and Solano; and the Napa Valley, which is Napa and Sonoma counties. The San Joaquin Valley is where the lowest quality grapes come from. Most wines made from these grapes are used in blends for generic wines. They also produce a lot of Thompson seedless grapes for raisins. The North Coast counties are the next step up in quality, and where a number of varietal wines are produced. The Napa Valley of course has the highest quality wine grapes. Grape prices and yields per acre in each of these regions vary greatly."

"Is that because they reflect the quality of the grapes?"

"Exactly."

"How much do they differ by region?"

"I thought you might ask that so I brought a copy of the California Grape Crush Report to show you. Let me get it out of the truck. Wine grape prices not only differ by region, but also by grape variety. I'll just look at the average of all varieties for each region. Let's see, last season in the San Joaquin Valley, wine grapes averaged about thirty-five dollars per ton, North Coast County grapes averaged One hundred sixty-six per ton and Napa Valley grapes were three hundred seventy dollars per ton. Of course these prices fluctuate from year-to-year with fluctuating supplies."

"Do grape yields also vary by region?"

"Yeah. In the Napa Valley, average yields are two to four tons per acre, in the North Coast Counties, it's about five to seven, and in the San Joaquin Valley, growers get ten to twelve tons per acre."

"Other than geographical region, what else affects grape yields?"

"Vine spacing and density per acre, pruning, soil fertility, altitude, temperature, management practices, and grape variety are most of the things that affect yield. Generally low yields, if they are the desired result of pruning and/or management practices, produce better quality wine because more of the vine's nutrients are directed into fewer grapes. The winemaker usually works with the vineyard manager to style the grapes, by pruning and other management practices, to make the grapes he wants for his wines."

"How much wine is produced from a ton of grapes?"

"About one hundred twenty gallons of wine is produced per ton in the Napa Valley and about one hundred fifty to one hundred seventy gallons per ton for the rest of California."

"Why are wine yields lower in the Napa Valley?"

"Some of the same variables that affect grape yields also affect wine yields. These include differences in temperatures, altitude, amount of rainfall and irrigation, pruning practices, and vineyard management practices. How hard the grapes are pressed when making wine also affects wine yields.

"Viticulture, from the Latin word for *vine,* is the science, production, and study of grapes, which deals with the series of events that occur in the vineyard. Duties of the viticulturist include: monitoring and controlling pests and diseases with sprays, fertilization, irrigation, weed control, canopy management, monitoring fruit development and characteristics, vine pruning during the winter months, replanting vines lost to disease, and deciding when to harvest. Viticulturists are often intimately involved with winemakers, because vineyard management and the resulting grape characteristics provide the basis from which winemaking begins.

"Vitis Vinifera is the species of grape used to make wine in California and Europe. I believe I described the most popular varieties when you were here back in May. In the northeastern US, primarily upper New York State, Concord, a species native to America, predominates. Popular varieties are Niagara, Catawba and Delaware. There are also French hybrids, which are derived from crosses between Vitis Vinifera and a number of American species, but mostly Concords.

"How many varieties of wine grapes are grown in California?"

"According to the 1958 California Grape Crush Report there are forty-seven white varieties and sixty-three red varieties."

"Which ones are the most popular for varietal wines?"

"Cabernet Sauvignon, Pinot Noir, Petite Syrah and Zinfandel for red wines, and Chardonnay, Gewurztraminer, Johannisberg Riesling, and Chenin Blanc for white wines."

"What are the main varieties used in generic wines?"

"Thompson seedless, French Colombard, Sauvignon Blanc, Chenin Blanc and Gray Riesling for white wines, typically Chablis or Rhine wine; and Zinfandel, Merlot, Gamay Beaujolais, Barbera and Petite Syrah for red wines, typically Burgundy or Bordeaux.

"What about muscadine and scuppernong grapes? I love to eat them fresh and I've even had some homemade wine from muscadines."

"They are from the species vitis rotundifolia, and native to North America. They are believed to have originated in North Carolina. The scuppernong is a white grape, colored light brown and the muscadine is a deep purple grape. They grow from New York State to Florida. Wines have been made from them since the sixteenth century. They are typically sweet dessert wines.

"The Vitis Vinifera wine grapes grown in California and Europe require deep well-drained soils," Glen continued.

"How deep should the soils be?"

"At least five feet, but deeper is better."

"How many years after planting before grape vines produce a commercially harvestable crop?"

"About three years, and anywhere from five years in the San Joaquin Valley to nine or ten years in the Napa valley before they are at full production. On average, the vines have about a thirty year life, although there are vineyards in California that are eighty years old. Pruning cuts the vine back so there is new growth. If the vine wasn't pruned, it would soon produce so many grapes it would die.

"The vine needs approximately thirteen to fifteen hundred hours of sunshine during the growing season and around twenty-seven inches of rainfall throughout the year in order to produce grapes suitable for winemaking. In ideal circumstances, the vine will receive most of the rainfall during the winter and spring months. Rain at harvest time can create many hazards, such as fungal diseases and berry splitting. The optimum weather during the growing season is a long, warm summer that allows the grapes the opportunity to ripen fully and to develop a balance between the levels of acids and sugars in the grape.

"Topography is important, too. Hillsides and slopes are preferred over flatter terrain. Vines growing on a slope receive a greater strength of the sun's rays with sunshine falling on an angle perpendicular to the hillside. In flatter terrain, the strength of the sunlight is diluted as it is spread out across a wider surface area. Additionally, a slope affords better drainage, obviating the possibility that the vine might sit in overly moist soil. In cooler regions of the northern hemisphere, south-facing slopes receive more hours of sunlight and are preferred; in warmer climates, north-facing slopes are preferred."

"I've heard that microclimates affect grape quality. What are they?"

"Microclimates are climates that differ in various spots that may range from a hundred yards apart to a mile or more. They differ as a result of air currents and temperature changes from day to night. Air drainage from canyons in mountains over a particular area often creates a microclimate. These make wines different even though the vineyards the grapes came from may be less than a mile apart. Columbia Creek helps create the microclimate for our vineyards."

"What are the major threats to vineyards?" Ann asked.

"When the vine is flowering it is very susceptible to weather hazards such as strong winds and hail. Cold temperatures during this period can also bring the onset of millerandage, which produces clusters with no seeds and varying sizes. Too much heat can have the opposite affect and produce coulure, which causes grape clusters to either drop to the ground or not fully develop. The main viticultural diseases include oidium, downy mildew, phylloxera, and plant viruses.

"Oidium is a fungus that causes powdery mildew on grape vines. It is a common pathogen of the wine grape. Infected plants display white powdery spots on the leaves and stems. The fungus is believed to have originated in North America. Oidium infects all green tissue on the grapevine, including leaves and young berries. It can cause crop loss and poor wine quality if untreated. This mildew can be treated with sulfur or fungicides.

"Frost from cold weather is a hazard in the Napa Valley sometimes. Frost is the solid deposition of water vapor from saturated air. It is formed when solid surfaces are cooled to below the dew point of the adjacent air as well as below the freezing point of water, about twenty-eight degrees. Sizes of frost crystals differ depending on time and water vapor available. Frost is also usually translucent in appearance. There are many types of frost, such as radiation and window frost. Frost causes economic damage when it destroys plants or hanging fruits.

"The initial symptoms of downy mildew appear on leaves as light to yellow spots. Infected vines become stunted with thick clusters of pale curled leaves. Severely infected leaves may drop from the vine. Infected immature grapes turn from green to light brown to purple and fall off the vine. Downy mildew is caused by a fungus called plasmopora uiticola. It is spread by wind driven rain. Control includes not planting susceptible cultivars, not planting vineyards in low or shady areas, and the use of fungicides.

"Grape phylloxera is a pest of commercial grapevines worldwide, originally native to eastern North America. These almost microscopic, pale yellow sap-sucking insects feed on the roots and leaves of grapevines depending on the phylloxera genetic strain. The resulting deformations on roots and secondary fungal infections can girdle roots, gradually cutting off the flow of nutrients and water to the vine, killing it."

"I read in a book I bought about the California wine industry that phylloxera almost wiped out the European wine industry," Ann added.

"In the nineteenth century, the phylloxera epidemic destroyed most of the vineyards for wine grapes in Europe, most notably in France. Phylloxera was introduced to Europe when avid botanists in Victorian England collected specimens of American vines in the 1850s. Because phylloxera is native to North America, the native grape species here are at least partially resistant. By contrast, the European wine grape is very susceptible to the insect. The epidemic devastated vineyards in Britain and then moved to the mainland, destroying most of the European wine growing industry. In 1863, the first vines began to deteriorate inexplicably in the southern Rhône region of France. The problem spread rapidly across the continent. In

France alone, total wine production fell from eighty-four and a half million hectolitres in 1875 to only twenty-three-point-four million hectolitres in 1889. Some estimates hold that between two-thirds and nine-tenths of all European vineyards were destroyed.

"Two major solutions gradually emerged: grafting cuttings onto resistant rootstocks and hybridization. Use of a resistant, or tolerant, rootstock involved grafting a Vitis Vinifera scion onto the roots of a resistant American native species."

"So American rootstocks saved the European wine industry?" asked Ann.

"California viticulturists have that view. In France, their view is that those American vines that were taken to Europe in the 1850s caused the problem."

"I guess both are correct," Ann observed.

"Maybe. But phylloxera also destroyed a lot of vineyards in California in the early twentieth century."

"How did they get it under control?"

"The same way as in Europe, by the use of a resistant or tolerant rootstock and grafting a Vitis Vinifera Scion onto the roots of an American native species because the rootstock does not interfere with the development of the wine grapes, and it furthermore allows the customization of the rootstock to soil and weather conditions, as well as desired vigor. Unfortunately, not all rootstocks are equally resistant. Modern phylloxera infestation also occurs when wineries are in need of fruit immediately, and choose to plant un-grafted vines rather than wait for grafted vines to be available.

"Plant viruses are intracellular parasites that need a host to replicate. Plant-to-plant transmission usually involves vectors such as insects. Viruses are very small and can only be observed through a microscope. Viruses of concern limit the plant's ability to absorb nutrients, killing it. Key viruses to grape vines include leaf roll, corky bark and fan leaf.

Appendix B. Enology

"The science and art of enology, or winemaking, has its roots in prehistoric times. The effects of alcohol were probably discovered when rotten fruit was consumed and found to have an intoxicating effect, which was viewed as pleasant. Fermented liquid could be stored for a long time without fear of decomposition, thus giving a reliable drinking source as well as a source of calories. Winemaking is believed to have begun about five thousand years ago in the Mediterranean basin. The first winemakers in California were the Franciscian Fathers, who founded a string of missions from San Diego to Sonoma that grew grapes and made wine, the last in 1823. Commercial grape growing and winemaking began in California in the 1830s. Phylloxera followed by prohibition pretty much destroyed the California wine industry, although a few wineries survived by making wines for religious occasions or by innovatively selling bricks of crushed grapes with specific instructions about what not to do to make wine. It was after World War II before California's wine industry really began again, which is when we started this winery. The University of California at Davis can be credited for its many contributions to viticulture and enology. Shortly after the war, it developed and published standards for grape growing and winemaking that have helped make California wines as good as they are."

"I read in a book I bought about the California wine industry that California can actually make better wines than Europe. Is that true? And if so, why?" Ann asked.

"That's true. California can actually make better wines than Europe. Our climate out here is steadier than in France, Italy, or Spain. They have about two good winemaking years in ten. We only have about one year in ten or fifteen that isn't excellent.

"Harvest is in many ways the first step in wine production. Grapes are harvested by hand. The decision to harvest grapes is typically made by the winemaker based on the level of brix, or sugar, and brix-to-acid ratio in the grapes. Harvest in the Napa Valley is mostly in September and October. We like a brix between twenty- and twenty-four, which is twenty- to twenty-four percent sugar content. Other considerations include ripeness, berry flavor, and tannin development, which are determined by skin color, seed color and taste. Overall disposition of the grapevine and weather forecasts are also taken into account.

"Up until a few years ago, wine grapes were picked into fifty-pound wooden field boxes and loaded onto flat-bed trucks for transport to the winery. Now most grapes are picked into small metal tubs that each hold about forty pounds. These are lower in cost than wooden field boxes. When full, the tubs are dumped into larger bins holding about a thousand pounds of grapes on a trailer pulled by a tractor which follows the harvesting crews down the rows. Each of these harvesting bins is monitored by two people, who sift through the arriving grapes and pull out any unwanted material such as weeds, grape leaves, tree frogs, and so forth. The tractor dumps these bins into one to two ton detachable tanks, or three to five ton mounted tanks.

Our grapes are loaded into two ton detachable tanks for transport to the winery. The use of knowledgeable labor costs more, but it pays for itself by enabling leaving behind the clusters that contain bunch rot or other defects. This can be an effective first line of defense to prevent inferior quality fruit from contaminating a lot or tank of wine.

"After being hand harvested and loaded into detachable tanks, the grapes are taken into the winery and prepared for primary fermentation. De-stemming is the process of separating stems from the grapes. Depending on the winemaking procedure, this process may be undertaken before crushing with the purpose of lowering the development of tannins and vegetal flavors in the resulting wine, or after crushing to let those tannins develop.

"Once the grapes have been transported to the winery, certain preparatory steps must be taken before the actual winemaking can begin. Cleanliness and sanitation are essential for good winemaking, as troublesome bacteria can cause disastrous results. Equipment must be sanitized with caustic soda, rinsed with water, and finally, treated with an anti-bacterial sulfite solution. To rid the equipment of excess sulfite, everything is rinsed with water a second time. It is estimated that approximately ten gallons of good quality water are needed for every one gallon of wine produced. Upon arriving at the winery, grapes are treated with fifty to seventy-five ppm of free sulfur dioxide. This process is called sulfating, and inhibits the unwanted microorganisms and wild yeast species on the grapes.

"Grapes can simply be stepped on to free the juice, allowed to sit and they will become wine and later vinegar. Winemaking is the process of controlling the many variables that influence the taste of the wine to get the desired results."

Ernest led her out to the cement-paved grape receiving area at the side of the winery where grapes were being unloaded. "Grapes are fed into a corkscrew-shaped auger where they are first crushed, then if desired, de-stemmed. Stems exit at the end while juice, skins, and seeds exit the bottom. At this stage, red winemaking diverges from white winemaking. All grape juice is white. It's the skin that imparts color to wine. Red wine is made from the pulpy juice, or must, of red or black grapes that undergo fermentation together with the grape skins. In addition to color, most flavor components of red wine are in the skin of the grape. White wine is made by fermenting juice that is made by pressing crushed grapes to extract a juice but the skins are removed and play no further role."

"I read that white wine can be made from red grapes," Ann commented.

"That's correct. Occasionally white wine is made from red grapes."

"How is that done?"

"By extracting the juice with minimal contact with the red grapes' skins. Rosé wines are either made from red grapes where the juice is allowed to stay in contact with the dark skins long enough to pick up a pinkish color or by blending red wine and white wine. White Zinfandel is an example of a rosé wine made from black grapes. It is essentially a varietal rosé. White and rosé wines extract little of the tannins contained in the skins.

"Exactly what is tannin?"

"It is a naturally occurring organic chemical found in plants, seeds, wood, leaves, and fruit skins. Grape tannin, most commonly found in red wine, adds bitterness and astringency as well as complexity to wine.

"To start primary fermentation, the juice is transferred to vats and yeast is added to the pulpy juice for red wine or juice for white wine," Ernest began as they entered the winery. Ann felt dwarfed by the giant stainless steel tanks inside the tall-ceilinged room. It was spotlessly clean, with no odor. "During this fermentation, which often takes between two and four weeks, the yeast converts most of the sugars in the grape juice into ethanol alcohol and carbon dioxide. The carbon dioxide is lost to the atmosphere. After the primary fermentation of red grapes the free run wine is pumped off into tanks and the skins are pressed to extract the remaining juice and wine. The press wine is blended with the free run wine at the wine maker's discretion. The wine is kept warm and the remaining sugars are converted into alcohol and carbon dioxide.

"White wine is fermented similarly, but there are no skins. After fermentation, white wine goes through cold stabilization. This process requires the wine to drop almost to freezing to precipitate out the tartaric crystals that can form. The crystals are harmless, but this process can improve wine flavor. It also keeps consumers from getting nervous if they see crystals in their wine bottle.

"The next process in the making of both red and white wine is secondary fermentation. This is a bacterial fermentation that converts sharp malic acid to mild lactic acid. This process decreases the acid in the wine and softens its taste. The tannic nature of high quality red wines is an important winemaking consideration. As the must is exposed to prolonged periods of skin contact, called maceration, more tannins are extracted from the skin and will be present in the resulting wine. If winemakers choose not to shorten the period of maceration, in favor of maximizing color and flavor concentrations, there are some methods that they can use to soften tannin levels. A common method is oak aging, which can mellow the harsh grape tannins as well as introduce softer 'wood tannins.' Fining agents can also reduce tannins."

"What is fining?"

"In winemaking fining is the process where a substance, called a fining agent, is added to the wine to create an absorbent, enzymatic, or ionic bond with the suspended particles. This makes them larger molecules that can precipitate out of the wine easier and quicker. Unlike filtration, which can only remove particles, such as dead yeast cells and grape fragments, fining is effective in removing soluble substances such as tannins, coloring phenols and proteins. Given enough time in a stable environment, many of these suspended particles would gradually precipitate out on their own. The use of fining agents speeds up the process at a lower cost. White wines are fined to remove particles that may cause the wine to brown or lose color as well as removing heat-unstable proteins that could cause the wine to appear hazy or cloudy should it be exposed to high temperatures after bottling. Red wines are fined for the same reasons but also for the added benefit of reducing the amount of bitter, astringent tannins which makes these wines smoother and more approachable sooner after bottling and release.

"What types of fining agents are used?"

"Gelatin and egg whites are commonly used. They are positively charged proteins that are naturally attracted to the negatively charged tannin molecules. These fining agents will bond with some of the tannins and be removed from the wine during filtration.

"What specifically does aging do for wines?"

"It improves the flavor of the best wines. As wine rests in an oak barrel it goes through subtle chemical changes, resulting in greater complexity and a softening of the harsh tannins and flavors present at the end of fermentation. Aging in an oak barrel does three things: It allows a very slow introduction of oxygen into the wine, but not at levels that would cause oxidation or spoilage, which acts as a softening agent upon the tannins in the wine; it allows a small level of evaporation, which concentrates the wine's flavor and aroma compounds; and it imparts the character of the oak into the wine.

"How long should wines be aged in oak barrels?"

"Wines that are higher in acidity and tannins benefit from longer aging in oak than wines that are not. Most red wines achieve all of the benefits of oak aging in one to two years. But some of the better ones continue to improve in oak for up to ten years. The only white variety that improves with age is Chardonnay,[19] and it is seldom barrel aged for more than a year."

"How does the winemaker know when a wine has aged in oak long enough?" asked Ann

---

[19] Sauvignon Blanc also improves with age, and is aged for up to one year in oak barrels. However, in 1959 when Ann got her lesson in Enology, the California wine industry did not make Sauvignon Blanc. In this novel, Ann changes that.

"Winemakers use an instrument called a *wine thief* to taste the wine periodically during the aging process. It is a glass pipette, or tube, about eighteen inches long. The stopper on the side of the wine barrel is removed and the pipette is inserted into the wine in the barrel, where the part of the pipette in the wine fills. Then a thumb is placed over the end of the pipette, and the pipette, containing the wine, is withdrawn from the barrel. The wine in the pipette is then transferred to a wineglass by removing the thumb from the end of the pipette, and the wine is smelled and tasted.

"Wine must be settled or clarified and adjustments made prior to filtration and bottling. It is then aged in the bottle."

"What does bottle aging do and how long are wines aged in the bottle?"

"Bottle aging continues to soften the tannins and the result, after a long enough time, is a wine with a blend of the fruitiness of the grape, the oak from the barrel, and the mellowed tannins. A heavy, robust red wine that has been aged in oak for two years may continue to improve in the bottle for another ten to twenty years. Most red wines that are aged, though, will be aged in oak for about a year and improve in the bottle for up to five years. Most white wines that are aged in oak improve with age for three to five years in the bottle."

"On average, considering both oak and bottle aging, how long is it from harvest to drinking for red and white wines?"

"That time can vary from a few months for simpler white wines to over twenty years for top red wines. However, only about ten percent of red wines and five percent of white wines will improve enough with age to make drinking more enjoyable after five years of aging than after one year of aging.

"Most of the wines I have drunk are around ten to twelve percent alcohol. Is that true for all wines?"

"The alcohol content of both white and red table wines and Champagne is ten to fourteen percent. Dessert wines are higher.

"Many wines of comparable quality are produced using different approaches to their production than I just described. Quality is dictated by the attributes of the grapes and not necessarily the steps taken during winemaking. Numerous variations on the procedures I just described exist. These variations constitute a winemaker's style. If five pieces of beautiful raw silk were given to each of five clothing designers, each would make a different dress from exactly the same material. But each would reflect the dressmaker's artistic talent. The winemaker is the same, and each will style their wines according to their artistic talent."

"Gladys has lunch ready," Cathy told them as she came into the winery. Lunch was turkey breast sandwiches, Caesar salad, and broccoli cheese soup.

After lunch, they went back in the barrel room and Ann asked, "What temperature should red and white wines be served at?"

"Red wines should be served at sixty-five to seventy degrees. Depending on the quality of the grape, reds should be allowed to breath after opening for ten minutes to an hour and whites from no time to about five minutes, to let off-odors dissipate."

"What is decanting and why is it done?"

"Red wines that have been aged for years may require decanting. This process entails slowly pouring the wine from its bottle into another glass container while holding a light or candle under the neck of the bottle to ensure none of the sediment gets into the decanted wine. Because they do not improve with aging beyond a few years, this isn't required for white wines. White wines should be served cold, at about forty to forty-five degrees. Chill by putting them in a bucket of ice and water for twenty minutes or in the refrigerator for one to two hours. Never chill them in the freezer because this will destroy delicate flavors.

"The taste of wine is usually described by comparing it to fruits or other things. For reds, many describe them as tasting similar to black currants, black cherries, plums, or bell peppers. And for quality reds, such as Cabernet Sauvignon and Pinot Noir, there will be the taste of oak because of oak aging. For whites, its apples, pears, figs, grapefruit, pineapple, or in some cases flowery or floral, particularly for Gewurztraminer. For quality whites, such as Chardonnay, there will also be oakiness. The less sweet a wine is, the more these various types of flavors can be detected.

"Next, I'll discuss making Champagne, beginning with *méthode Champenoise*. After primary fermentation and bottling, a second alcoholic fermentation occurs in the bottle. This second fermentation, which gives Champagne its carbonation from carbon dioxide, is induced by adding several grams of yeast and several grams of rock sugar. At this time, the Champagne bottle is capped with a crown cap. After aging a minimum of from one-and-a-half to three years, the residual yeast sediment, called lees, must be consolidated for removal. The bottles undergo a process known as riddling. In this stage, the bottles are placed on special racks at a forty-five degree angle with the cork pointed down. Every few days the bottles are given a slight shake and turn and dropped back into the racks. Eventually the angle is increased. The drop back into the rack causes a slight tap, pushing sediments toward the neck of the bottle. In about six to eight weeks the position of the bottle is pointed straight down with sediment in the neck of the bottle. The neck is then frozen, and the cap removed. The pressure in the bottle forces out the lees, and the bottle is quickly corked to maintain the carbon dioxide in solution. This is the most expensive method of making Champagne.

"Another method for making Champagne is known as the transfer method. After fermentation in a tank, it is then transferred to bottles for secondary fermentation. When this is complete, it is transferred to a tank, filtered and bottled. This method allows for complexity to be built into the Champagne, but also gives scope for blending options after the Champagne has gone into the bottle. Cost of the transfer method is between *méthode Champenoise* and the third method, the charmat bulk process.

"In the charmat bulk process, the wine undergoes secondary fermentation in stainless steel tanks, then is bottled under pressure. This is the lowest-cost method of the three.

"Styles of Champagne are from very dry to sweet. Their color ranges from white to pink to deep red, depending on the grape variety used. Champagnes require no breathing time and do not improve with age. They should not be stored for more than two years. They should be chilled in the refrigerator for two hours or in a bucket of ice and water for twenty to thirty minutes and served at forty to forty-five degrees, the same as white wine.

"Dessert wines are sweet wines typically served with dessert, although they can be enjoyed alone as well as with fruit or bakery sweets. There are three types, Sherries, ports and late harvest wines. They contain high levels of sugar and are fourteen to twenty percent alcohol. They are made by ensuring that some residual sugar remains after fermentation is completed. This can be done by harvesting late, making late harvest wine, freezing the grapes to concentrate the sugar, also called ice wine, or adding alcohol, called fortification, before fermentation is completed. For example, wine spirits in the form of high proof brandy is added when making Sherry and port. In other cases the winemaker may choose to hold back some of the sweet grape juice and add it to the wine after the fermentation is done, a technique known as süssreserve.

"Sherry is made from white grapes. Before the fermentation process is complete it is fortified with grape brandy, called wine spirits, to increase the alcohol level, then baked at one hundred thirty-five degrees for ten to fifteen weeks. This makes Cream Sherry. If the wine is allowed to complete fermentation and go completely dry before fortification it is a dry Sherry. Some Sherries may be oak-aged for twenty years or more. Sherry has a nutty-like taste.

"Port is made from red grapes and is not baked. They are always made sweet. There are two kinds: tawny which is deep red to purple in color, and ruby, which is light red. Some tawny ports may be oak-aged for twenty years or longer. Ruby ports are light and do not improve with aging. Ports are often said to taste like raisins.

"Some of the most popular dessert wines are made from moldy grapes. But not just any mold. The mold is called Botrytis cinerea or noble rot. It sucks water out of the grape while imparting flavors of honey and apricot to the future wine. It typically occurs in over-ripe grapes left past normal harvest, usually into November. The weather conditions to produce noble rot occur only a few years out of ten. Many wines made in this way are called Thanksgiving harvest wines, and many are made from the Johannesburg Riesling variety of grape. They are deep gold in color, complex in nature and are often described as tasting like apricots or peaches. Late harvest dessert wines improve with age up to and sometimes beyond ten years.

"Sherry and port should be served at sixty-five to seventy degrees like red wines. Late harvest wines should be served at fifty-five to sixty degrees. Chill in a bucket of ice and water for ten to fifteen minutes or in the refrigerator for an hour. Dessert wines should be allowed to breathe for ten to fifteen minutes.

"The main by-product from making wine is pomace, which is the pressed grape skins and seeds. It is sold as cattle feed.

High proof made from wine stock is brandy, usually made from bad wines that are distilled into ethyl alcohol and sold to industrial users. Brandy is made by distilling and then barrel aging good wines.

"Wine vinegar is made from the fermentation of ethanol produced from wine by acetic acid bacteria. The process usually takes from several weeks to several months. A faster method entails adding a bacterial culture to the source liquid before adding air using a pump system or a turbine to promote oxygenation to speed fermentation. This process produces vinegar in one to three days.

"The label on a bottle of table or dessert wine contains important information about that wine. It will of course have the name of the winery that's selling the wine; the wine class, which is the variety of grape it was made from if it is a varietal wine, or the name Burgundy, Chablis, or Bordeaux if it's a generic wine; its appellation, which is the country, state, county, and/or viticultural region where it was made; date of vintage; alcohol content; quantity of contents, such as seven hundred fifty milliliters; and the term 'Reserve' may be used to designate a special bottling or limited production. Finally there will be terms that tell you how it was made. 'Estate Bottled' means that one hundred percent of the wine was made from grapes grown in vineyards owned and managed by the named winery. 'Produced and Bottled by' means the named winery purchased, crushed, and fermented seventy-five percent or more of the grapes and aged and bottled the wine. 'Vinted and Bottled by' or 'Made and Bottled by' means that for seventy-six to ninety percent of the wine in that bottle, the named winery bought bulk wines made by another winery and aged, blended, and bottled them. 'Cellared and Bottled by' means the wines were produced by another winery and aged, bottled and marketed by the named winery. 'Bottled by' means the named winery only bottled and marketed the wine. For Champagne, the method used to make it will appear on the label along with the same information on wine labels.

Appendix C. Tasting Wines

"It goes without saying that wine is an acquired taste. The more a person knows about a subject, the more they enjoy it, whether it's art, music, literature – or wine," their teacher, Alexis, said as he began their first day's lesson.

"There are four major components that make up the taste of a wine. These are alcohol, acids, tannins and sugars. The major alcohol in wine is ethanol, the same as in beer, or distilled spirits like scotch and vodka, although obviously not nearly as much as in distilled spirits. Acids give wine longevity, balance and crispness. Chemical pH, or level of acidity, in wine affects a wine's color, taste, flavor and long-term stability. Tannins are present in all wines, but most notably in red wines. They come from the skins, stems and seeds of the grapes during fermentation, and also from oak barrels in which the wine is aged. Tannins are important in extending the life of wines, and supply a harsh, dry taste characteristic often described as puckery or astringent. This quality is reduced as a wine ages, giving it a mellow taste. Sugars are also present in all wines, and provide a detectable sweetness when they exceed one-half percent. When a wine is described as completely, or bone dry, the sweetness is undetectable.

"The five key stages to wine tasting are those that make up sensory perception. These are color and clarity, the aroma of the wine in the glass, taste, the 'in-mouth' sensations, or mouth feel, and the finish, or after-taste. These five stages are combined in order to establish the following properties of a wine: complexity and character, potential or suitability for aging or drinking, and possible faults.

"A wine's overall quality assessment, based on this examination, follows further careful description and comparison with recognized standards, both with respect to other wines in its price range and according to known factors pertaining to the region or vintage; if it is typical of the region or diverges in style; if it uses certain wine-making techniques, such as barrel fermentation or malolactic fermentation, or any other remarkable or unusual characteristics."

"What is malolactic fermentation?" a man in the back row asked.

"A process in which tart-tasting malic acid naturally present in grapes is converted to softer-tasting lactic acid.

"Whereas wines are regularly tasted in isolation, a wine's quality assessment is more objective when performed alongside several other wines, in what are known as tasting 'flights.' Wines may be deliberately selected for their vintage, which is horizontal tasting, or from a single winery, which is vertical tasting, to better compare vineyard and vintages, respectively. Alternatively, in order to promote an unbiased analysis, bottles and even glasses may be disguised in a 'blind' tasting, to rule out any prejudicial awareness of either vintage or winery.

"To ensure impartial judgment of a wine, it should be served *blind* — that is, without the taster having seen the label or bottle shape. Blind tasting may also involve serving the wine from a black wineglass to mask the color of the wine. A taster can be prejudiced by knowing details of a wine, such as geographic origin, the winery that made it, price, reputation, color, or other considerations.

"Scientific research has long demonstrated the power of suggestion in perception as well as the strong effects of expectancies. For example, people expect more expensive wine to have more desirable characteristics than less expensive wine. When given wine that they are falsely told is expensive they virtually always report it tastes better than the very same wine when they are told that it is inexpensive. French researcher Frédéric Brochet submitted a mid-range Bordeaux in two different bottles, one labeled as a cheap table wine, the other bearing a grand cru etiquette. Tasters described the supposed grand cru as 'woody, complex, and round' and the supposed cheap wine as 'short, light, and faulty.'

"Similarly, people have expectations about wines because of their geographic origin, producer, vintage, color, and many other factors. For example, when Brochet served a white wine he received all the usual descriptions: 'fresh, dry, honeyed, lively.' Later he served the same wine dyed red and received the usual red terms: 'intense, spicy, supple, deep.'"

"Vertical and horizontal wine tastings are wine tasting events that are arranged to highlight differences between similar wines," Alexis began after lunch. "In a vertical tasting, different vintages of the same wine type from the same winery are tasted. This emphasizes differences between various vintages. In a horizontal tasting, the wines are all from the same vintage but are from different wineries. Keeping wine variety or type and wine region the same helps emphasize differences in winery styles.

"Tasting flight is a term used by wine tasters to describe a selection of wines, usually between three and eight glasses, but sometimes as many as fifty, presented for the purpose of sampling and comparison. A tasting note refers to a taster's written testimony about the aroma, taste identification, acidity, structure, texture, and balance of a wine. The temperature that a wine is served at can greatly affect the way it tastes and smells. Lower temperatures will emphasize acidity and tannins while muting the aromatics. Higher temperatures will minimize acidity and tannins while increasing the aromatics. General rules of thumb are that white wines and Champagnes should be served at forty to fifty degrees Fahrenheit, and red wines at sixty to seventy degrees.

"The shape of a wineglass can have a subtle impact on the perception of wine, especially its bouquet. Typically, the ideal shape is considered to be wider toward the bottom, with a narrower aperture at the top, or tulip or egg shaped. Glasses that are widest at the top are considered the least ideal. Many wine tastings use glasses that are egg-shaped. Interestingly, the effect of glass shape does not appear to be related to whether the glass is pleasing to look at.

"Judging color is the first step in tasting wine. Without having tasted the wines, one does not know if, for example, a white is heavy or light. Before taking a sip, the taster tries to determine the order in which the wines should be assessed by appearance and nose alone. Heavy wines will be deeper in color and generally more intense on the nose. Sweeter wines, being denser, will leave thick, viscous streaks, called legs or fingers, down the inside of the glass when swirled.

"There are five basic steps in tasting wine: color, swirl, smell, taste, and savor. These are also known as the 'five S' steps for see, swirl, sniff, sip, and savor. During this process, a taster must look for clarity, varietal character, integration, expressiveness, complexity, and connectedness.

"The wine should be bright and clear, with no particles in it. A wine's color is better judged by putting it against a white background. The wineglass is put at an angle in order to see the colors. Colors can give the taster clues to the grape variety, and whether the wine was aged in wood.

"Varietal character describes how much a wine presents its inherent grape aromas. A wine taster also looks for integration, which is a state in which none of the components of the wine, acid, tannin, alcohol, is out of balance with the other components. When a wine is well balanced, the wine is said to have achieved a harmonious fusion. Another important quality of the wine to look for is its expressiveness. Expressiveness is the quality the wine possesses when its aromas and flavors are well-defined and clearly projected. The complexity of the wine is affected by many factors, one of which may be the multiplicity of its flavors. The connectedness of the wine, a rather abstract and difficult to ascertain quality, describes the bond between the wine and its land of origin, or terroir.

THE WINE QUEEN

"A wine's quality can be judged by its bouquet and taste. The bouquet is the total aromatic experience of the wine. Assessing a wine's bouquet can also reveal faults such as cork taint, oxidation due to age, overexposure to oxygen, or lack of preservatives and wild yeast contamination due to Brettanomyces or acetobacter yeasts. Although low levels of Brettanomyces aromatic characteristics can be a positive attribute, giving the wine a distinctive character, generally it is considered a wine spoilage yeast. The bouquet of wine is best revealed by gently swirling the wine in a wineglass to expose it to more oxygen and release more aromatic etheric, ester, and aldehyde molecules that comprise the essential components of a wine's bouquet. Sparkling wine should not be swirled to the point of releasing bubbles.

"Pausing to experience a wine's bouquet aids the wine taster in anticipating the wine's flavors. The 'nose' of a wine, its bouquet or aroma, is the major determinate of perceived flavor in the mouth. Once inside the mouth, the aromatics are further liberated by exposure to body heat, and transferred retro-nasally to the olfactory receptor site. It is here that the complex taste experience characteristic of a wine actually commences.

"Thoroughly tasting a wine involves perception of its array of taste and mouth feel attributes, which involve the combination of textures, flavors, weight, and overall structure. Following appreciation of its olfactory characteristics, the wine taster savors a wine by holding it in the mouth for a few seconds to saturate the taste buds. By pursing one's lips and breathing through that small opening oxygen will pass over the wine and release even more esters. When the wine is allowed to pass slowly through the mouth it presents the connoisseur with the fullest gustatory profile available to the human palate.

"The acts of pausing and focusing through each step distinguish wine tasting from simple quaffing. Through this process, the full array of aromatic molecules is captured and interpreted by approximately fifteen million olfactory receptors, comprising a few hundred olfactory receptor classes. When tasting several wines in succession, however, key aspects of this fuller experience, length and finish, or aftertaste, must necessarily be sacrificed through expectoration.

"Although taste qualities are known to be widely distributed throughout the oral cavity, the concept of an anatomical 'tongue map' yet persists in the wine tasting arena, in which different tastes are believed to map to different areas of the tongue. A widely accepted example is the misperception that the tip of the tongue uniquely tells how sweet a wine is and the upper edges tell its acidity.

"As part of the tasting process, and as a way of comparing the merits of the various wines, wines are given scores according to a relatively set system. This may be either by explicitly weighting different aspects, or by global judgment, although the same aspects would be considered. These aspects are one, the appearance of the wine, two, the nose or smell, three, the palate or taste, and four, the overall effect of these three aspects. Different systems weight these differently. That is, appearance fifteen percent, nose thirty- five percent, palate fifty percent. Typically, no modern wine would score less than half on any scale, which would effectively indicate an obvious fault. It is more common for wines to be scored out of twenty, including half marks, in Europe and parts of Australasia, and out of one-hundred in the United States. However, different critics tend to have their own preferred system, and some gradings are also given out of five, again with half marks.

"Because intoxication can affect the consumer's judgment, wine tasters generally spit the wine out after they have assessed its quality at formal tastings, where dozens of wines may be assessed. However, since wine is absorbed through the skin inside the mouth, tasting from twenty to twenty-five samplings can still produce an intoxicating effect, depending on the alcoholic content of the wine.

"Today, we will discuss red and white generic wines, red and white varietals, desert wines, Champagne, matching foods and wines, and wine etiquette," Alexis said as he began the second day of the wine school.

"Generic wines are a blend of a number of grape varieties, and can be divided into two classes: ordinary wines and premium wines. Ordinary wines may simply be called red table wine and white table wine, or they may carry the name of a grape production region in Europe. Thus, the reds may be called Burgundy, Bordeaux or Chianti, and the whites Chablis or Rhine wine. Ordinary generic wines are made from blends of lower-priced grapes. For reds these include Barbera, Carignane, Gamay Beaujolais, Petite Sirah, Ruby Cabernet, Grenach, and others. For whites, Burger, Chenin Blanc, Thompson seedless, French Colombard, Palomino, Sauvignon Blanc, Gray Riesling, Semillon, and others. Premium generics are made from higher quality grapes, and also carry the name of grape production regions in Europe. Again, Burgundy, Bordeaux, and Chianti for reds, and Chablis and Rhine wine for whites. Grapes used in premium Burgundy and Bordeaux include Cabernet Sauvignon, Merlot, Pinot Noir, Zinfandel and Petite Sirah. Grape varieties used in premium Chablis and Rhine wine include Chardonnay, Sauvignon Blanc, Chenin Blanc, Johannisberg Riesling, and Gewurztraminer. Prices for generic wines cover a very wide range, from fifty cents to a dollar for an ordinary wine,[20] a dollar-and- a-half to two dollars for premium whites and reds,[21] to over a hundred dollars[22] for the highest quality aged Burgundys and Bordeauxs, equal to prices for the highest quality red varietals.

"Premium generics can be either dry, with a very clean, crisp taste, or less dry, with detectable sweetness from residual sugar."

---

[20] The same as $4.00 to $8.00 in 2014.

[21] The same as $12.00 to $16.00 in 2014.

[22] The same as $800.00 in 2014.

"What is residual sugar?" an American woman asked.

"Any natural grape sugars left over after fermentation ceases. Dry wines usually have less than 0.3 percent residual sugar, medium wines one to three percent, and sweet wines have more than three percent residual sugar.

"The highest quality premium generics are dry, full bodied, and intense, with an expansive bouquet.

"Less experienced wine drinkers often believe that ordinary generic wines are inferior, and only drink varietals or premium generics, but that's not necessarily true. We don't have filet mignon or roast duck every night. A nice Burgundy or red table wine can go well with a hamburger or ham sandwich, as can a Chablis with a turkey sandwich or grilled chicken salad. There is relative value in a five dollar[23] bottle of wine and in a one dollar[24] bottle of wine. Drink the ordinary generics to appreciate the premium generics and more complex varietals.

"Rosé wines are made from red or black grapes, but left in contact with the skins for only a short time – a few hours. Otherwise, they are made like a white wine. They may be blends of several varieties, such as Zinfandel, Gamay Beaujolais, and Barbera, or made from only one variety, Zinfandel for example.

"Rosés are typically light, fruity, lively and delicate. Colors range from light pink to light red, and taste from very dry, to medium body, to sweet with residual sugar. They should be served chilled like a white wine. Two hours in the refrigerator or twenty minutes in a bucket of half ice and half water.

"Champagne has the reputation of being the beverage of kings and queens, and for special occasions. In France, it is made from grapes grown in the Champagne region, while in the United States, it is called both Champagne and sparkling wine, and is made in New York state and California. It may be a blend, or made from a single variety of grape. Some Champagnes are

---

[23] The same as $40.00 in 2014.
[24] The same as $8.00 in 2014.

made completely dry and some with residual sugar. However, extra dry refers to a Champagne that is slightly sweet. Pink Champagne is a rosé Champagne. Champagnes are made in a limitless range of styles, from dry to sweet, white to pink to deep red. Taste is light, fresh and fruity.

"Dessert wines consist of Sherries, ports, and late harvest Riesling. Sherries are sweet or dry. If the wine is fermented until it is dry before adding wine spirits, it is a dry, or cocktail, Sherry. If fermentation is stopped while there is still sugar in the wine before adding wine spirits, it is a cream Sherry. Sherry may be an aperitif as well as a dessert wine. It is nutty in flavor and usually amber in color. The best Sherries are oak aged, which makes them brown in color.

"Ports are always made sweet. They are produced from red or black grapes, and the style is fruity and mellow. Ports may be made from a blend of varieties, or from one variety. Tawny port may be aged in oak for five years or more, and bottled aged for ten years or longer. Some of the best tawny ports are over a hundred years old. Ruby port is light and fruity, and not aged.

"Late harvest Rieslings are deep gold in color, luscious and sweet. Taste is often compared to peaches, apricots and even honey. They improve with bottle aging for up to ten years.

"Serve Sherries and ports at sixty-five degrees F., and late harvest Rieslings slightly colder – at fifty-five degrees. "Today's lunch is roast game hen with wild rice, green beans, and fresh baked bread," Andre, the cook, announced after he had entered the barrel room. And for a treat to go with the meal, we have a nice Sauvignon Blanc from this winery."

"Now we will cover the white and red varietals," Alex began after they had finished lunch.

"If fifty wine experts were asked their opinion about Chardonnay, all would agree that it is the best quality white varietal. Chardonnay has a buttery character, rich and full-bodied, and is pale gold in color. It lends itself well to a variety of winemakers' styles. It's a work horse grape, but also a grape with finesse. You can make a delicate Chardonnay, fresh, light, crisp, and fruity, or just the opposite, rich, oaky, complex, and powerful. It ages well in oak, which adds complexity. The best Chardonnays will be aged in oak for a year, and improve with age for up to another five to ten years in the bottle. Most however, do not improve in the bottle for more than three to five years. The taste of Chardonnay is often compared to herbs, lemons, apples, apricots and peaches, with a woody taste from oak aging. It is always dry.

"Sauvignon Blanc, if aged in oak for up to a year, is a close second to Chardonnay. In fact, some feel that Sauvignon Blanc offers a formidable challenge to Chardonnay for white wine supremacy.

"Why is oak aging so important for Sauvignon Blanc?" Ann asked.

"If it is not aged in oak, Sauvignon Blanc has a grassy flavor, and overly aggressive aromas that many don't like.[25]

"Sauvignon Blanc is a very distinctive wine that is different from all others. It has a very intense, spicy flavor, herbal and fig-like. People either like it a lot, or not at all. It ranges from light yellow to medium gold, and after being aged in oak, improves with bottle aging for another five to ten years.

"Johannisberg Riesling is the classic grape of Germany. It is perfumy and grapey in character. Styles range from slightly sweet, with one to two percent residual sugar because of the higher acidity of Johannisberg Riesling grapes, to fresh, fragrant and crisp, to dry. It is pale straw-colored, with a green tint. It is not aged in oak, and improves in the bottle for up to five years.

---

[25] In response to the unpopularity of Sauvignon Blanc in California, in 1968 Robert Mondavi developed Fume Blanc. It is Sauvignon Blanc aged in oak and made in a fruitier style. Now, most Sauvignon Blancs are oak aged, so the only difference in these two wines is the winemaking style. They are both made from Sauvignon Blanc grapes.

THE WINE QUEEN

"Chenin Blanc is a good introduction to white varietals, or to varietal wines for new wine drinkers. It is simple, soft, and fruity, and does not have the intensity of character of Chardonnay or Sauvignon Blanc. It is a very light straw color. Chenin Blanc does not improve with age, and is best if consumed within four years of when it was made.

"Gewürztraminer has a unique, floral, perfumy character. Many say that it tastes like a rose smells. Its flavor is intense, very fruity and spicy. A good wine for new wine drinkers. Styles range from dry to sweet with one to two percent residual sugar. It is light straw-colored. Gewürztraminer is not oak aged, and improves in the bottle for up to five years.

The red varietals we will cover are Cabernet Sauvignon, Pinot Noir, Merlot, Zinfandel, and Petite Sirah."

"Cabernet Sauvignon is considered the king of the red wines. It is also the most elegant of the red wines, and is the most consistently well-made red varietal. Cabernet Sauvignons are among the world's best wines. The grapes need a cool climate to keep the acid high enough. They are small and berry-sized, which results in more skin per gallon, and more color and flavor. Its intense, powerful character lends itself to many styles. The amount of tannin and the ratio of fruit to wood taste are the biggest variables in style. Cabernet Sauvignon has a wide variety of aromatic descriptions. From spicy, fruity and plumy, to herbaceous and bell peppery. Almost always made dry, its complexity and elegance of flavors is what makes it so desirable. When young, Cabernet Sauvignon is harsh and needs at least five to eight years of aging. Lighter styles age gracefully up to ten years, while heavier, outstanding vintages will improve up to fifty years. Cabernet Sauvignon needs to breathe at least fifteen minutes, with the more complex wines requiring up to an hour of breathing time.

"Lighter in color and taste than Cabernet Sauvignon, Pinot Noir is considered the queen of red wines, second only to Cabernet Sauvignon. Pinot Noir is velvety in mouth feel, and chemically different in color than any other red wine. Its taste is minty, toasty, oaky, and earthy. It is soft in body and very dry, but with age, develops a seemingly sweet quality. It is best if consumed five to ten years after it is made and needs fifteen minutes breathing time. It is difficult to make well. Many experts believe that a winemaker's skill can be determined by how well they make Pinot Noir.

"Merlot is primarily a blending grape, but also makes a good varietal.[26] It is moderate, soft, and mild, with a light, fruity flavor. Its taste is like ripe cherries or plums. Aromas are cherry fruitiness, herbal tea, and orange rind. The aging time for Merlot is about half that for Cabernet Sauvignon. It needs fifteen minutes breathing time.

"Zinfandel is an extremely versatile grape. It makes good red wines as well as rosés, often called white Zinfandel. A good port can also be made from the late harvest of Zinfandel grapes. Zinfandel has a great deal of berry-like character. It has a full taste, well balanced, and not high in acid, so it can be soft. It has a rich, berry fruit taste, with a peppery quality. Its taste is often compared to raspberries, blackberries, cranberries and boysenberries. Zinfandel is medium red to deep purple in color. As a table wine, it does not improve with age, but as late harvest desert wine, it can improve for ten years or more. It needs only about ten minutes breathing time.

"Petite Sirah is the last of the varietals we will examine. It is primarily used as a blending grape for body and color, but is also made into a varietal. Very dark in color, it is almost black like India ink. It is direct, simple, and full-bodied, with a narrow range of styles. Petite Sirah has strong tannins, and thus an astringent taste, but it develops well from aging. It will benefit

---

[26] By the 1980s, Merlot was second only to Cabernet Sauvgnon as a high quality red varietal. It is my favorite red varietal because it is softer and fruitier than Cabernet Sauvgnon.

from three to six years of bottle aging, although some may continue to improve for up to ten years. It is usually too strong to drink without food, such as lamb shank, prime rib, aged cheeses, and other strong foods. It needs 15 minutes to an hour of breathing time.

"Wine is good as an aperitif, or cocktail, without food, and certainly with food. The best practice is to eat the foods you like with the wines you like. However, a general guideline is to match complex wines that have a more robust flavor with heavier more powerful foods, and softer, simpler wines with lighter foods. Thus a Cabernet Sauvignon or very high quality Bordeaux would go well with lamb, beef, venison, Italian sausage, and so on, while foods that would go well with Chenin Blanc or Chablis would include fish, shellfish, poultry, and salads. An example of foods that would go well with wines between these two extremes, such as Chardonnay, Johannisberg Riesling, Pinot Noir, and Zinfandel would be roast pork, duck, veal, tuna salad, pasta, and quail.

"Next we will discuss wine etiquette," Alexis told the class. "We will begin with opening the bottle.

"Corkscrews date back to the sixteenth century, and there are many different kinds. A basic corkscrew consists of a pointed metal spiral, called a helix, attached to a handle, which is a horizontal bar of wood. The user grips the handle and screws the metal point into the cork. Its point should puncture the cork with a small hole and penetrate smoothly, without damaging a lot of cork tissue. Once the helix is firmly embedded into the cork, a vertical pull on the corkscrew extracts the cork from the bottle. The wing-type has metal levers or wings on each side of the helix. As the helix is twisted into the cork, the wings are raised. Once the helix is embedded in the cork, pushing down the wings pulls the cork out of the bottle in one smooth motion. The most common design has a rack and pinion connecting the levers to the body. A sommelier knife, or waiter's friend, is a corkscrew in a folding body similar to a pocket knife. An arm extends to brace against the lip of the bottle for leverage when removing the cork. A small hinged knife blade is housed in the handle end to be used in cutting the foil wrapping the neck of many wine bottles. A corkscrew of this type is less intuitive to use, and requires more skill in order to be used without damaging the cork, but can be used more quickly and with more show than a wing-type corkscrew. The twin prong cork puller can extract a cork without damaging it, to allow for sampling the wine before re-inserting the cork. The cork is removed by first inserting the longer prong between the cork and neck of the bottle, and pushing it down until the shorter prong is inserted between the cork and bottle neck on the other side. The device is then rocked first on the side of one prong, then on the side of the other prong, while pushing down on it until the prongs are inserted the length of the cork. The cork is then twisted out of the bottle. The twin prong cork puller is also known as the butler's friend, because it enables wine to be removed from its bottle and replaced with a less expensive wine without knowing the wine bottle was opened.[27]

"In opening a bottle of Champagne, safety is the key because there are about six atmospheres of pressure in the bottle. You don't want the cork exploding out of the bottle because it could break something or hurt someone, and you don't want Champagne foaming out of the bottle either because you want to drink it instead of lose it. Peel off the part of the foil that

---

[27] Another very good corkscrew is the screwpull developed by Herbert Allen. It wasn't developed until 1979, so would not have been in Ann's wine tasting class. The screwpull has a Teflon-coated helix, which enables it to more easily penetrate the cork without damaging much cork tissue. It has plastic grips on each side of the helix. When removing the cork, the grips are held firmly against the neck of the wine bottle while the helix is screwed into the cork. As it penetrates the cork, the cork is pulled out of the bottle.

covers the top inch of the bottle. Then, holding your thumb firmly on the top of the cork, twist the loop on the wire hood to loosen it, and lift it off. Next, hold the bottle at a forty-five degree angle and, grasping the cork with your hand, turn the bottle while pulling upward on the cork until it comes out.

"Champagne should be served in a tall, narrow glass flute, not the bird bath-type glasses that it is often served in at parties. The flute directs the bouquet to the top of the glass where it can be enjoyed instead of around the sides where it is lost, like the bird bath-type glass does.

"When a waiter brings you the wine you have ordered in a restaurant, the waiter will show you the label prior to opening the wine. Be sure it is the wine you ordered. After removing the cork, he or she will show it to you. Squeeze it to be sure it is pliable. If it is hard, split, or cracked, and not pliable, it could have dried out when the wine was stored and let oxygen into the wine, which oxidizes and ruins it. Wine should always be stored on its side, to keep the cork from drying out. Once the wine has been allowed to breathe, to let any off-odors dissipate, if appropriate for the wine you ordered, the waiter will pour a small amount of the wine in a glass for you. Swirl the wine in the glass and smell it, then taste it. If it is bad, it will have a heavy, grassy, musty smell and taste, or a sour smell and taste like vinegar. This is rare, but if the wine is bad, refuse to pay for it.

"Are there any questions? If not, that concludes our class for today."

About The Author

Robert Allen Morris is an agricultural economist with more than thirty-five years of experience in agribusiness. He spent most of his career working for large companies. These included Duda, a company with agricultural operations in Florida, Texas, and California; The Coca-Cola Company; Tropicana Products; Cutrale, one of the world's largest citrus processors, growers and exporters, based in Araraquara, Brazil; and Prudential Agricultural Investments. In 2007, Allen joined the faculty of the University of Florida in the Food and Resource Economics Department, with responsibilities for both educational programs and research. In April, 2012, he resigned his faculty appointment and joined Blue Lake Citrus Products as vice-president of sales and marketing. Blue Lake Citrus Products produces and markets the Noble brand of high-end specialty citrus juices as well as bulk citrus juices for other brands and labels. Allen has published more than thirty articles on agribusiness and has given numerous presentations world-wide. When he worked for The Coca-Cola Company in the 1980s, his responsibilities were in The Wine Spectrum, their wine subsidiary. The Wine Spectrum, which was comprised of The Taylor Wine company in New York State, and Taylor California Cellars, The Monterey Vineyards and Sterling Vineyards in California, was the second largest wine company in North America. While working there, he was sent to wine school, and taught the basics of viticulture, enology, and wine tasting, experiences that provided much of his background for writing this book. Allen currently resides with his wife, Kate, in Winter Haven, Florida, and can be reached at Allenmors@aol.com. Visit www.OrchidSpringsPublishing.com for more literary works by Allen.